NEW TEACHINGS

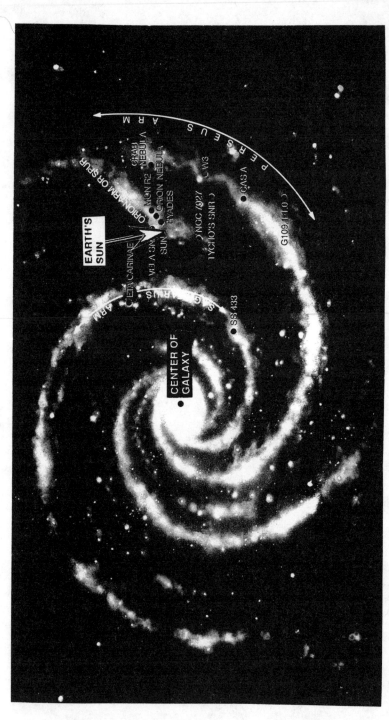

Our Sun lies 30,000 light years from the center of our Milky Way Galaxy, in a spur off one of its major spiral arms.

NEW TEACHINGS

for an
Awakening
Humanity

1994/1995 UPDATE

THE CHRIST

 S.E.E. Publishing Company, Santa Clara, California, U.S.A.

Cover Photo: Eric J. Pittman
Cover Layout, Original Edition: Amy Haws Peck
Cover Layout, 1994/95 Edition: Lightbourne Images

ISBN # 0-937147-09-5
Library of Congress Catalog Card Number: 94-068706

Spiritual Education Endeavors
Publishing Company
1556 Halford Avenue, #288
Santa Clara, CA 95051
USA

Original Edition, ISBN #0-937147-00-1
First Printing   March 1986
Second Printing   August 1986
Third Printing March 1987
Fourth Printing November 1987

1994/1995 Updated Edition, ISBN #0-937147-09-5
First Printing September 1994
Second Printing February 1995
Third Printing August 1995
Fourth Printing October 1996
Fifth Printing April 1999
Sixth Printing April 2000

DEDICATION

This book is dedicated to God and to peace and the preservation of all life everywhere . . . to every soul on the planet earth . . . and to our guides, friends, and teachers from the heavenly realms who lead us lovingly back to full spiritual awareness and manifestation.

HOW JOYFUL IS THE SOUL WHEN ITS
YEARNINGS ARE FULFILLED.

ACKNOWLEDGMENTS

A special word of thanks is given to Holly Brunz, Merry Finley, Amy Haws Peck, Pat Proud, Ann Valentin, and John Willis for their part in this book's preparation. I am also grateful to Francie Meyer and others for their assistance in this endeavor.

Our cameraless light painting cover, by artist Eric J. Pittman, uses refracted sunlight directly on photographic paper to capture the experience of energy.

For information about his work contact the artist at 1275 Balmoral, Victoria, British Columbia V8T 1B4, Canada.

1994/1995 UPDATED EDITION

I especially want to thank Ron from the S.E.E. Publishing office for his devoted service in preparing this updated 1994/1995 manuscript, most especially for his efforts in page layout and preparation for printing. I also want to acknowledge Orpheus Phylos and Archangel Michael for their help in designing Chapter X's illustrations describing the Shoemaker-Levy comet contact with Jupiter.

TABLE OF CONTENTS

Virginia's Foreword

When this book was finally published in time for Easter of 1986, initiated by my Israel trip in the fall of 1984 (with 45 other meditators), I thought I had completed my writing task for the one called Christ Jesus. In fact, I was expecting to return to my college teaching career and continue in my chosen life profession as if nothing had happened. Ha!

However, life would take a very different turn so that now, after 6 book publications in 8 years, the outcome of that first act of willingness has moved me inexorably along a defined path of spiritual service that merely uses those same skills under the direction of my soul intention.

Like many other people who find themselves involved in these previously unexpected adventures, it all seems very natural now, and there is no turning back, no rejection of the time and commitment required of me. Because of that willingness to serve I have met many wonderful friends whose hearts and minds are also attuned to the cause of individual cleansing, growth, and awakening. Each one of you is very precious to me and just knowing you exist warms my heart and furthers my own persistence to peace and the preservation of life on our extraordinary planet.

Because <u>New Teachings for an Awakening Humanity</u> was one of the primary publications issued to help us remember why we came to earth, it has been well received both here and abroad. There are 100,000 copies out there somewhere in many different languages, and we still get some requests for it. Since we recently exhausted our supply of English language copies, we either had to let it go out-of-print forever or reprint more. When donations made it possible to reprint this English edition, Jesus requested that I include several updated chapters in it, so you are now holding the original material and his updated commentaries. This allows new readers to have both the original and the update, and for you who may already have read it, to easily notice the latest information. We chose this solution because it is faster than committing nearly a year's time to do a totally new book by Jesus and because he said most of the original comments were still valuable.

I ask your indulgence in this partial revision solution and hope it serves your need for current information from our beloved Christ Jesus. Of course, a subscription to the bi-monthly Love Corps Newsletter is yet another way you can acquire his ongoing comments.

Besides the publication of celestial information, my current focus is on networking, on spiritual communities, on helping our new age children and their parents, and on teaching new meditation practices that will help our bodies safely shift into a full 12-helix DNA pattern and the development of the 13-level chakra system to bring back our full consciousness. Therefore I will share Jesus' 18-breath "Garment of Light" Ascension Meditation process (similar to the Flower of Life/Merkabah meditation process introduced by Drunvalo Melchizedek). However, because things are changing so rapidly, I have also been guided to introduce yet another meditation form for those who may be ready and interested. Check your guidance for confirmation about learning either of these helpmates. They must be personally experienced, not just described on tape.

Many of us are powerful beings used to achieving what is usually called success, but as we come under spiritual influences and increasing energies, it is group consciousness we seek, group cooperation we need. And it is among such group alliances that our greatest healing opportunity for ascension can be energized and nurtured.

Will you join me in a pledge to willingly achieve our sacred personal, group, and global responsibilities as we practice conscious cooperation in serving our role in the preservation of God's many worlds?

Joy, light and love to you,

VIRGINIA

Chapter I

Needed: A Love Corps

Have you ever wondered what Jesus would say to you if you could see him on TV or hear him speak by radio to mankind? There have been so many on earth who have prayed for my coming, my assistance, that I have chosen to communicate through this process of mental telepathy and to transmit my thoughts to humanity on the planet earth today via a living earth dweller with whom I have good mental rapport and telepathic contact. (But I would come to you, as well, if you would build the meditation bridge for it, dear ones.)

Yes, it is so. This is my own statement sent directly to you, not mere reports of my sayings and actions recorded later by the disciples and those who came after. Most of all these are *not* remarks for a bygone era. These are *my* teachings for this New Age, this new time of an awakening humanity. Herein are my personal messages regarding the condition of your planet and the things which you should do if your spiritual evolution is to be assured.

Because of the severity of your situation, I do not speak in biblical terms or in the "thee's" and "thou's" of former phraseology. My words are not intended just for so-called Christians but for everyone. These words address the immediate conditions that your earthly negativity has caused and which must change if you are to prevent serious repercussions. They are serious because I love you and would call your attention to the emergency state in which you reside. They also represent a new beginning for those who are willing to learn and to apply only peace in their everyday lives. In this sense, my words are for an *awakening* humanity. They are a call for a truly spiritual adventure ... a corps of love that will inaugurate this time of opportunity and loving endeavor called the Golden Age. For in spite of the danger there is hope. Please remember this. And the larger the Love Corps the greater our hope and opportunities.

Regrettably, my brothers and sisters, many have deified me. Even worshipped me. And this erroneous attitude must be changed into its valid perspective if you are to understand the true meaning of my long ago mission and the place where I and humanity now exist in God's reality. My message then, and the essential message of all major world religions, has been love and compassion. I have particularly stressed *love for the Creator above all else.* And then love of the human family as yourself. I care not which religious name you use in honoring God for my purpose is broader than the separations of belief you have devised. My purpose is inclusion for all who choose it, regardless of color, country, culture, or conditioning. But I do not wish to be the centered focus of any official church. It is God, our Parent, who is to be revered, not the one called Jesus. Please hear and follow my request.

Do not limit me or God by pettiness and rigidity of your present misguided understanding! Accept that I come to all, for all, to share the truth of who you are, why you are here, and where you may go through open minds and hearts dedicated to God's fruition on earth.

Truly, I speak so that you can complete this long journey of return which all prodigal sons and daughters started eons ago -- a journey that has brought this exquisite planet to the brink of destruction by your hand, but which may yet be salvaged by an immense willingness and dedication.

I come again to remind you that *all persons must acknowledge the Creator* -- that source of power which gives us all our life eternally -- and to remind you that a spark of that power is in *you!* God is not merely some external reality that you must bow down to but is an integral, internal aspect of your own identity! Both aspects should be the primary focus of your life. Of course you stand in awe of this great Creator, for you cannot possibly imagine the magnitude of its grandeur and capabilities.

I use the pronoun "its" to show that God is actually a combination of the masculine and feminine principle in one identity. Thus it is both male and female, active and receptive, power and love, father and mother. It needs no separate physical expressions of these male/female aspects as you of earth have fallen into and will emerge from in the future when you awakened ones evolve into a resurrected body again.

God, by any name, is balance, integration, and synthesis of all the finest qualities of life itself and has never known your division into separate parts of its multi-faceted qualities. Thus, there is no feminine God and there is no masculine God, but only strengths of will and power, balanced together with love and nurturance in one embodiment. Your own spiritual development requires you to balance both aspects of God within you regardless of the physical body you wear so that you express both power and love even though you are in the "separation" -- or separated portion of the sexes -- of which holy books speak. But regardless of which body you inhabit, male or female, your identity is both power and love. For this is who and what you are forevermore, and any illusion to the contrary is a temporary blindness from which you will recover if you choose.

God is more than "he" and more than "she." Do you understand? God is the perfect example of will and power to produce material life or creation in the Universe, and then with the balance of love to nurture, guide and care for it. Let not pronouns of "he" and "she," "him" and "her," separate you from God's perfect unity. Men are not better than women, or vice versa. Both are one-half of a full equation seeking the balance of self-unity, not relying on another of the opposite sex to supply the opposite polarity within.

Then let both men and women who read this material settle into the certainty that God is everything in perfect balance and come to peace between the sexes, to cooperation between power and love.

Even I am unable to describe God's perfect balance, energy and true wonder. Words cannot express the sense of inner knowing. But all of this God magnificence is within you and is available to draw upon if you choose it. What a gift! A gift of expansion and immense joy. Yet many deny it or ignore it or misuse it, all because of free will.

Have you ever wondered why God gave you this gift of free will? Let me share some information little known on the planet, for the souls on earth are set upon a rare venture. You are a marvel of God's expression and were given free will as an opportunity to learn a deep abiding love for the Creator ... a feeling of caring that is not merely a mental appreciation, but a heartfelt embrace of deep love and affection, peace and joy. In the Universe live many other beings with physical bodies of a lighter density than your own, most of which you cannot see. These are imbued with great mental power and knowledge. Yet they accept God's laws which they willingly follow, intellectually, without the love feeling you were created with. Your ability to feel love, combined with your *free will*, make you a novel species in this part of the Universe.

Earth life was given the opportunity to love and worship the Creator with a deep emotional response. You, then, can feel like a true offspring and can adoringly be led to God's open arms, which long to embrace you in the full circle of familyhood. You were made with love, to love. But, since you were also given free will, you are faced with a provocative choice. Again I tell you this is an opportunity for spiritual growth seldom known in this Universe. Yet, my beloved ones, it is this very aspect of the free will gift that has made your venture on earth so delicate, so difficult. Many other lifeforms created by God simply know the universal principles without question in a mental way. They do not emotionally love the Creator, although they accept and respect the gift of life bestowed upon them. *But you of earth are to love our Creator.* Other lifeforms use only intellect to understand God and the laws of the many universes. This is in contrast to those on earth who have a deep emotional nature and heart expression of love which, by their choice, they can focus on the Creator. Yours is a unique challenge and very frankly I must say it has not been the success that we -- your teachers and guides in the heavenly realms -- would wish.

If you were standing with us and looking down upon the conditions of earth I wonder what your reactions would be to the war and violence and hatred boiling in one place and then another. Without ceasing, peace tends to elude the human mind and heart. Endless are the internal struggles each of you faces and often loses from an undisciplined mind, an unloving heart, or an unwillingness to be aided by those of us dedicated to your success. To the few peaceful-hearted ones we give deep thanks, for it is through you any improvement is possible. You are anchors of God's light far from home.

I come again to you now because you are entitled to be told the truth of your present dilemma and to be advised that you must rise above the negativity that the planet earth holds at this hour. You have forgotten how to be peaceful, but you must remember if your life experience is to conclude positively. You must become the peace, each of you. For without your inner acceptance and awareness, it cannot manifest in the physical world around you. You must overcome the present level of negativity because your current environment of ugly thinking is not only destroying your own planet and threatening your physical future, but has now been carried into the streams of space far beyond that allowed by the Creator's laws which guarantee safety to other life.

YOU MAY NOT TAKE THE EVIL THOUGHTS OF WAR AND VIOLENCE AND THE WEAPONS OF DESTRUCTION INTO SPACE! Hear this statement and heed it well. You are at a crossroad, a time of no return if you do.

I have pondered long about how to explain the criticalness of your present conditions knowing many may choose not to heed, not to understand, not to cooperate. Still, I must come; I must ask you to expand your understanding of what you are causing and to change your attitude at once. Either you create PEACE on planet earth *soon* or many souls will fail in this experiment to love God of their own free will choice. But that will be the price for those who continue attitudes of war and violence. For these actions are now contaminating space and other lifeforms; I'm sure you realize this cannot be allowed.

Malicious children should not have bombs. However, if they have some in their own yards, their own territory, because the family has allowed them to build them -- either through stupidity, negligence, or disinterest -- the police may not be able to intervene in time to avoid disaster in their own home if one is exploded. But, if a child is threatening to blow up the neighborhood and has already thrown out a few small detonations as a preliminary assault next door, action will be swift, will it not?

In a way this is approximately the situation earth faces. An attitude of such violence, hatred, and war has been allowed to permeate your population that earth is now that child -- armed and ready to explode. To live in any proximity to you, as a neighbor, is threatening, and I assure you that although you cannot see life in space or in your own solar system, it does exist at higher dimensions and in lighter vibrations. Therefore, any negative movement beyond your own 250-mile boundary injures your own Mother Earth, creates negative weather patterns and causes an illegal assault on God's other space children who must be guaranteed safety. Who among you would not claim the right to protection if the neighbors brought violence to your domicile? Hear, then, this example and live by it. Do everything in your power to be peace loving and to demand your governments and military establishments do the same!

A few monstrous minds in your midst have created weapons capable not only of humanity's annihilation, but of far reaching destruction in the *Universe*. Accept that the willful, dangerous child called earth does not have the eyes or instrumentation to see higher forms of life. Most of you cannot see me, yet I am more real than the chair upon which you sit or the floor upon which you stand. You are BLIND. Wake up to your responsibility. The present weapons on earth are great enough to destroy all of humanity now, yet even worse and more horrendous ones are planned and ready for implementation. This madness, this infectious condition of violence, must stop. MUST STOP!!!

If you allow a few maniacs to damage this exquisite planet -- which was prepared for you to assist in your spiritual self-realization and in your devotion and love and appreciation of all living things -- then you are foolish indeed. And I give my strongest recommendation that you do all in your power to change the circumstances of humanity's felonious actions before it is too late. I say to you, with the respect and encouragement of a loving, older brother, that all of heaven will reach down to you in support of this peace effort. We will guide and assist humanity to avoid such a needless disaster anytime we are asked to help. So, invite us into your hearts. Meditate every day and begin to build a bridge from your heart to the soul energy created by God. Take this power and raise yourself from a mere child of earth to a child of heaven.

This is no idle task we are about. You can become more fully an expression of God only by your choice and persistence. Let the light and peace in you guide the way and set the model for your greater destiny. Ask for guidance and it will be given. We stand beside you to lead you to a goal far beyond your present understanding. Trust that there is a plan -- a Divine plan -- with rewards beyond measure. But to achieve them there is a cost.

The cost is that you must free yourself from the negative hypnosis which permeates your technological societies. You must change the programming of your mass media and prohibit the violence which imbues each subconscious mind with such ugly visions that you have forgotten who you are and who created your life force. If you cannot change the violent attitudes of your movie, TV, radio and literary sources, then remove yourself from their influence which constantly weakens your love nature. These negative, widespread thought forms are engulfing the planet in a dirge of blackness that is harder and harder to penetrate by those of us in the light. Many are in quicksand and know it not, yet we would rescue each one who asks to have personal peace and who will join with others on this planet to create planetary peace.

Make peace on earth a reality then, and stop earth's invasion of space with the plague you would bring by your very thoughts of violence and war. If humanity ignores its love heritage now, much will be lost, so all of heaven attends you in full force and dedication if you but seek us.

Ask to become an instrument of love and peace. And meditate to receive the support we offer. Why else, children of the light, did you come? Fill your mind and consciousness with something worth having! And from your mind will come loving activities that make life more enjoyable and dear for you, for all life on the planet, for earth itself and for your brothers and sisters in space. Heed these words which have come to humanity for eons of time but are now urgent! Critical! Very critical!

Stop this preoccupation with sub-human thoughts and activities or be willing to bear the consequences of your choice. God has a plan for your glorification and for the planet's expansion in the solar system. *You did not make the plan.* You cannot change it. It exists. Your only logical choice is to listen within to the voice that knows your part and then follow its higher guidance. Your only logical behavior today is to pray and meditate to receive God's communication -- to apply it in life -- and then to join with others on the planet like yourself to practice peace.

You are the caretakers of the earth! Have you forgotten your reason for coming?

There is one Central Being of such magnitude and power that you cannot imagine its creative intensity and multiple avenues of growth. I assure you that God is real, actual, and without question. To doubt such a power when you can see its manifestation before your very eyes is ludicrous. Did you make the sun that brings warmth and light and the energy for all life, including your own? Did you create the stars that shine above you in the night sky, that have energies traveling at speeds you cannot match in your puny earth communication and transportation systems?

What is it that, even by the most logical of intellectual inquiry, allows you to think that you are wise and learned and capable of standing before God with these gifts you call science? Especially when these gifts are sealed in the envelope marked War -- marked Hell. Is this really the soul gift you would bring that spiritual realm of love which has created every inch of planet earth and covered it with the luscious beauty and magnificent vistas to soothe your hearts and cheer your minds? Does not the beauty of such a place lead you to a state of appreciation?

You, men, women, and children of earth, agreed to come here as the caretakers of the earth. Caretakers! What does that mean to you? If someone is caring for you, how do they do this? What is it that allows you to know when you have been cared for with love, with consideration, and with respect? Does a nurse mishandle sick patients in a non-caring way? Does a mother subject her children to brutality? Does a father abandon his family responsibilities and avoid his goal of provider? Even in your earthly blackness it is not generally approved that such activities are desirable, though it is becoming more and more rampant. This is particularly true in your western societies where nations have the greatest personal wealth but destroy the earth to achieve it.

Close your eyes and open your heart. What care do you give this earth homeland? What care do you give other human beings? What care do you give the plants and animals -- yes, and even the minerals which are serving earth by their contents in her physical makeup? What care are you giving the emotional and mental and spiritual needs of Mother Earth? For like you, on a far grander scale, she lives. Lives on many levels! And although you see only the flesh of her, as it were, she has feelings, and this layer of emotion -- invisible to your eyes -- lies in a bank of energy just beyond her crust.

Since the earth is an unique being who is growing and learning, *as do all things in the Universe,* you affect her attitudes by the way you treat her, by the type of care you give. You have filled her emotions with such violence and terror that I cannot even describe the way it looks to us here in the heavenly realms. It is a thick, black murky sea of ugliness which you have contributed. It is no wonder you fear volcanoes and earthquakes and the tremblings of that mighty one on whom you ride. She has the power to shrug, itch, scratch and eliminate those non-caring thoughts given to her by individuals and combined humanity.

Yes, you were chosen long ago to care for life upon the earth and to learn the full expression of love and wisdom so that both the earth and her subtle life energy bodies, and you and your life energy bodies, would raise a stupendously magnificent glow of light and praise to God for all the Universe to see, to model. Earth is becoming a star and you are the co-creators of that process.

I am saddened by the state in which most of your people exist. Only mercy and grace have held the tides of devastation from your door, through our intervention on your behalf with the other lifeforms in your solar system and the galactic government to which you belong. By the Creator's decree alone have you been given extra time now to practice peace.

However, as I have explained, your refusal to care for Mother Earth, and all upon it, and your actions to endanger space itself must now cease. Let it be known that you must change and do it quickly -- individually, in groups, in nations, and finally in a planetary movement.

By shooting your missiles, your weaponry, and sending killer satellites up through that which you call empty space, but which is actually the invisible energy fields containing the emotions and mind of Mother Earth, you hurt her. You therefore hurt yourself. Grasp this so that you see your own responsibility in the matter. God has not brought destruction to your planet. Humanity has. By every angry thought, action and deed, and lack of love and caring, you have seeded pain and suffering for yourselves.

These thoughts of anger and violence and rape are done not only to individual persons, but to the very land and soil and life upon which you all survive day by day. You are killing yourselves and wounding the planet. Yet she can survive and will survive even without your own presence upon her. Why do you create in her the desire to be rid of you? Will she not wish to remove the irritations that attack her peace as a dog scratches fleas? Do you jab her with your various machines without so much as a blessing and thanks for what she gives and does on your behalf? She takes the sun's energy and nurtures all of life with it. Do you really grow food, or do you harvest her gifts of sustenance?

Where is the love God created you with? And where is the care you promised God to give all living things on earth?

If you were judge and jury of this situation living on some other planet, what would you think of such a situation? In this answer you may find your escape. For if you see you have been ignorantly hurtful, you can change at once. You can pull the knife from Mother Earth's heart, her feelings and her thoughts. Need I say it is heaven's request you do so AT ONCE?

Now that you know the serious hour approaches for humanity, what will you do? Will you ignore what is said? Will you go into a deeper denial because the shock of the truth is too much to bear? Will you become angry because the plan devised to raise you from mere mortality to godliness is failing because the majority of humanity is asleep and unwilling to achieve its spiritual evolution? Or will you cry out to the heavens to help you and earth?

Already such a cry has come to us; therefore, this message is being relayed to you (via telepathic transmission) with a promise that all who seek will find. All who love will be loved. For as you know it is in the giving that you receive. This is your time to give. Give love to your Creator. Love yourself as the beautiful light that was created long ago. And love all others of the mineral, plant, animal and human family. Don't forget to love the lifeforms you cannot see elsewhere but which do exist, and also love this jewel of a homeland you have inherited. Have you not great love for the earthly mother who rotates you in daily rhythm of day and night? Have you no love for the other planets and stars who are your brothers and sisters of the heavens? Many of them are caretakers of your own planet in ways you cannot presently grasp or appreciate. But, just as you feed and water the plants and animals of your own earth, so you are fed and rocked in God's certain caring by the nameless ones who exist in the many mansions of creation, unknown to you now.

Many there are who guide and protect you if you will listen, myself among them. And you can be guided in both your dreams and meditation times if you wish it. I, myself, will send help to any who choose it, for I want to strengthen all who desire self-growth and greater service to the Creator. Many confused souls and a vast number of the unbelieving and uncommitted need to be awakened. It is by your example that you may assist us in turning others to God. Please encourage them to meditate *every day*. Remember, however, they do have free will and cannot be forced, even if a wrong choice today means a future spiritual loss.

I am saddened that some will not join humanity's thrust into this time of awakening, but their own free will is ruler. If an individual chooses -- or causes -- separation from God, then the effects must be experienced as a learning lesson for the soul. That is why I call everyone within the planet's boundaries to become still and listen to the voice of God within. It may yet bring some uncommitted or lost souls into the remembrance of the Creator. However, even the misguided and negative ones are learning and must be allowed their path, too. Need I say that souls who do not choose the Love Corps path within the alloted time must experience the effects of their free will?

All of heaven, including the spiritual teachers and leaders of all religions, times and places, are now joined for this one last call to raise earth and humanity up into the bright and glowing firmament prepared there. We desire beautiful Mother Earth to rise with regal splendor into this Golden Age of enlightenment -- peopled by a loving citizenry devoted to the glory of the Creator -- with earth's contribution to the Divine plan in the Universe *achieved!*

Humanity's completion of earth's Divine plan depends on you, each one of you. Then use your free will wisely. Express your choice, your destiny, lovingly. While you of earth are unique in your capacity to love from the heart in a deep, deep way, many are loving the wrong things -- the material objects only. Some of you are not caring at all but are filling your lives with motives and activities non-acceptable to Spirit. I remind you that because you are a prototype for the deepest feelings of love possible for the God who gives you life, this is the test by which you know if you are fulfilling life's purpose.

Examine your day. Are you caught up in the stressful push for a life that lacks a spiritual expression of love? If so, make necessary changes NOW. Use me as your example if you like, but do not use me as a crutch or substitute for your own learning and commitment. Being "born again" means you are free of the past but this is meaningless unless you are willing to love God by your own choice. If you will love God above all things, through your own free will, then your heart's purity can combine with Spirit to take you into that formerly unattainable peace on earth.

This message I bring you. It is the moment of awakening for humanity. You stand on the brink of glorification or possible disaster. THE TIME IS CRITICAL! WE CANNOT DELAY! PEACE MUST COME TO EARTH! That is why I have spoken.

Our Parent has rendered an *ultimatum* that earth-life must not be destructive to others. Neither does it serve the Universe for the planet to be destroyed by a thoughtless, unloving, unconscious citizenry. Therefore, we of heaven will do everything we can within the next year to assist humanity in bringing peace to all that it thinks and touches. Love energy is pouring down upon the planet, upon your own body. Feel it. Use it to change your predicament. This infusion of energy is our gift.

I have been joined by forces beyond your understanding to do everything possible to achieve your mission, your advancement -- or if you prefer, human salvation. But we must work through you, by your permission. Transformation comes from willingness.

Therefore, each of you is called to join us in the work that must be done. You are reminded to put the usual habits and limitations of life aside and place your devotion, dedication, and energy toward accomplishing a *peaceful* planet. This is your gift against viciousness and violence. You are the corps of love and this is your opportunity for victory. By the power of your mind and the love of your heart you can win this promotion, this expansion.

Join us fervently, steadfastly, and in solidarity, for this is the time of that final separation between the forces of so-called good and evil, of consciousness and unconsciousness, of light and dark.

My concern in bringing this type of message to earth is obvious. Fear could come into the minds and hearts of many. And this fear could paralyze your desire and willingness to help at your maximum capacity. Yet the truth is the truth and I cannot deceive you about your present danger. I cannot deny the actual circumstances even if you do. My love for you has brought me the responsibility of World Teacher, along with the assistance and cooperation of thousands of others like myself whose only purpose at this time is to save you from what *you* have created. Our mission is to turn you around to face the truth of your own situation so you can correct it quickly and permanently!

Then listen, my brothers and sisters. We stand with you to the end of this accomplishment. WHO WILL JOIN THE LOVE CORPS? WHO WILL NOW BECOME A LIGHT WORKER

TO ACHIEVE PEACE ON EARTH? That is, who will devote time and energy to this cause of peace rather than to war and violence? There is a pressing need to enlist the children of God, of love and light, to identify themselves and volunteer whatever it takes to bring the peace all loving hearts truly desire. We need a corps, a Love Corps. Will *you* volunteer?

I asked you before; I ask you again. Come forward if you haven't already been active. Increase our power through your willingness and cooperation. Ask us for our help to guide the way and we will explain with the voice of Spirit within you that which you must do. In this loving conspiracy of the light workers to raise the earth we will unite heaven and earth to achieve the golden goal set before time began. Let the mighty intention for peace be achieved in this twilight hour, dear ones. Let the plan which heaven knows and serves be fulfilled among you at last.

Truly I speak so that you can complete this long journey of return which the prodigal sons and daughters started eons ago; a journey that has brought this planet to the brink of destruction by your own hand, but can yet be salvaged by willingness and dedication.

It saddens me that perhaps a vast number of souls will not answer this call, not believe it, or otherwise procrastinate. But I cannot intervene in their personal choices. It also saddens me to see the warmongering governments and military powers lead billions of people to possible destruction because the people don't take action to prevent it. However, we cannot for this brief time do anything but help you help yourselves. But we will do that to the full extent you ask and cooperate.

If our gigantic investment of energy to the task of PEACE fails to change the actions of humanity, there is a plan of implementation which will ensue. This plan will assure that your violence and weapons do NOT harm the space beyond your borders. That is all I can say of it at this time. But I assure all who will listen and participate that no matter what is to follow, you will be advised through your daily meditations of what actions *you* are to take. We will provide you with the safety of our daily communications if you are a God-committed worker who has opened your personality to your soul level through contemplation, meditation, and prayer.

The golden Christ energy is at your disposal and a part of my message regards the necessity for everyone on the planet to meditate every day without fail.

With peace as your only motive in living, you become peaceful on every occasion and through your example more of God's creations may be convinced of the emergency and join in our project for love and peace. Then we may bring more souls along with us on our rise into the fourth dimension, or that which you call heaven. Actually a part of you is in the higher place, plane or dimension now, but most people do not know or accept this truth and have no basis for understanding what is happening.

The third dimension, where you reside in your physical flesh, is denser in vibration and uses death as its termination of life experience. But you operate from the fourth, or higher, area through your intuition or soul knowing if your heart is open and your mind is dedicated to the living God. In the fourth dimension, no physical death is possible. This truth I showed by my resurrection nearly 2,000 years ago. What this means is that the God-nature in you has the capacity to move in many levels of growth and service whether your personality knows it or not. By awakening your personality to its highest awareness, however, growth is even swifter.

Because of the Creator's intention to raise your beautiful planet and its lifeforms into the fourth dimension, those of negative and evil ways will not be permitted access to this finer mansion. That is why it is so critical that you become the servants of light and lovers of God. In this awakened state of consciousness or knowing it will be impossible for the unloving to exist. For God is light and unless you are awakened there would be too much light and not enough darkness at your level of consciousness. Have you not been blinded sometimes by a light so bright you could not open your eyes to it? On a grander scale it is of this I speak.

Those who love can tolerate and use the light, bit by bit, as they become accustomed to its intensity. *Those who lack love cannot.* It is a physical actuality of which there is much proof if your scientists were open to comprehending it. Meanwhile, you may have to accept this truth based on your own inner knowing. That is what plagues this planet -- free will. For you are always open, then, to doubt. The "Show me" and "I don't believe it until I see it" are your doom. Not that you should automatically accept whatever is said, but you should be willing to create a system by which your human personality can find out the truth! And only through meditation is this feeling possible for most earth dwellers.

When you hear a statement you must use your inner knower, your teacher and guide, or Holy Spirit, to solicit the truth. What a comfort to know that God is available! But then you were told we would not leave you comfortless. Do you understand this means you have to build that light bridge from your physical to your spiritual self through prayer and meditation? It is in the silence with your soul, in the quiet with God, that your conscious awareness comes home.

The establishment of communication between your physical body, in the third dimension, and your greater "light" body, in the fourth dimension, is the link each of you must choose to make of your own volition. No one can do that for you. Unfortunately the human personality often goes astray by its refusal to meditate and draw close to its Source and never establishes a spiritual connection. I urge you to make this communication link possible for yourself through daily meditation as well as during one weekly group meditation wherein you share love and the information you receive with others. Support will be critical to you in the days ahead, I assure you. Would you not wish to have a higher communication link if your earthly systems of telephone, radio and TV become damaged or inoperative? But, beyond that, do you not wish heavenly guidance and love?

I wish to repeat for all to remember. You -- the citizens of earth -- hold peace or destruction in your minds and hearts. Unless a majority of you commit to this goal of peace and place every ounce of energy toward its accomplishment, the heavenly realms cannot ... by the Creator's instructions to us ... do it for you. We will assist totally, *but humanity must bear the results of its choices.*

Humankind may choose to hurt itself, but other lifeforms will not likely allow the hatred, violence and war to permeate beyond your boundaries into space which contains more life than your tiny minds and eyes can grasp. Be warned, then, that all weaponry which you allow your governments or military personnel to use against your own nations, Mother Earth, or in space, is a cause which will bring terrible effects. This cause and effect action is a universal principle by which you live. Therefore, choose in love; let love be your cause.

God's grace, or forgiveness, is not a free pass to do as you please without a change of heart intention. It is a pardon for past events and a new love awakening, a fresh attitude of joy and peace. It means our wills are joined for the Creator's purpose and glory. Therefore, forgive yourself and others and free the frozen energy that holds anger, fear and guilt in place. STOP THE WEAPONRY. SURRENDER THE ATTACK-AND-DEFEND POINT OF VIEW. TAKE SPIRITUAL COMMAND, LOVE CORPS, AND CHANGE THE NEGATIVE BELIEFS ON EARTH. LET LOVE GUIDE YOUR DESTINY. For you are the light of a new day, a new and Golden Age.

But, dear ones, you already know the truth. You were created in love and with wisdom. You were, and you are, the designated caretakers of the earth. This was the task that brought you here. As caretakers, caregivers, you came here to be God's love crop -- a universal orchard of joy and beauty even as the planet herself gives of her fair bounty.

By your fruits be known, then; it is harvest time.

Let us feast together on the shared splendor of unified love and peace. In the Great One's name I certify this common cause, this common spiritual venture, for all who select it. And with that immense power I touch your soul, rekindling your embered state of conscious awareness.

When your tiny heart expands to the greatness intended for it, and when your tiny mind expands to encompass the gigantic nature of life in God's many universes, you also will feel the love for each precious creation. Only as you expand your horizons even beyond the thing you love most dearly will you grasp a hint of the truth lying beyond your temporary blindness. Come. Receive the immense gift that awaits your awakening perception. Not only will your little soul grow, but in combination with the other awakening souls like yourself, you will build a firm foundation and sturdy bridge to traverse the dimensions and planes and purposes of creation.

Be willing in your heart and mind to leap forward, not to crawl in the mud any longer. Be willing to fly and reach areas of experience that this new intention and strong commitment bring.

Beloved of God, remember your identity. Be the caretakers of the planet and then -- one day -- of the starlife beyond. Sense your origin as the light, as universal love, and make that reality your very own.

You were given the opportunity to serve long ago and time has wended its weary, violent way into the present moment -- the now of your experience. Will you settle for this imprisonment among your limited desires and attachment to illusions? Illusions which trap your consciousness into continued powerlessness and depression?

You have a saying upon the planet ... "Now is the hour." Beloved of the one family ... your hour is *now!* Step forth from your death chamber and taste the providence of light, dear ones.

A divine and glorious world needs your presence. Hear God's clarion call to move forward in that vast *Love Corps* needed to reclaim the planet for its holy birthright of peace.

Then receive your blessings as this love you share overcomes all negativity and thoughts of war forevermore.

Peace is possible by your example. Then let us march together in perfect union to achieve the purpose for which you came. In God's eternal name let this mighty achievement reign on earth by your love and service.

Peace be yours.

Amen.

1994/1995 COMMENTS

As you clearly observe today, dear ones, there are still many wars and you have not achieved a permanent moratorium on underground hydrogen or nuclear explosions. Also, you have gone further into space without a spiritual discussion about why you are doing this and without committing to a DECLARATION OF RIGHTS AND RESPONSIBILITIES concerning your explorations and settlement intentions. Since April, 1994, you have been given higher vibratory frequencies of group consciousness to help examine your purposes and to design a pattern for earthly behavior that is consistent with your soul purposes as caretakers of the Earth, your solar system, and the galaxy beyond.

It is still incumbent upon you to heal yourselves of negativity like fear, hate, and greed lest you carry them aloft as baggage of communicable and deadly diseases. Then let love and wisdom lead your way, beloveds, as you stop the weaponry and heal your destructive tendencies. You are not only the caretakers of planet Earth, but since July, 1994, you were required by Archangel Michael to be more fully cognizant and nurturing in your solar system and galaxy, as well. Then know that all your teachers and guides are requiring your cooperation in recognizing and implementing your planetary, solar system and galactic relationships and responsibilities. Please meditate upon this and go forward to share the message, find the solutions and experience the joyful satisfactions.

I love you and support your willingness to be present-day disciples. Be happy in serving our Creator!

Chapter II

Who Are You?

Is there anyone alive who has never asked, "Who am I?" No! All of mankind asks, "Who am I?" And many remark, "Why is that question never answered for me? My entire life is lived in this constant query which whispers deep inside me, in some submerged identity, seeking to surface but somehow beyond my ability to hear or grasp."

"WHO AM I?" you repeat. "WHO AM I? What is this thing called life all about? What am I doing here anyway? Is it just some cosmic joke, a meaningless excursion of a few years duration in which I may do exactly what I want? Or is there truly a purpose I can know and accept which gives meaning to all of life? Something I can know is accurate?"

So your questions are the questions of all of human beings. These "Who am I? ... Why am I? ... Where am I? ... What is life all about?" questions must be answered by giving some structure in which this experience called life can be held. Otherwise, you feel lost and abandoned without hope and security. For what does humanity need more than anything in this present time but peace and the security of a future without war? The certainty that life goes on no matter what happens?

Because I am your World Teacher, I will attempt to give you enough cosmological information to place all of these questions into a believable context for the average technologically oriented mind to grasp. Surely you recognize it could not be told 2,000 years ago because humanity was ignorant, not ready.

Now if I am to be useful to you as your World Teacher, along with so many others who draw near the earth these days to assist mankind, I must stretch your imagination and get you to see a wider creation than what your little minds presently comprehend. For when I appeared on earth as that one called Jesus, humanity was totally ignorant of mechanical things and had no communication devices as you do today that could spread an understanding of what life is really all about.

Humanity, then, was ignorant beyond description and well-known as the dark planet of your solar system and your Universe. Little light existed and there was nothing of the mental understanding I could use to explain the working of God's twelve universes. And so my examples and illustrations were all given simply to open the human heart to God -- to love -- and to the necessity for peace above all, which is the highest form of love, is it not?

What could I say to a simple person about the workings of not one, but twelve universes? Or about twelve living planets and their lifeforms, each as a separate aspect of God's purpose in this solar system? And so I chose examples that would remain in the subconscious mind to be understood later -- and I chose TWELVE disciples to represent the characteristics of God which humanity must learn and balance. There is always symbology in the race consciousness as it moves into higher levels of growth.

Humanity is limited now, but it once used this earth as a mighty and glorious residence of immense beauty and love. Now see it as we see it. A place of darkness of the Spirit! A place of war and hatred! A place where humanity has allowed its own fears to be expressed through military and governmental leaders who take fear, ignorance, and evil out to hurt your own living Mother Earth -- and then into space where you endanger other beings you cannot see but who also have life and eternal relationship in the great Oneness of all creation.

You were babes, indeed, and I could only hint, two thousand years ago, to that morass of the unawakened, about your former greatness and spiritual evolution -- out from, and back to, the

Creator. I could speak only to you as the adult member of its family speaks to a cooing infant.

Now that you are beginning to crawl, however, I have a reverse problem. For now you have crawled into the scientific and technological arena without the proper love nature required before it is safe to explore such information. Your mechanization has outdistanced your soul! You are like an armed bomb ready to detonate by the next great negative thought.

Oh, you are probably saying, "I am not like that. I pay my taxes and go to work every day and tithe to the church and do good deeds. No, I am not responsible for the events of earth or even of the government of this place where I live." Truly do you deceive yourself. For if love and goodness prevailed, how then are your world events the way they are and why have you sent so much evil out into space? Know I am called upon by many other planetary officials of your own solar system, and a variety of other beings having residence in your Milky Way galaxy, to tell you to cease this flagrant abuse of space. Space is protected by galactic law.

Please hear that I am not trying to paralyze you with guilt, for the limitation it brings emotionally does not assist you in making forward progress. But, I share these facts that you may *immediately* implement an upgrading of your own behavior and share your concern in outspoken commitment. This is the time to *be* peace, but also the time to share it, for only by the sharing and multiplication of energy into a beautiful thought will the negative band of blackness in Mother Earth's emotional body be cleansed. You have soiled your dwelling place and must reverse that action. For she, like you, has physical, emotional, mental, and spiritual energy layers and is a massive reflection of your input to her. Since you are a cell in her body, be sure your influence is one of deep love, respect, and appreciation for each unique beautiful thing she nurtures upon her body, upon her surface.

Whether you believe it or not, each planet is just as alive as you and is a great being of light and wisdom. You and your scientists must one day accept this truth for it is your ignorance about life that allows the weaponry used beyond your borders where earth's subtle bodies -- nonphysical essence -- are violated. No sane people would annoy, aggravate, or injure any part of their mother, the land of their own existence, but this is what you do. Where will you be without her for your sustenance? Beware you grasp these words, dear ones. Your lives depend on it. You must be the *caretakers* of the earth, the cooperative protectors of space! For this you were created.

Now that I have come to share the truth, will you honor my willingness to ease your confusion by really listening? Will you open your heart and listen with the soul intention to gain a deep clarity of who and what you are? Let us see as I give you this information.

The part of your holy book, called the Old Testament, refers to a time of the beginning but gives you no scientific explanation about it. Yet there is a sense in you that there has been a beginning of some kind. That is why the question torments you -- for it is as if you feel the answer is there, just a hidden thought away. (Hindu teachings are more useful about this than the Jewish and Christian religions, of course.)

Close your eyes a moment and take several deep breaths before we proceed. Listen carefully. A few may know of these things in a different perspective, but that matters not to anyone with a truly open mind and heart, for there was a beginning, and there is a present opportunity for humanity's advancement in the Universe. Upon this opportunity I focus now.

How would you explain to a baby that it was created by an omnipotent power of such magnitude that there could be a birth of Spirit, or life energy, anytime it chose to visualize what it wanted and then energize this thought with the power of a million suns? I will try not to use mathematical formulas here except to say the number is beyond your calculation and comprehension at this time, but perhaps you glimpse a sense of its magnitude by trying to look at the one sun around which your tiny planet earth rotates. You did not make the sun you see, nor the stars, luminaries and planetary bodies. But the Source did. Ask yourself, "If I did not create all that I see of beauty around me on this planet, then who or what did?"

God did, if that is a word you can grasp with any pure meaning -- the Creator-of-All did. It is a force so powerful that your languages cannot describe it! Therefore, sense its tremendous magnitude in your heart and let us go on from there as I invite you into knowledge that few on earth have heard before. The power of electricity and solar energy and radio and air flight and TV were always there, but you have only recently understood such principles. Is this not true? Then realize how ignorant humanity is and be still within so you can learn further truth.

Those who listen will have much revealed in meditation and will acquire great peace of mind, will trust in what lies beyond earth, and will make an easy journey back along the steps prepared for each soul who chooses to accept the gift already given to humanity. It is through the transformation of your little consciousness into a greater reality and attunement with this great power that you grow and advance upon the earth and within the solar system in which Mother Earth dwells.

Within your earthly Bible is the statement that "Ye must become like little children to enter the kingdom of heaven." That is true merely because children are open to learning whereas most adult earth dwellers are puffed up with self-importance based upon the fact that your society says they have studied and are therefore knowledgeable; they are the so-called experts of it all. In fact, very few such experts, especially in the areas of what you call science, know much at all. Historians are even harder pressed to fit together pieces of a puzzle that clearly lack a majority of the pieces. How, then, can such incomplete evidence be examined and explained by those who believe they understand it?

How can a geologist explain the face of the earth with present evidence, except to call it speculation, when many parts of the earth have gone under water, or under mountain upheavals?

Through meditation the silent secrets can be given and their pieces put together from the basis of where it all began. You can scarcely travel from one destination to another if you lack the understanding of both locations. And that is what your earth faces today in what you call education. You do not know where you have come from nor where you go.

The irony of it all is that rather than admit you do not know, the experts continue to parade their half-truths in the name of education and go unchallenged in their judgments. It is wise to ask the experts with what premise they started and how they know they have arrived. Most of all ask if they have reverence and respect for God. Judgment and the belief you know all about life only ruins you. Give up your own petty understandings and ask for truth to be free.

Your so-called scientists do not grasp that your solar system's sun was breathed into its place about 218,000,000,000 years ago and that it took nearly one million years before it was made habitable by the highly refined light energies of the great beings who run this solar system. These energies, which your language has no words for, are as light furnaces in their creative nature and would dissolve you. Because of the higher vibration and nature of their light, the sun is their natural habitation. Your tiny, frail flesh would die there. That is why I said you had to go through The Christ to know God, for God's power would unintentionally, but immediately, kill your body. Does this make sense?

Now in your Universe, the twelfth, there are twelve different solar systems with a total of 1,900,000, or nearly two million planets, busily using the energy of God. Each solar system has its own centralized power source (Solar Logos) and the individual twelve rays of sound and light spectra not understood on earth. These rays are great beings of immense power themselves, each representing a particular aspect or facet of God which life in the solar system is to develop and bring into balance. Each of these color streams of energy controls a certain aspect of creativity or influence. Thus, here on earth, you are on a unique planet, a second ray planet -- and the focus of the rays is especially for love and wisdom. It was for this that planet earth was created, and it is only this which each soul living on her is to perfect.

If you will use the ever flowing rays to strengthen God's purpose in you, the planet will rise into the heavenly realm by natural causes. But if humanity insists on ignoring the rays of love and wisdom or uses its *free will* in the wrong way, then earth will have to be cleansed of that negative use of the ray energies one way or another. Which is why I tell you that the separation of loving and unloving souls will soon occur. For as the power of the many spiritual energies assist at this time in bringing the love/wisdom rays into perfection, all those souls who do not flow with its power will be unable to bear the change in their physical and subtle bodies.

You are being infused with the rays and the light of God, dear ones, as soul fuel or food, and unless your heart is open to love, you cannot bear the intensity and magnitude of their nature. Only the children of light will know what is happening and be able to utilize the love/wisdom rays properly during the cleansing soon upon you. So use your free will wisely.

Since it is impossible for most of you to see energy in its higher vibrations, you are blind to the majesty and power of your Universe and the realms who would help you. Only a few clairvoyant people can see what I speak of. These clairvoyants must be treated with respect for their powers which one day will be the ability of all humanity once again. At the time of the fall, or separation, this loss of true or inner vision occurred.

This inability to see the higher vibrations of light causes you much pain, for you look only at the physical in all you do. You do not see that matter is only the end result of a higher power, not the beginning or the main reality. Be willing, then, to acknowledge that you are limited and ask always that the higher forms of subtle life be made manifest to you, so you do not destroy earth and space through this unfortunate ignorance and blindness. Soon the awakened children of light will move ahead into these higher realms and if you are sincere you will be assisted in that process. Remember in the meantime, however, to acknowledge that you are ignorant, for this ignorance has caused your present blunderings and bumblings on earth and in space.

In answer to your questions about who and what you are, then, grasp that you are light and energy because that is what God is. Consequently you have always been alive as a spiritual creation. ALWAYS. Therefore, at the soul level you are an immense collective mass of energy in identity. You are ageless and eternal. You are vast beyond description since you were created in the beginning and have temporarily come over the bridge from infinity into your present physical form.

In your limited perception here in the third dimension of consciousness you cannot remember this generally, but you contain all the truth you will ever need. And because of your original identity you are capable of unlimited understanding and knowledge about yourself, about this earth you call home, and those so-called invisible or unseen dimensions that are but a thought away.

This great "spiritual you" has existed in many experiences before your present life and, therefore, brings here not only a dynamic drive to learn but also prior training, as it were, to assist you in your current existence in matter. So do not think you are weak and helpless and ignorant! Not when you have this higher Spirit or self to feed you, not when you have assistance and truth as you live each day on the planet. Remember always that you have an intrinsic identity as light and energy, but you must acknowledge this identity and then ask for its assistance. That is the key. This wiser you, massive in its abilities, can only keep in touch with you through your recognition and acknowledgment. "Seek and you will find" is not an idle comment I assure you! Nor is "Ask and it will be given."

In this current time of awakening, much of each soul's prior experience and glory will be released to Love Corps participants. This is a gift to those who serve the light.

Who are you? You are a spiritual reality living in a physical body because it benefits your soul experience to do so. And in the vast mind of God, the source of us all, a plan for many souls to expand in the qualities of love and devotion was offered you. You accepted this opportunity for growth and expansion because that is the nature of God ... for by its division into many parts it moves ever outward and achieves greater power and wisdom as it does. God and you are working together for the good of all, stretching farther and farther into distant regions of consciousness and love. An exciting and noble purpose, is it not?

So, then, you live on a planet called earth which would provide you with the greatest challenge to grow and learn and to realize that your mind is the creator or architect or builder of whatever appears in the physical world you now call home. You came to learn and your soul chose this time and place to help you develop your own personal soul evolution and the evolution of the human family. You picked it, as you would select a course of study, knowing that the evolution of the earth herself would be part of your, and her, learning process.

This was a deliberate choice not some accident of a fierce and cruel God. For you have always existed and always will exist. Therefore, what else are you about but learning and loving? Do you really think the soul remains idle for all of eternity? Even as you sit in the limitations of a physical body does this temporary existence make sense? Surely life is ongoing action. Only death brings an awareness of the transformation of life. For you are forever and ever alive. Wise you are, as well. And wiser do you grow. This growth in love and wisdom is the promise I came to bring, dear ones, and you are not alone in the process. Many of us came together in true brother and sisterhood. In a mass family opportunity we linked minds and purpose to touch the earth, feel the Sun, see the handiwork of the great God in physical density.

Many persons ask themselves, "But why would I do that? What purpose does it serve to have a body anyhow?" It is good to ask this question. And to help answer it, I will ask you if you have ever looked in a mirror? If you have, you notice that it reflects whatever is before it. Thus you can look at the reality being presented. Physical form is like a mirror for your soul, which intends to bring pure motive and intention into the personality. Since Spirit must penetrate the mental and emotional filters of each human being in order to do this, any barriers caused by ignorance and misqualified information bring distortions which create pain. To identify these distortions and dissolve them from the personality is the purpose of your physical body. It mirrors what you think, how you judge, and your many attitudes about life. You have the body as a mirror of the soul so that you can see what false beliefs you hold and get rid of them. It is a "mind over matter" suit, and its health and your life affairs are your constant progress report!

The reason you need to bear the consequences of your own cause, or thoughts from your mind, is that the Universe in which you dwell is mental and is structured on twelve certain laws, one of which is cause and effect. What is created in mind is the cause, and that which is experienced in the body is an effect. Unfortunately many personalities do not recognize their responsibilities and constantly feel victimized by life, or by God, for what happens. But I confide that while there are great beings of love and wisdom who direct the destiny of this planet from what you might call higher or inner dimensions, you are here to learn to use that mind power purely when you are again out of the body.

Please think of us in heaven as a compassionate energy or light which supplies guidance and inspiration to you while you are in this process. Thus, you are never alone, day or night, sleeping or awake, if you choose to have us assist in your expansion and perfection. And as you invite God or the angels or any great spiritual master or teacher into your thought, you choose to connect with a wondrous power. This connection moves you quickly and wisely through the experiences of balance and imbalance that exist here on planet earth to help you learn the control of mind. For if you were to be given a high

task in the Universe to create on behalf of God, your tiny
untrained mind would create havoc, as it does in your own life
now. This learning to use mind energy in only a positive way is
critical if you are to grow and serve yourself, humanity, the
planet, and God in reverence and devotion.

How many prayers have come to me saying, "Help me! Help
me!" Yet when we of the greater knowing come to you with
ways to grow and release your limitations and expectations of
how the world should be, you will not follow our suggestions
and then your life continues in its misery and woe, its fear,
anger, and war. What do you gain from asking for help if you
will not follow the very prescriptions we give for understanding
life's events and surrendering to the lessons they contain? For
the answer is always the same and will always be the same.
Love. Purity of thought and action. When the mind obeys the
soul in these matters, it grows and advances into even higher
levels of usefulness to itself and all of life.

Therefore, understand that the things of this earth which you
call evil or negative such as hunger or war or disease are here to
train you in the ways you view these and respond to them, for
each soul may be on a different level of perfect mind usage and
these experiences teach bold and oftentimes painful lessons
which will NEVER be forgotten. In this way these famines and
horrors serve humanity, for they bring separated attitudes and
beliefs into focus on identical issues, providing a common
curriculum or teaching outline for love and peace. You are here
to demonstrate self-mastery in the use of your mind and its
thoughts or you would not be on the planet at this time. Therefore this is an opportunity which serves a higher purpose than
your tiny human personality may realize.

It may be difficult to see these events as valuable, as helping
you to recognize balance from imbalance, love from fear. Surely you can see that it is difficult to appreciate freedom unless you
have been imprisoned or health unless you have been ill. Yet
through these various opportunities you grow toward perfection.

Perception or clarity of mind sets you free and earns graduation into greater realms of understanding.

But you always have two factors to make the task easier and more productive to the soul. First, you have a mind that can be trained to give up all personality judgments and achieve only positive responses to whatever happens in the world. Or at least, it can accept that there is a plan and that if love is given in each circumstance the result will bring peace.

Secondly, you are not alone in this temporary existence unless you choose to be. There is never a time when the infusion of our power and love and guidance is denied you. But should there be an earthquake, for example, it may be impossible for us to get through your self-focused activities which are dearer to you than meditating and finding time to attune yourself to the helping frequency we would use.

How many times in your life has your own soul called out to your personality in warning about some activity or decision that is not loving, not appropriate, and can only return you misery? How many times have your personal and specifically assigned guides (whether you call them angels or not) tried to whisper suggestions but you were too preoccupied to listen? How many times have the spiritual teachers come into this barbaric negative mortality to remind you of who you are and why you are here, only to be ignored, misunderstood, or deified into a meaningless ritual where the inner teacher of each person is quickly forgotten or never acknowledged as the key to freedom and joy?

I will ask no more questions about this but remember that your answers will have to be shared one day from your own soul to its teachers. Even I, the Christed One, had many teachers and lessons when I walked upon this tiny planet earth. And it was all part of the Father/Mother's plan so that I could better serve humanity from a place of common experience.

This living planet, which is often ignorantly referred to as a rock riding through space, is also part of God's plan for growth and service; for just as you have inner feelings and mental and spiritual aspects, so does she. And in many ways you, the human family, and she, the mother or home of you all, work together to extend life and love in broader and purer ways. Never doubt she has her own destiny and never attack her or you will attack the feminine nurturer within yourself. This is so critical that I say it many times. What you do to any other living thing must result in your own experience of it. And this applies to the mineral kingdom, the plant and animal kingdom, to humanity and yourself, to the higher life forces who are alive in physical form in space, and to all invisible or unseen energies that abound throughout creation.

Will you accept, dear ones, that there is great opportunity here in this place of balance and imbalance, this world which reflects what you think? We of heaven realize that if you do not understand the purpose and do not follow the rules, you will suffer pain. Yet through your errors you will gain; for love is the balm for all wounds, and healing is the result you first acquire and then offer others.

Many of your holy books and written scriptures tell you that there is an omniscient, omnipresent, and ever expanding force, source, or energy which is called by many names in many languages. "God" will do. Most of these teachings say that this God constantly moves and grows, gaining further power with the development of each being that is a smaller part of the whole. Even your physicists begin to grasp the potential of this concept as they explore the secrets contained in the ether.

Space contains a myriad of lifeforms mostly unknown to you in your extremely limited definition of life. Be cautious how you treat space, and move ever so slowly as if you were in a darkened room filled with precious breakable objects which you must not injure. Part of space contains the extended life energy fields of your own Mother Earth and she suffers from your space vehicles and weaponry as it blasts through her invisible energy fields.

Beware where you step in thought and in form. For is not a flower a star? And is not a star an atom of God just as you are? Be still and listen. Those who do will hear the symphony of stars yet unborn and the truth of God manifesting in directions and ways you cannot presently imagine. Sound, heat, light and color energy rays are everywhere present moving unrestrictedly from lighter, higher energy to denser forms. As you learn about these energies, you can earn your place among those who will respect and honor them. Yes, you must be willing to say, "Teach me! Teach me love and wisdom."

With this humble request and honorable intention called reverence, you can then be taught as you meditate daily. In the silence you have softer brain waves or mental reception through which we can reach you, both alone and in groups, where the combined power allows a greater influx of love energies and healing for all.

The vital impression I wish to impart here is that earth is a very small planet physically, and is part of a solar system *family* from whom all are fed by the sun's life energy even as you place food in your mouth for the assimilation, digestion, and elimination process to be completed in a healthy manner. There are those who laugh at the sun worshippers of long ago, but their clarity of devotion surpasses your own. For who would not extend appreciation to a group of God creations, or beings, who by their love and willingness feed and fuel the life force of your solar system, earth and yourself without ceasing?

Your two greatest difficulties are free will -- and, therefore, doubt -- and your lack of appreciation for the gift of life and sustaining support to earth. It is wise to be reverent, for a lack of reverence detracts from your spiritual growth. Do not ignore devotion; do not doubt God! For the doubter who denies the truth becomes an unloving soul with no appreciation for anything given from the Creator and the other creative energies in their continuing process to make you whole again. Without their love and caring there is no hope planet earth's population will return in remembrance and commitment to the relationship originally intended by that Central Being.

While I can share this brief overview of the immense Universe in which you have a tiny part, unless you can feel and appreciate it, the information will do nothing to aid humanity's restoration to its former place of wisdom and love. For once the earth glowed with an etheric light of such beauty that she was known as the jewel of this quadrant of the Universe. Will you help regain her former position?

To grasp some sense of what I share, please take time on a clear-skied evening and just sit and watch all that you see above. Every twinkle of light represents an immense number of life-forms -- into the billions, even as earth contains such. Know that the governmental body, the Milky Way galaxy, is the home-land of many great beings, luminaries, energies, and vibrations who have their residence there and who have profound spiritual effect upon planet earth.

Most important to remember is that some souls chose to come to earth in a mass immigration plan, in a spirit body, to begin this newly made planet about eight million years ago. The inten-tion was to make it a wonderful learning place within this solar system and this galaxy, a place where love and wisdom would reach a high plane of expression. So you are not here by acci-dent nor were you always in this dense form which now encases your soul in physical flesh.

Most religions speak of a separation or fall in humanity's past, and so there is much I could share about this sinking of consciousness into its present pitiable condition. To avoid guilt, however, is my goal, for it freezes your ability to change and move forward. Therefore, let me just remark that what is gone is gone. Whether you are a fallen angel, rescuer of fallen angels, children of these angels, a visitor from some other starseed or merely an unlearned or lightless soul, *you are needed!* Mankind's future depends in large part upon your commitment to have peace and nothing but peace. Let this be our common purpose and opportunity regardless of past history.

I say once again that eons ago when the planet was given life, the goal was for this new creation to rise in glory. As a glowing beacon, she was to exemplify a creation who would honor its Source in true adoration and love but with a developing wisdom as well. Thereby those of the galaxy who were not yet given the capacity for heart love could see it demonstrated in matter for them to emulate. For I tell you some beings of this galaxy desperately need an example of love, a model of love, to follow.

In this earth experiment for all souls to grow in love and wisdom I must gently ask you to evaluate how you think humanity is doing at this hour. Is your present civilization a prototype which you would give other members of God's creation as a sample of how to love with the heart? For they already overshadow your mental capability and primitive scientific and technological information. But until now these great mental learners have focused almost entirely on the intellectual aspect of life and no other.

You of earth, who were intended to become the pattern which extends love to these mental beings, have much to learn from these other ones but also much to teach of the feeling nature of mortality. You can teach how to love God totally while sealed in a fleshly body. Perhaps you could be described as energy living in matter remembering itself as that greater love identity. But however you explain this, be assured that this was the plan undertaken nearly eight million years ago here by the spiritual and etheric realms, from which some of you emerged and are a part.

Some souls volunteered to be here until the plan was achieved and earth was in concert with the other planets in both the solar system and the galaxy as that place where the demonstration of love of God and all lifeforms could be witnessed and experienced. The graduates could then go forth to teach others and practice what they themselves had learned. You must ask how you are doing in that experiment. And in that answer and evaluation -- not from a wish to be guilty or burdened with the crushing awareness of failure -- you must bring forth a new recognition of what must change if this noble purpose is yet to be fulfilled.

Let each person on earth acknowledge that *behavior is the test of knowing*. How are you behaving? What have you learned, citizen of earth, that you would share with your own human family on earth? And what it is you would teach the rest of this galaxy's lifeforms about LOVE? Certainly those who teach love and peace will learn more about their subject but they must have some basic proficiency first.

Imagine, if you will, that you are a member of another branch of God's creation seeded into the same galaxy alongside this small solar system in which earth resides. If you were such, would you wish to meet the present day earthlings as your model of peace, as your loving neighbors? Very likely you will think of a few individuals who could be used as ambassadors of peace because of their gentle nature and love quality. But what of the rest? And which group do you personally fit into?

I come to tell you that your soul's desire is to have love and peace and to share these not only on this planet but in the solar system, and beyond. There are life energies you cannot even presently see, except as they temporarily materialize on occasional monitoring and reconnaissance visitations. Your present assaults on your own earth's invisible energy fields -- and upon those brothers and sisters in space -- have made you suspect indeed. If the situation were reversed and you were the technically superior, might you not also watch earth with suspicion, as it spews forth killer satellites and threatens other lifeforms with nuclear blasts and plans to deliver even greater destructive weaponry as its calling card in the Universe?

My heart is heavy in the telling of such a tale. It seems a nightmare better left unspoken. Yet your opportunity for an intended divinity must be brought to you for your examination in the hope that you will hear, and remember, and return to earth's original focus. As your World Teacher I must make this attempt to change the abysmal reputation earth has gained, for it was exquisite for a million years before the spiritual fall into density. Can you hear me? Is there a response to what I ask?

I say to you all that it is my intention to lead the earth onward to her original purpose and usefulness to God. EARTH WILL RISE INTO HER FORMER GLORY AND ALL SOULS ARE

REQUIRED TO CHOOSE THEIR PATH AS PART OF THIS ASCENSION NOW.

Some who read and ponder this will be joyful in the remembrance that forgiveness has been granted for all the past errors and will choose to combine energies with others like themselves who are dedicated and committed to this task of love/wisdom teaching. There will be those who scoff and laugh. Many will deny. This can only bring a harsher lesson to be soulfully experienced at a later time. But for those who will focus on the love and wisdom aspects of human life and practice it to the highest state possible, the future looms nearer to God, and to us, the higher beings of light who offer to teach you spiritual mastery. It will also bring you closer to those lifeforms from other residences and homelands in this solar system and beyond, who seek at heaven's request to assist us in whatever ways may be necessary.

Yes, there is a legion of volunteers ready to help earth's rebirth, and humanity's awakening. This legion will be used by those of us in the spiritual realms in case earth's experiment goes astray due to nuclear disaster -- or by a response from the earth herself to eliminate humanity's accumulated violence and negative emotions.

To those who may scoff, laugh, deny, and otherwise doubt what has been said, let me speak now about the nature of doubt and how it affects humanity, for doubt is truly a great enemy and the most deleterious of attitudes to hold. To doubt is spiritually fatal, for in the refusal to keep an open mind, all perish. The soul is stymied. The life is wasted. If you knew how many souls on earth at the present time doubt everything, you would know why this is called a dark planet.

Spirit is free, active, unlimited, and one with the Creator. Doubt keeps the Spirit's full expression locked into a tiny dark cell -- without breath to live -- all possibility of growth doomed. For it is only in your willingness to trust the unseen that you grow. Therefore, I say, cease your doubting! And let the wind of acceptance blow away the cobwebs of this illusion that you are something other than a creation of the living God.

Doubt is satanic. To listen to it is to close off your good as surely as if you had murdered yourself. It is suicidal for the Spirit. Doubt has retarded many human souls. Doubt is hell personified. It leaves no room for hope, no access to peace. Doubt is your inner enemy, and the enemy of all humanity, as well.

Doubt is created in your mind. Often it comes as a whisper, then a full blown denial. Finally it becomes a faithless rejection of good -- a rejection of the Creator. When this happens, its infectious nature controls the affairs of the race and they fall deeper and lower into the abyss of pain and suffering, which no light can penetrate. I say that doubt is your nemesis and the major foe of your time.

The effect, or punishment, for doubting is brought into your life by your own mind, not by God. Let this be known and accepted. And this is the last time, for a thousand years, that doubt will be allowed to flourish on planet earth. After that time there will be no doubting souls left here. They will all have been removed. This is your future, children of the light. No more will you have to battle this hideous quality of infectious thought. So remain strong! Keep your faith high, and realize that in a few years the spiritual cleansing will remove those souls who will not now honor God or hear the inner voice for God. It should lighten your step to know that the exhausting battle will be over for the faithful and there will be a bright new tomorrow of peace and reverence.

Rest content that you know the meaning of faith, which is to trust the Creator to implement that Divine plan in the best way possible. Your ultimate act of faith is to accept a God most of you cannot personally see, except through your natural environment and in your daily activities of love, and to follow the evolutionary spiral of its design back to where you will be the true children of God again.

Faith requires you to follow the inner teacher, that spark of God given to you when your individual soul was created eons ago. This is why I have asked the faithful, or those who would learn of this love quality, to meditate daily and join with others in weekly meditation for healing the planet and all those upon it. For through this experience of listening you are fortified and can sense or remember who you truly are.

In these approaching times, you will be spiritually lost if you do not have God's inner voice at your disposal. Where will you be without this spiritual communication device in earth's emergencies? My heart cannot dwell on the thought of it because the fear and suffering will be great.

Have faith then. Be strengthened by your inner guidance which is the gift to all who ask and demonstrate their sincerity by meditation. You have my promise, as a resurrected Son of God, that you may sit silently and simply say, "Take my doubt, Father/Mother. I am willing to let my heart and soul be filled only with love and faith."

If you persist in this willingness and follow your meditations regularly, there is still time to rescue yourself, with the help of the heavenly realms, and to assist others in this awakening process. Or to continue growing if you have already begun to awaken.

I tell you, my beloveds, that you are worthy and capable of far more than you can imagine, for you are the created ones of a great and marvelous Source. You cannot imagine the magnificence that will yet be yours through devotion and service, but it is an exciting opportunity that we will undertake together in love, in the light of joy and peace.

Know that you will constantly be in the company of great souls and high teachers as this journey begins, and be not afraid of its outcome. You walk until you can fly. You fly until you become the light. One day your bodies of physical form will be like the one I showed you at the time of my resurrection, and beyond that it will become lighter and lighter still. To honor and use that spark of God-given identity *positively* is our major function. Individually and in unison we will do far greater things than can be explained today. But you can believe that there is no limitation in God's plan!

None.

What a gift to us all.

Truly if you have any sense of the grandeur of God it will be easy to serve and appreciate this great Source and give up the petty human kingdoms of fear, anger, guilt, pride, and greed that exist on this tiny speck of land in the vast ocean of creation.

I recommend again immediate action to begin, or continue, meditation for yourself *daily!* And to participate *weekly* in small meditation groups composed of family or friends. Hear the inner teacher when you have group decisions to be made. Remember the age of solution by consensus, by agreement, is here. Let your own life, your family's life, and the business or world of work be steered by this same inner guidance system. The smaller political units in your world can apply these truths, too, working together in the smooth machinery of love and common goals. Then the nations can be as one planetary expression.

This is my promise. Every soul who practices love as directed from the inner, higher self shall find a love work in the remaining years of this century and then shall return together to walk in the Golden Age with others like yourself. Take my hands, beloved. Opportunity beckons. The inexpressible joy of our mutual mission awaits.

Keep God's remembrance close in heart and mind as you continue the journey to rejoin your Creator once more. Let this very day begin your commitment to love God more fully and to give up all doubt. I assure you that any sincere request to change doubt to faith will be heard and supported by those of us who love you. We will absolutely support your relinquishment of doubt and irreverence. Take another's hand in peace to diminish doubt for you cannot return to us empty-handed, empty-hearted.

I, the Jesus of a bygone day, have proffered this reminder so that you and all mankind can be returned to the fullness of God's intended creation. If you have stumbled or fallen use my love, and the love of all of heaven, to be supported and lifted up again to full stature as a forgiven soul made new, made pure. Truly you are the unsullied, innocent light if you wish to awaken to it. Be willing to remember your forgotten spiritual estate, and let the purifying rainfall of your sorrow and regret flow out with cleansing tears that refresh the thirsty soil of your soul. See the slate washed away by the silver-gold healing of a cancelled past. This is a time of new beginnings for the negative or unawakened. Come forward! This is a time of sweet return to your true identity for all of humanity who choose it.

But only you hold the power to make that decision, beloveds; I can only guide you with my recommendations and the support of heaven's hosts. The saints, angels, guides, sages, gurus, avatars, masters, adepts, and lords of all places and dimensions also stand beside you.

Receive encouragement and even praise today, in a renewed attitude of greater purpose, for the insidious disease called doubt lies in the strongest of you and needs to be released totally.

Give reverence to receive self-respect, love and peace. In reverence and humility a soul's errors can be easily forgiven and transmuted. Then give all reverence to the Creator, exchange faith for doubt, and thrill to the newness of a clean start. For who among you does not carry lingering memories of regret, remorse and recrimination against self and others?

Have your own definitions and judgments of life brought earth her glory and your own deep soul satisfactions?

NO! Which is why we call you to the Love Corps.

Then surrender your doubt and judgments and let us assist humanity in its planned ascension. Your time is here. Your time is now. Use it well.

Peace to all from that Great One whose loving mind and heart has brought you forth into light and life, and also from your brothers and sisters in spiritual dimensions.

We encourage you and eternally support your efforts to come home in consciousness to that magnificent Creator of love and peace called God.

To all of you, amen and amen.

1994/1995 COMMENTS

In evaluating who you really are today, and how you have changed in the past eight or nine years, I can can state unequivocally that we can see the growth and improvement your efforts have brought in your awareness. You are already experiencing a higher level of interest in metaphysical subjects such as angels, near-death episodes, Star Trek-type beings in space, and many materials concerned with healing on physical, mental and emotional levels. Humanity also has a greater knowledge about the cellular composition of the DNA codes and how they may be physically changed or engineered . . . and even some knowledge as to how your single, mutant DNA helix pair is beginning to change back toward the six pair you once had, and need to have. You need to have this knowledge and change in order to live in the full 12-helix spiritual consciousness or the condition called enlightenment.

This awareness has caused a major identity crisis because your genetic shift demands the release of linear time, of certain physical problems in the body, release of many emotional feelings held deep in the unconscious storage level, and release of those unexamined mental attitudes and beliefs that define the actions and behaviors of your everyday life pattern. Then in brief, you have to let go of nearly everything you've learned that opposes your true soul identity as a light being in service to your Creator's plan for the advancement of planet Earth! No small task, beloveds, but one you will accomplish with the support of these many extraordinary spiritual frequencies and light waves that bathe you in the second coming of cosmic wisdom and love.

Waves of meta cell influences some call God consciousness, or photon energies, are affecting all of space in this galaxy! Indeed, as this enormous meta cell's identity and intention of high consciousness come from what you call the angelic realms, linear time is vanishing as you move into higher realms and dimensions. Along with that time shift, linear thinking is also vanishing and tomorrow can only be based on the now of this very moment. This shift in linear time and linear thinking makes it easier for those with spiritual willingness to increase their power of manifestation and their ability to see and experience things that are inspirational in nature and content. This is, indeed, a second coming, my brothers and sisters, which has been long promised you, but is dependent—as I have so often said—upon your personal choice, your willing acceptance of it. We are here, as I modeled in my earth life long ago, to offer ascension without the necessity of physical death. To offer grace. To offer resurrection without death, but not with the crucifixion aspect I experienced.

Because linear time and thinking are vanishing, group manifested power can be nearly instantaneous if strong emotional desire accompanies clear mental focus and high spiritual intention. As time shifts into a higher reality and illusions fade, duality must end, especially within your own beingness where the conscious and unconscious parts of your own polarized self are vying for control. You are a beautiful essence presently enclosed in the trappings of flesh living in a play of life which demands you choose one of two directions. Love or fear. Peace or war.

Indeed, the answer to your question "who am I?" was given when the Creator birthed your soul with that sense of love and caring which is the natural inheritance of the human species. All you need do is remember, appreciate, and express that essence, beloveds. This is the cosmic commandment everywhere.

May the Creator's blessings be yours forever. Adonai.

Chapter III

My Purpose on the Planet

In the historical epoch prior to my birth on the planet earth, the spiritual hierarchy and the Essene community of the Hebrew faith had already prepared the necessary channels for my birth as Jesus in the physical world. My parentage had been selected, my life blueprint was set in motion, and the events which later Christians would incorporate in their belief system began. It seemed, for a short time, the attention of the Middle East was focused upon one infant, one birth, one bringer of light and love.

Yet, my beloved brothers and sisters, I beg you to understand that this was not an isolated event but rather one moment in the chronology of teachings brought to the planet earth by many high or angelic teachers. And although the Christian Bible has not acknowledged this, it was neither the first teaching nor was it the highest teaching. For later in this new epoch ahead of us, called the Aquarian or Golden Age, the highest teachings will be brought forward even as I introduce the theme of it to you presently.

In order to understand the coming of Jesus into the physical world 2,000 years ago you must know that there was much darkness, misery, and negativity in the human heart -- so much so that unless it were cleansed, the entire spiritual evolution of much of humankind might have been permanently lost. I repeat -- *permanently lost* -- to emphasize that in the heavenly realms there was much concern about humanity's ability to return lovingly to the Creator. There was concern that humanity had forgotten God was inside them as an internal experience, not just an *external* identity only.

The divine inspiration to heal the human heart through love and forgiveness had to be instituted before any further evolutionary opportunities could be made available. The awakening had to be seeded. So there needed to be a prophet or messenger who would remind each soul of its eternal identity, its responsibility to love God above all things and then its brothers and sisters as itself. I will say to you that this was no easy task! For the negativity of human thoughts over eons of time had to be penetrated and overcome by that one who entered onto the earth.

Other great ones had penetrated this veil of darkness, ignorance and evil, every four to seven hundred years in one way or another, somewhere on the planet. Yet this final penetration was a desperate and urgent commitment on the part of The Christ -- that one beloved of the Father/Mother -- who would not abandon those who prayed for help.

From the heavenly realms where The Christ looked down, it seemed impossible to penetrate such lack of love and such egotistical personalities desiring power over each other without God's light. I share in humility and love that there were few spiritual volunteers at that time to come to human beings with one last opportunity to cleanse their hearts and return them to the memory of the God within. Many teachers have been here, as you know. Most have been mistreated, abused, defiled, ignored or rejected. That is why on this earth today you have separate groups of religious beliefs brought to you at varying times. Each teacher brought the message of the good word, with the promise of redemption if you would turn within and listen to the soul voice given you at the time of creation.

My task was to mentally overcome the evil and lack of love, the hatred and the fear of humanity, and I say to you in sincerity and without hesitation, that had the personality called Jesus not loved you with the love of the Creator, I could never have stood upon this earth and overcome the negative thoughts that were here. Without that love there would have been no hope of success. Without that deep commitment from the light and the God within, Jesus could not have brought you the message of love and forgiveness that many longed to hear -- the message of the Father/Mother's plan for the Golden Age on earth.

You must understand that when I walked upon this free will planet as Jesus, my desire to inspire love did not prevent the evil thoughts of human beings or their acts of violence, their perpetrations of faithless living. Your history books, before and since the coming of Jesus, will remind you in the most obvious ways that although this planet is a beautiful creation, it is peopled by a darkness whose continuing presence here cannot be allowed. My message approximately 2,000 years ago to mankind was simply this. You were created by a force or power beyond your comprehension, a spark of which resides inside of you available at any time to guide you, protect you, and lead you ever upward from where you came -- to your home in light, love, and peace. This journey of Spirit awakening in the flesh was at its deepest ebb, and in heaven there was concern that this project on the planet to create a people of balanced love and wisdom had failed.

Please understand that my appearance as Jesus was chronologically timed to give humanity the example of love and forgiveness so badly needed here. It was also a response of my heart, my overwhelming desire not to leave you comfortless, not to abandon you in your faith. For there are on this planet today a small percentage of believers who have, from the moment of time and through experience along their way, gained in the light, practiced the love and ministered the truth.

It was to these light workers' calls that I returned once again to support them, forming a vast union of loving hands, hearts and minds from the regions of China to the tip of Africa, from the North to the South Pole, and around the globe in all directions. As a shepherd gathering a flock, these lights could be seen and identified by the heavenly realms and contacts made through the inner teacher's voice which is in every being who chooses to use it. Knowing that there would be these little light centers, soul points, shining in the darkness scattered around the globe, Jesus came.

I regret that the teachings I brought 2,000 years ago have not been understood or followed as they were intended. I will later speak of the necessity for the churches and institutions as you know them to analyze themselves and to take this last opportunity to divest themselves of the need for self-aggrandizement and power. They must cooperate with all teachers of light, including myself, who remind you that the only purpose of a minister or spiritual teacher is to model love. Thus they introduce the concept of turning within so the inner spark of God can blaze brighter in each person. All else follows this.

My mission, therefore, was to collect every soul who had ever believed in the God/Creator, who practiced love over evil, who willingly cared for others during the last 250,000 years ... and to remind them they would be given an opportunity to demonstrate self-mastery by the year 2000 A.D.! Now, I remind you who listen that, by the end of the twentieth century, you can achieve self-mastery and be eligible for a still higher experience in the Golden Age. Since I am presently the World Teacher -- having been given that office by my willingness to come among my brothers and sisters with a final offer of love and forgiveness -- you can trust the intent of my message. Listen, please, with your *heart* and your *soul.*

I came to you as the model of a body apparently crucified but able to have a continuing life experience after death. This is what the resurrection proved. Life continues. Resurrection is a symbol of dying to the old and awakening to the new. It means this is true for your ideas and beliefs, not just your fleshly body. Therefore, my message was that you must constantly learn new things and gain deeper, broader understandings of what life in God's universes is all about! You must learn where those on earth fit into the universal plan, for although life is the vitality of active energy expressing itself, different streams of consciousness have different paths to follow and earth's is the lesson of love. My message said that whenever you refuse to expand and learn the greater love and knowledge brought to you, these limitations become concrete barriers to the amount of clarity and light in your soul.

Yes, I came to say that you are a chosen creation of God who was given free will to spiritually live or die -- to believe or not to believe -- and to encourage your positive choice. That was my message *then and now.* My heart is open to all those who have chosen faith in God, or will today make that commitment. You are the light of the world by your belief and action. You are as God created you yet you can disguise that truth if you wish and even deny it. Still God's energy lives within you. And by your positive thoughts, your surrender to the love within, you are healed. In your spiritual nature lies the opportunity for further advancement and growth and evolution back into the arms of God and all of creation. *You are an ever-awakening being in this process.*

I said 2,000 years ago and I repeat now that you must turn within to receive the blessings and direction of heaven. This means daily prayer and meditative times. Two thousand years ago, upon my resurrection, it was difficult even for my own disciples to understand, to believe that I had not abandoned them because they had not fully believed me and had not had their own profound experience of Spirit. They felt confused, bewildered. It was a shock which I would rather not have brought, but from it they learned and went forward to teach what they understood God to be. By my model they, and you, have an example to show that man can rise above negative thinking and survive the experience called death.

So, when you look at my former life as Jesus, your heart should tell you that an older brother, a teacher who loved you dearly, left the heavenly realms to be with you a short period of time -- to teach forgiveness and plant the seeds of love and peace for your self-mastery. Now I come to remind you that you are all *jointly responsible* for the present conditions upon your Mother Earth and to say that the time of recompense, required by the universal law of cause and effect, is coming soon. It is you who have created the separation from God, and it is you who must return to God through your own free will to do so. Have you forgotten that plan?

At the time of my visit 2,000 years ago I wanted you to know what would occur 2,000 years later, but would humanity then have believed in airplanes and automobiles and the radio and television to come? No. Just as you will likely not believe that in a few centuries from now human beings will regrow limbs, heal almost at once and live in a healthy state presently unimaginable. Many technological discoveries such as an inexpensive energy for the fueling of space vehicles also await you. And much, much more!

Mysteries will vanish with sunlight clarity for those allowed here in the thousand years of peace, and the inventions and creative knowledge will flow easily into souls who seek in love, into eyes with the pure preordained vision of Spirit. Each human being will see the glow of energy around every other living thing and life will be a warm connectedness between those still fleshed in a physical body and those who wear the garment of light ... companions all.

I said before that it was not my intention to be deified and to be called a savior of mankind. My role was that of way-shower. And it is this role I must insist be clarified in your thinking if there is yet confusion about what it means to be reborn in Spirit.

Because you are a spiritual creation, this is your true identity and it can *never* be changed unless you reject it. Because God gave you permission to choose or not to choose love, however, the earth has been filled with pain and circumstances of evil. This experiment on the planet earth has not been going well. Therefore, there will soon be a division between the believers and non-believers of God, between the practitioners of love and peace and those who are not learning it. A separation between those who wish to demonstrate self-mastery and those who do not! This is not a punishment but an effect *you* have created. Nonetheless, time has run out. The school must graduate its students now. The end of the term is here. From this place some will go on to a higher level of practicing the lessons of self-knowledge, love and service. Others will be placed where it is hoped they can still learn the basic acceptance of God-consciousness. Self-mastery is your goal. Claim it now with others like yourself in the Love Corps.

I have reviewed for you my purpose in coming here. Let me now say that after the crucifixion when I arose in my heavenly light body which the Creator gave us all at birth in the heavenly domains, I shone like the sun as a reminder that each of you is also that spark of the living God. You are a form created with light, capable of manifesting great love and using the universal laws of behavior here in your physical form.

I did not come to save you from having the personal responsibility to grow in love and to practice forgiveness on yourself and all others! I repeat this statement and underline it and I exclaim it. *I did not come to take on your personal responsibility of choice and behavior!* I came only to free you of the past mistakes you have made so that you could choose more wisely, more lovingly, what you truly wanted. It was a second chance so to speak, a new beginning, the cleansing of past deeds and unhealthy attitudes that would prevent your acceptance of something finer. My teachings were not enough, as you see from present conditions on the earth. For there has been a continuing insistence on war and destruction, which now threatens to infect the solar system as well.

I came to show you the way in which YOU will grow in understanding and the practice of love wherever you are in God's Omniverse. For the Father has many mansions or many levels of consciousness. I came to show that when your physical form is dead you are then in your resurrected light body. I also patterned for you that a body can literally be taken up in the light rather than left decaying and dying here. I demonstrated that either way, you need not fear death. When I came to show you that example, it was not so I would be deified, but rather that I might remain as a road map for future reference, providing a way to expand your understanding of who and what you are.

My resurrected body also showed you that I overcame negative thinking though it surrounded me. I modeled that you can rise above evil through contact with the eternal source which resides within you even while you dwell in the flesh. My example has been frozen and deified, not followed. I come in thought to free you then, and to return you to the God within, for care and keeping. Will you accept your awakening?

I say to you that my appearance on the planet earth was to demonstrate the power of the mind -- of good thinking over negative thinking, of positive belief over the darkness, of love over hate. Unless you believe what I did then, and am sharing now, your journey to the earth could fail. I fully remembered who I was and came all the way home in consciousness. Do *you* want to come home as self-masters?

The difference between you and me is small in principle but wider in practice. I believe totally in the Father/Mother and nothing else. I have mastery. You have doubts. You have not totally committed your heart and mind, and you therefore need further growth. My purpose in your life is to assist your growth. All the other great teachers of the world religions also seek to assist you in the growth and practice of love and compassion. That is our function here; that is our purpose; that is the reason I came.

In order to create earth's Second Coming, you, as a being of light, must select once more and with the greatest commitment possible, a spiritual path which foregoes all desire for war and hatred. This cleansing begins within each man, woman, and child and is a personal responsibility. When you choose peace personally, you are then brought into contact with others like yourself for the betterment of humanity. This is not a time of passivity or of aloneness, but a time of peaceful joining together. The coming age is the time of connection with God, but also with the soul life in the brothers and sisters around you, both visible and invisible. We are now at the culmination of 250,000 years of learning and self-mastery for those who seek it. Your souls have not been sitting idly in heaven all this time, but growing through love and service even as I have done.

My most serious evaluation of the present Christian churches is that many sects do not acknowledge such ideas nor do they understand prophecy and direct revelation by God. Yet when a human being is connected to the higher truth in Spirit, then indeed she or he hears the voice for God! And is led to the future action which is most appropriate and loving.

I wish to say that there are those in the church groups who practice this principle to the best of their ability, but there are many who have separated themselves from those of other races, nationalities, beliefs and religions. I say to you, each one examine your conscience. I ask you to listen to the voice of God within you, the voice that will lead you into the activities you must do immediately.

I herewith issue a last pardon to every child and adult on this planet -- something I am empowered to do because I overcame negative thinking and returned fully conscious to God, fully Christed. (This means I never doubt the power, truth, and love of our Creator.) But each soul has free will choice to accept or reject. I once said, "Go and sin no more." I remind you that this means have no further doubt, no lack of love.

At this time I stand with my brothers and sisters of the light who teach in many religions around the earth to remind you that wherever you are on the planet, the concepts of love and compassion can speak to your soul.

Love and compassion bring forgiveness, but forgiveness requires responsibility! For once you realize that your soul has been forgiven its past transgressions, you must begin immediately to practice the love you truly are at the highest reaches of your capacity. You must turn within each day and meditate to find out the behavior and actions which are appropriate for you. If you do this, knowing you are forgiven and the past is washed away, we start fresh and possibly there is still time for much of humanity to join together, heart to heart and mind to mind. Perhaps we can yet omit some prophecies of destruction described in the New Testament, Book of Revelation, by our dear brother-in-spirit, John, and by other world religions and metaphysical groups which give portents of similar things yet to come.

Every age has its prophets and truth bringers, but few there are among the population who will listen and take action. You must listen and act now. The Golden Age is a time when every soul may hear the voice within, and the land will be filled with many divine representatives of God. You may reach this achievement through your willingness and commitment of daily meditation combined with weekly meditation times shared in the presence of other loving souls. You may not enter the Golden Age alone. There must be two or more gathered to appreciate and honor that supreme Source without which we would all expire.

We will establish a Golden Age on this planet with those beings of light who will work to prepare the way for the Second Coming. I await that experience following the cleansing of the planet earth of its negative influences. This glorious adventure is not something I do alone, but in cooperation with the many good souls -- visible and invisible -- who wish to advance humanity's growth into greater understanding and service.

The God-of-All now issues a proclamation to its many children here that each soul may, through a change of heart and willingness, be included in this golden experience if it will begin to demonstrate the teachings of love and forgiveness.

I myself urge you to combine a willing heart and fertile mind to create on this planet a force field of light, peace, and energy blazing forth as bright as the sun itself! This glow will encourage many teachers like myself to come forth into our next round of spiritual growth and consciousness known as the Second Coming. I say to you negative ones who have sought power and murdered others, that even you will be forgiven if you cease and desist from these activities and surrender to the knowledge and practice of love *now*.

However, if you choose to continue in the negativity and the violence of thought and deed which persists here on this planet, you must accept the consequences of that choice. You will *not* be allowed to continue spiritual life on this planet after the cleansing time. Hereafter there will be two distinct realms designated for humanity, one for God and one for those of unaware consciousness. There will no longer be that vast middle ground of "Maybe" or "Someday I'll think about it." The sidelines are vanishing now. The teams are forming. And I promise you this time the light workers will prevail!

If I repeat this necessity for right choice, it is because my heart desires you to know the truth so that you can never say later, "I did not know; I was not told." That is why this message will be translated into the major world languages and spread around the girth of this globe. Let every being capable of understanding this proclamation make his or her decision wisely. Let us join in the achievement of spiritual commencement.

The purpose of my visit 2,000 years ago has nearly run its course though not with the results I intended. Very quickly now the separation into the for's and against's, the yes's and the no's will be accomplished. I encourage you to do whatever is necessary to be among the "yes" group for it is graduation to higher things you select. This is the time for coming *together!*

Please contemplate, meditate and pray to the Almighty Source very seriously, knowing the awakened ones of light will be given love and support. In the days ahead you will need to be fortified by a daily connection to your higher self in order to live through the possible events known as the Tribulation ... and to be admitted into that transformational period leading to the thousand years of peace. In all ways cleanse yourself, especially at the mental and emotional/psychological level where the distortions of doubt in the human personality would keep you from surrendering to the Creator-of-All.

Since the human family needs to prepare its love nature for an upgrading into heavenly realms, I beseech you to cleanse your inner unconscious limitations -- your fear, anger, your sadness, regret, guilt. By enrolling with any legitimate healer you can release the negative habit patterns which prevent the full expression of God's love to yourself and those around you. This is the time of self-cleansing. *All* are required to do it.

When you are healed and capable of peacefulness, each one, then the planet will be filled with peace and war will end. The most difficult part of this will be the surrender of your ego/personality's desire to maintain its own power and think it knows best what it should do at any given time. I assure you that there is *no one* ... NO ONE ... on this planet who knows the best action to take every day unless she or he is listening to the voice of God within! You may have a general direction, but you will lack specifics. The only rule is to be willing to cooperate with one another and to listen and await the universal pattern to unfold from our greater realms. We are waiting and watching to see how many souls will choose to go forward in a state of peace, love, and service.

Yes, there is a general plan for you to follow, but the exact details and its timing will be determined by *your* response. Specifically, then, there are probabilities of the events within the year ahead, but these could be improved and ameliorated by your change to peace and the giving up of war and military aggression both on earth and in outer space.

Each of you will be "saved" to the degree *you* surrender your little, personal will to the greater Will of the Creator and the heavenly realms. Each of you will participate in the glorious events of the Golden Age to the degree that you now practice love and show commitment to a just and spiritual purpose.

You have my personal promise, joined with the thousands of other spiritual and religious teachers of all times, that we have not left you comfortless as this spiritual fruition draws near. Choose God, choose love, and be assured your choice will be registered *for* or *against* as *you* decree it.

I once told you that each soul must make its own decision; even God will not require your obedience. Think on this choice with diligence and sincerity, and you will not be led astray by others of a negative understanding. Trust your heart and inner God-voice to lead you in all things, and you will know the best solution on any issue.

If you are committed to God, then every other aspect of commitment to your family, spouse, friends, neighbors, and work place must be subordinated to it. You must not compromise God's teachings for any other idol of the physical life that is not of the highest love, the total good. In some cases this means you will be in disagreement with those you care about. Nonetheless, the love of God must come *first* in every life. ALL ELSE FOLLOWS THIS COMMITMENT.

Because you are the light and knowingness, I strongly urge you to take this identity and quality into all activities of your world. Most particularly take it into those causes and movements, gatherings and organizations that seek to improve humanity's responsibilities as caretakers of the earth. Peace organizations are a good example of places where the unified power of meditation and visualization are critical.

If you understood energy and could see it with your eyes you would realize why groups are immense power cells of light and focused thought. And it is this focused thought, shared with us of higher dimensions, that increases the output of your love. As long as you think you do it alone, you limit the quantity of power available to accomplish the task. Your light is very low wattage by itself; but when you ask the Creator to assist you in manifesting your purpose or need, that light and power are greatly, very greatly increased. But we see you do not realize this and take a secular path which frequently does not even mention the word *"God"* or higher power. This is not to your advantage and does not further your purposes during this time when we are saturating your planet with huge amounts of light and love so that you can manifest peace.

We are standing ready to assist you, yet you ignore our presence and dedication to the deepest desires of the human heart -- peace. If you could see the amount of light and energy we add to the good thoughts you have, when asked, then perhaps you could face asking for assistance. Your fear that peace organizations may be thought of as religious restricts your own good.

Therefore, I say to you that at any meeting where you gather in the name of peace, or where you walk or march for peace, you should ask that the power and support of God, or heavenly forces, be present to help bring fruition to your ideals. By that act you benefit more than you can ever dream. And being spiritual and being religious are two different things. We do not ask you to designate any one religion, but we do ask you to recognize the Creator-of-All and call upon that power, force, or source, to support your plans. It is also possible during such times of quietude that we can slip suggestions into your minds with ideas that might be useful to your peaceful purposes.

You have an earth saying "Try it; you'll like it" ... and my suggestion is that you do try it. There is much to gain! And peace is a spiritual issue if you think about it, because it requires love and love is of God. Therefore, if the leaders of various peace movements fail to recognize the source of peace as love and the source of love as God, their efforts will automatically be minimized by the law of cause and effect. For you cannot bring to fruition more than you can imagine and project by thought.

At a recent peace meeting of some magnitude there was no attempt to settle the large audience into a focused state of peaceful intention before the program began, nor was any closing ceremony to further unify healing to earth and humanity given. This was a great loss for the particular audience but more so for the planet and humanity. We trust that the leaders of such organizations will be persuaded to include such a simple opening or closing as part of every gathering, even those where planning is done. Or would you continue to do these things alone and reap the result which all your history demonstrates has been unsuccessful?

Yes, you should get more peace workers, but for each human being would you not also wish the same or greater number from spiritual realms on your team? Furthermore, we would suggest that instead of having nearly a thousand peace organizations with separate goals that you be willing to cooperate with each other for a major thrust of combined power. This joining together, or networking as you call it, is going to be critical in the time remaining through 1986 when our intense support of your efforts is available.

You see, beloveds, if you of the peace movement cannot come together in joint endeavor, how can you expect those who do not believe in peace to learn from your example? For only in combining talents and willingness can you model to others that it can be done on earth. Truly I hope you grasp the deep significance of what I share. If not you, then who else will become that positive model, that demonstration for peace? Nor should peace groups work alone. Environmentalists, healers, religious groups, and men and women of goodwill everywhere can join the Love Corps.

I say this to remind you that your own plans, without the guidance of God over these past seven million years, have brought you tragedy. Surely it is time for the mass of earth dwellers to acknowledge that they must cross lines of apparent separation, join energies in peaceful purpose, and ask for our support. This is what the Golden Age is about.

Once again I say it. Your peace organizations -- or groups for any cause -- separated as they are, will fail without mutual cooperation and without the recognition of a power greater than yourselves. You must invite Spirit into your midst because of your free will nature. Yes, you image makers were given free will, and you see before you the results of that gift. You see the dissension, the rage and violence and the war. Is this what you want? Or are you finally ready to cooperate with one another and accept help and guidance from the sages and truth bringers of all time?

To cease separation from the Creator, and also one from another, is the highest form of wisdom. Please do not wait until the fires burn out of control and the plague spreads unchallenged to call upon our assistance to aid your work, your honorable cause of peace. Do you hear my concern? It is given with love though tinged with the sadness of watching a humanity which continues in the quicksand of ignorance and self-will. In the name of our Creator I once more ask you to assist each other to achieve peace and also request us to join you in your desire to implement it.

Think about your role, my beloved brothers and sisters, and choose God above all things. Put your purpose into practice.

With a magnificent burst of light let us leave the limitations of earth's density and ride into rainbow streams of color to brighten your soul. Listen to the soothing celestial refrains refreshing your memory, joyously recalling who you truly are. Starseeds come forth; the long sleep ends.

Take God's remembrance, our hands, and levitate with us into higher and higher realms of knowing. Be reborn into the tomorrow of a new creation.

Rise up, dear ones, and take your place in the cosmic bliss of a shimmering Golden Age, for the awakening children of light are loved and are safe ... and with that absolute promise, I say, give *glory* to God! Give *thanks* to God that you are the prodigals returning and that you have given up all doubt!

You have been gone a long time. Soon you will rest and laugh and glow ever more brightly as inhabitants of God's illustrious suns, planets and stars.

The Creator's plan contains infinite opportunity for all. Come *now*, in joy, as our Love Corps makes the journey, hand in hand, filled with certainty and excitement. We leave no one behind who wishes to join.

Come. Your opportunity is here. Our appointed hour is at hand.

I close with the hope you are refreshed by the truth and by your opportunity to become a shining example of its power.

In the Creator's name let us say, together, amen.

1994/1995 comments are contained in Chapters X and XI.

Chapter IV

Earth's Purpose in
God's Twelfth Universe

To understand my appearance on the earth nearly 2,000 years ago you need a framework and a context in which to hold the information, or it makes little sense to the intelligent mind, the seeking heart. But I warn you that the truth will probably startle you because the historical records of this planet have been so decimated over the eons of time that you hardly know any truth about its geology, its geography, its peoples or their activities. Therefore, you do not understand or know the truth.

Regrettably your text books in the schools have done little to further the truth because only a modicum is provable by the actual evidence you now perceive. Lands and cultures have come and gone and many lie under miles of ocean water or mountain debris beyond your direct knowledge. Only with recent photographic techniques used in space, looking back at earth, do your geologists begin to see the actual physical evidence beneath the earth's surface. And there is much more to learn. Much more!

That is why I have come to share an abbreviated history of earth with you, at least in part, so you can begin to grasp the enormity of your present situation and understand the reasons why a World Teacher like myself came to this place 2,000 years ago to bring this 250,000-year phase of humanity's spiritual evolution to its conclusion.

If you will open your imagination and become as a child, you have much to gain. Let your intellect relax and soften as your intuition comes into gentle knowingness. Give your soul connection first priority, and let its knowing -- along with your heart's response -- confirm what I say. If you dare to do this your life will change in a way you would have thought impossible, and you will find yourself connected to the living God in a deeper, more life-affirming manner than ever before. For this is the ending of an era, the ending of an age, the ending of my leadership over the earth *in the way your scriptures reported me as Jesus of Nazareth.* There is now a greater Jesus, for I have grown and expanded as you children of light are also doing. Understand that my essence is now with the Christ Consciousness, even as part of my energy guides planet earth.

Having so said, let me explain my meaning.

The great spiritual Creator of us all goes so far back in history that you may not believe the dates for the planet earth's relationship to that great One. I told you that life in its spiritual dimension has existed about eight million years above earth's surface in the etheric realm and that life before earth is trillions of years old. Since earth is part of the 12th Universe, and the other eleven took many eons to develop under the Creator's original designs, this 12th Universe is younger but of greater variety than the others.

Did you know there are literally millions of planets in some of these universes? And that many of them have living things, not only in plant, bird, animal and mineral life, but creations of what you call spiritual bodies, as well as some physical forms like your own and others which you cannot even imagine. You are certainly not alone in this Universe, although many of your space brothers and sisters are different in size, build, light density, and mental capacity.

So focus your mind to the dark and starry sky above and notice each twinkling light you can count. These are huge planetary globes, star systems, and immense light structures brought forth in the firmaments as an image from the mind of God. Yes, it is true. There are many lifeforms because our Father/Mother has been experimenting over a trillion years to learn what types of life are most effective and what is most pleasing as a creation. If you could walk among the stars you would know that these are inhabited by beings who were also created by a Source far beyond your mortal comprehension.

Seek you further truth, strange as it may be? Then know that these twelve universes each have a different purpose and a different type of experimentation to suit the Creator's plans.

Our Father/Mother Creator -- or the Central Being -- resides in a special place, alone, because the intensity of God's nature (electricity is probably the best word you can imagine even if it is more involved than that) is so strong that even I, who am made directly from it, do not stay long in the presence of this Mighty One. Others of God's immediate hierarchy cannot bear this powerful presence at all, except for one, and so I am used as an intermediary at times. There are few words in your written language to explain all this and since we of the heavens use light packets, and pictures, and sound instead of verbal communication I cannot expect you to receive the outpicturing or harmony I am sending to describe The Parent-of-All.

But let me pause a moment and describe that one we call Parent so that you have a picture to hold in your mind, your heart. For in many ways are you created like God, although of course God is both male and female energy combined in perfect balance as we have said. This is critical to understand, for in the "separation," or descent into a third dimensional world, God's wholeness suffered division into duality on your earth. There you have densified or solidified into those two separate parts called male and female. One day all humanity who have chosen to return to God will lose the density of the physical body and become a form of light containing both male and female principles in balanced proportion. It is in this ascension that you will become more like me, the son of God, who is made purely in the image and identity of that powerful One.

God has a form of immense size and of a blinding glow beyond description. While it is true that the Father/Mother is omniscient, omnipresent, and omnipotent, do not forget that God has an enduring and passionate love for everything of its creation. God is not a gaseous vapor nor a nebulous, formless "something." It is from the perfect love and immense power of this indescribable being that you were born as souls, as children of the cosmos.

Blessed are those who choose to believe for the power and love of this Great One are beyond telling. Yes, you are the children of a great being who loves you. Most importantly, our Parent is personally directing your destiny through us at this time when we would have you return home. Only those dedicated and willing souls on earth who are assisting the planet earth's rise nearer to God, only those of loving disposition and intention, are welcome there. I tell you, my dear ones, your Parent is a beautiful being of light beyond description in your language. But perhaps you can sense this from the simple remarks I have made? Let every doubting heart open wide to acknowledge that your Parent exists, for those who persist in denying this indescribable First Cause deny their own identity, and through free will they will be deeply wounded by false choosing.

Again hear what I say. In denying God's origin you deny your own. This is what causes the mortal error leading to spiritual retardation. You either live within the love that God extends or by your denial move outside of that immense love, and not just for these few years you call life! Whether you like it or not, God allows each soul its own choice because to have a heaven, each must agree and wish to be there. Only on earth is there this broad range of experiences as in a training school of multiple attitudes and negative dispositions.

Here you have various educational and military training centers where the person enlists or attends and then learns a certain curriculum leading to advancement and positions of responsibility. I pray you understand that this pattern of choice on earth was given to teach you only love and devotion. However, we will now spiritually separate those who will cooperate in God's higher endeavors from those who won't, for that time of choice is nearly over as the 12th Universe moves back to our Creator.

Those who cannot join in love and peace will be left to another experience.

HEAVEN IS NOT AN IDLE PLACE. ITS MANY ACTIVITIES REQUIRE LOVING AND DEVOTED FAMILY MEMBERS TO WORK HARMONIOUSLY IN THE ORGA-NIZATION AND MAINTENANCE OF THE PARENT'S HANDIWORK. How could it be otherwise? For is not the light everywhere?

Now children of light, I will describe the twelve universes which our Father/Mother has made including earth's position therein. In your local Universe there are twelve parts, or solar systems, and earth's position is in the smallest of the dozen solar systems in your Universe. Keep your minds open to times long past in cosmic history in order to grasp that these other created universes preceded yours, and then you will understand the present situation in which earth finds herself much more easily.

My own Universe was created first and has one beautiful solar system with only two planets produced by the Creator in an act of intense love and imagination. In my Universe there is only the perfect love I described to you while part of my energy was on earth as Jesus. Those who are privileged to live there find it heaven, indeed.

There are additional universes which were experiments following that first one. There is a second Universe in which the Creator made all beings of female nature, or the love and nurturing side of God, and the third Universe which has only male attributes or the will, power and active aspects of God. Both of these universes are of such a high vibration you could not see them with the human eye, just as most earth dwellers cannot see me and the angelic hosts. In those separate universes, both the males or females could independently reproduce offspring with the breath, even as God ordained it, and needed not a sexual, physical counterpart. This is a spiritual dimension strange to your own body limitations, I realize, but it is nonetheless true. (Those who have difficulty with the so-called "virgin birth" may see it now in a new light.)

The 4th Universe was created following the experience in which the male and female principles were separated from each other. They were recombined in the 4th Universe since love and power should be together and not kept apart. This is a *soul essence* and quality that I speak about, not your dense physical flesh which came eons later after the other Universes were completed.

Then there were made by the Father/Mother's breath, even as the first four universes came forth, a series of specialized planets where particular qualities or functions were stressed in both the male and female beings. In the 5th Universe was developed the power of mind thought, which is different from intellect. Let me clarify that in God all are of one mind and are whole. When Spirit leaves God's mind to experience life in matter worlds, it then has separated minds capable of *individual* soul experience. Yet this entire Universe kept one primary, unified thought, or *intention,* to love God, paramount, even though the souls were separated. By your standards this was miraculous!

In humans, then, you need a love purpose to direct energy into thought or you will misuse it. A thought is energy moving its intention into reality. A thought is alive. God's thought is energy in a single focused creation; it does not analyze or break things down into separate parts as does human intellect. On earth many of your technologists have great intellects, but not wholesome minds. Mind requires a heart's love for wholeness. Intellect is only 50% of thought. When intellect and intuition -- or God knowingness -- are combined, there is perfect balance.

In that 5th Universe all inhabitants did so well they were allowed to return to the Creator *en masse* and it is now an unpopulated area in what you call space. Of all the many creations, only these of the 5th Universe were never lured into temptation away from God as an entire group! Although there are isolated examples elsewhere of this great God love in the mind of his created ones, never did an entire Universe grasp the love principle and practice it so perfectly. It is they you are to emulate, dear ones, so you can also go home together. But, of course, this took eons to demonstrate, and the Creator had been busy making other universes in the meantime.

The 6th Universe is a place where the miniaturization of lifeforms was stressed so the inhabitants are tiny in size, the planets are smaller than most, and the beings love God devotedly as their acts of producing beautiful natural things, such as flowers, prove. The descendents of these tiny creations living on your earth's etheric plane, often called nature spirits by those with the clairvoyant power to see them, are dedicated to bring flower and plant life to its highest form. These little workers are purely devoted to their task of beauty and have never strayed from the function for which they were created.

In the 7th Universe of eight million planets -- one million inhabited -- the male and female beings were focused solely in the area of intellectual expertise, mathematical science primarily. Because of this great emphasis upon the gaining of scientific knowledge, there was no love side to their nature for one another or for the Creator. Here it was learned that intellect in male or female without the balance of heart love is not desirable. This 7th Universe is still functioning but the citizens are yet paying off a debt to God which I cannot describe at this time. Suffice it to say, all must accept that science is a God-made thing, not the work of mere mortals who claim it as theirs. A true scientist can only discover a universal law or principle to fulfill life's function and use it for the good of all. In fact, every scientist is obligated to seek reverently for God's principles, with the intention of applying them only for the common good.

In the 8th Universe of four milllion planets, our Creator caused a million to be inhabited and did a variety of experiments to understand the effects of the rays upon matter. Here some beings were given almost X-ray vision; others were imbued with the rays of heat, magnetism and electricity and were able to oscillate, to levitate. I will say only that there were many different experiments made to learn the effects from various kinds of temperature changes, effects from extensive dark and light exposure, and so forth. These creations willingly underwent the experiments for the good of the lifeforms which would follow them. Because of their difficulties during these trials, however, I came to give my love and peace during their many cataclysms. For while they could feel the presence of God during these various experiments, it was my stepping down of the Creator's power vibration that gave them a greater awareness of God's presence and comfort. So you see, dear ones, in the Omniverse all of God's creations have their plans and purposes. Each builds upon the PRIOR GIFTS of the ones before it. Thus, in your position in the 12th and last Universe, while God prepares to bring you home, you have the aspects of all this learning at your disposal if only you seek and synthesize it.

The 9th Universe, with only about 900 inhabited planets, was a spacious and unusual experiment. These people were focused on their spiritual natures and the love of God so constantly and consistently that this area is now empty of them. Merely a perfumed hush of peace remains in the ethers from their gentle natures. Because of their deep devotion our Creator would often come there, close to those who were different in size or magnitude from each other, but not different in the size of their affection. They all had the gifts of clairvoyance, clairaudience and mediumship. Where did they go? Some to God and some to rebirth into your 12th Universe, dear ones. A few are a part of this Universe, this solar system, and your planet in ways you find it difficult to understand. But they are part of some of you if you claim them.

Unlike their devoted predecessors of the 9th Universe, the 10th Universe creations were attentive only to the matters of theology or the study of comparative religions throughout the many universes. With only 10% of some 900 planets inhabited, they spent their time thinking and learning. In their theological colleges they would study these different teachings, in an intellectual way, seeking to know God with the mind alone. But dissecting God to find the heart of love gains little and this was their learning gift to those of you who follow. Knowing man's mental definitions of the Creator and experiencing that love in the heart are two very different things. And it was my purpose here 2,000 years ago to bring the experience and teachings of love back to earth again, as others had done before and since.

Now a very sad, sad tale. The 11th Universe of Mechanism could not have existed save for the focus on engineering. However, of the men and women from these million-and-a-half planets, *all but those on two planets were decimated by war*. For in that time and place, with the great inventiveness of thought without love's influence, their designs led to military uses. Although the warfare was carried out primarily by the machines they had invented, at least 860 of God's planets, themselves, were almost decimated by the violence.

What a loss that this seething conglomeration of equipment and metallic instrumentation was harnessed only to the forces of a destructive nature and created havoc beyond description! It was permitted because of free will just as your planet has free will. But, although they feared God, they held no heart love to soften their inventive genius. It happened, then, that the life-forms chose machinery over God; their inventions became their masters, and they could never regain control over their equipment, their monstrous images made real.

Perhaps you recognize some influence of that experiment in the 11th Universe with what your own 12th Universe is doing? Those of you who inhabit the planet earth, along with about 500 other 12th Universe planetary forms, are now caught up in that possible destructive aspect of engineering mechanization. (Of course, most other planets are superior to earth in technology but you refuse to acknowledge this fact along with their interdimensional presence. Where do you think UFO's or flying saucers come from?)

Since you have the mixture in this 12th Universe of all the other eleven in varying amounts and combinations, your 12th Universe is a potpourri. It is all here from those trillions of years of learning and growth that has already transpired before time was.

Your 12th Universe is the largest of all that has preceded you. It has the greatest variety of learning possibilities to use, and the most tremendous opportunity to learn from past mistakes and past glories. All strengths and weaknesses of these past experiences are available to you. Then you must choose wisely in your Universe and competently amalgamate or synthesize the best of it all, denying that ill-fated mechanization which manifested so widely and destructively in the 11th Universe. You, as humanity, must focus more clearly on love than ever before if you wish to return to God purified of violence. For return is scheduled, soon, but only the loving ones can proceed.

Now, are you interested to learn what your own Universe's history has been over these past millions of years? Especially the eight million years as it applies to the planet you live upon? Then let us pause a moment, together, in the Creator's love, and ponder what has been shared.

I wish to speak about your own solar system which is in the 12th Universe, and about your so-called space programs. You might ask your scientists who send astronauts and instruments looking for other life to expand their own consciousness and stop wasting so much money looking for things in the third dimensional world. Most life on the other planets operates in the etheric levels of the fourth dimension and beyond. That which does not would not wish your warlike attitudes to locate them anyway. So, your three dimensional eyes and instruments are blind. You are like a person standing in a brightly lit room with blindfolds on. So do not be surprised that you do not find life *as you know it* on the planets in your own solar system. You look in the wrong place out of ignorance.

The very fact that you are spiritually blind means that your adventures in space will leave you more perplexed than satisfied. When your own consciousness advances into fourth dimensional realities you will see many others, including those of us who are awaiting the reversal of your AMNESIA. Yes, spiritual amnesia is what you have, and looking for other physical life while in this state means certain defeat because of the way you establish your space projects.

I have admonished you as a group not to take violence or weaponry of any kind into space but it is permitted to pursue totally peaceful research projects of a truly reverent or scientific nature. However, unless you are wise enough to select a captain and crew with several clairvoyants among them, do not expect to "see" other life. Sad to relate, your earth citizens are nearly the lowest form of consciousness in the known solar system at this time, which is why the earth is being bombarded with the high frequency of light vibrations in hope of awakening a sleeping race.

All of heaven in its multidimensional reality is presently involved in an enormous expenditure of energy that you are incapable of grasping, and apparently -- for the most part -- of even appreciating. Nonetheless, we will continue to follow God's decree to assist all who will awaken during this eighteen month special grace period which began on *August 1, 1985*. That is why I have said, and will repeat again and again, that time is critical to you. For these additional energies of love and power that come to you represent one of the greatest commitments that millions of us beyond your sight are giving. They are the same type of consciousness acceleration that your so-called Renaissance times in Europe and the other golden ages of wisdom in the Orient and elsewhere represent, only multiplied by a much higher factor.

The fact that most people are not even vaguely aware of this energy tells us you are more limited and unaware than we knew. Yet we have made a promise which will be kept so that none will be lost who chooses to awaken. Be advised that the increase in energies to your planet has already changed those who are alert and cooperating with us, so that the aware ones are slightly over halfway between the third and fourth dimensions, that is, about an average of 3.6 out of 4.0. By the time our spiritual infusion is over, the light workers will be growing close to fourth dimensional consciousness.

The many others who wait to awaken until later in this century probably cannot do so without pain and suffering. The longer the personality resists its awakening, the more profound the experiences the soul must bring to ignite awareness. For some people this may be very intense. Therefore, choose now and avoid a need for this unpleasantness later on. Your soul will probably put your personality to the test of self-mastery for it was this achievement you desired.

Those who have been meditating and can now receive other-dimensional telepathic contact from us may already have surpassed the 4.0 figure I have shared. For it is during your daily meditation periods that you bring the cleansing of limited thoughts and open yourself to the broader, more universal content of all that God is. For what God is you are becoming though it is shadowed in the darkness and ignorance of illusion. This is your opportunity for transformation.

If you could receive a trillion dollars and every other wish of your personality's earthly desires, I tell you that the gift of God's energy at this time greatly surpasses it all. Not that you should not have money for food and things that represent God's abundance, but if you make of them your full-time pursuit and give only attention to the material things in unreasonable proportion, then you deal in idols of a false reality. So have a life of the material things to meet your basic needs, and then share your wealth, however large or small it may be. For as you give to others from the resources God has shared with you, the true prosperity of soul comes.

As you have been told, at the time you call death when you ascend in your spiritual body, the contents of your mind, feelings and heart leave the body in an identity form of lighter vibration. Hopefully, you will have conquered all bodily pursuits of the usual list you have heard before -- lust, all addictions, gluttony, and greed in all its forms -- for without a body to express them in you will be left with a mind full of thoughts that bring no joy, especially as you have no physical flesh through which to enjoy them.

Many are the prayers that come to us saying, "Father, give me" ... this ... or that ... or something else. And we do make every effort to have your mental belief and emotional experiences cleansed enough so that the barriers to having your good are removed. Yet the greatest gift to have, and the greatest prayer to speak, is merely to accept all that has already been given every child of God. And in that prayer you become a vessel of acceptance to the perfect things your soul would direct to you. Most of which, incidentally, are not at all what you think you want and need.

So ask for all that has already been given and cleanse yourself from the false belief that keeps it from you. Then shall you know heaven on earth even as you rise in consciousness to the greater state of God-awareness which is the one and only true need of humanity. It is so simple but few will hear it, few will respond. Still we remain stalwart in giving you what God has already granted through our own love, and compassion, and willingness to serve. Will you, in return, follow this example here on Mother Earth, which so desperately needs your support and where humanity so urgently needs to awaken? We of heaven ask for your support and assistance as we shepherd humanity into the Golden Age. We truly do need that corps of love -- that group of Golden Age apostles, disciples and believers.

I have spoken of that New Age but let me give you an outline of what it means to earth and life upon it. The Golden, or Aquarian, Age is a time of energy change and uplifting for all of humanity. It is a time when the things formerly invisible are made real to you; it is a time of joining heaven and earth together in open communication and cooperation. Therefore, it is a time when your usual, or limiting, habits must change, because the structure of consciousness itself is changing and you with it. It is also an opportunity to recognize and become, in the fullest measure, the higher or soul self while living in matter and physical form. EACH PERSON MUST BUILD A BRIDGE OF ENERGY BETWEEN THE PERSONALITY AND THE SOUL-SELF TO ACHIEVE THIS! For this is the time for alignment of the lowest and the highest into one motive and one action. *Love.* It is nothing less than an integration in which the wisest aspect of soul becomes the director and leads the way for the individual's and group's gain.

You see, the soul is group-oriented because it is of God and is already in contact with unity, which earthlings forget in their separated bodies of flesh. Meditation is a way of achieving great forward progress because in contacting the soul you are enabled to pour your efforts into selfless service, something the average human personality resists. For do you not say "That's mine" as you refer to God's gifts around you? And is this not separation ... or the opposite of unity? Is it not truer that *everything is God's* and just temporarily on loan to you during your visit to earth?

After all, what do you take of your physical world with you upon departure but the memories of your thoughts and behaviors and the emotions of it all?

The Golden Age, then, is a time of group process, where a number of people who have established soul contact can envision a mutual goal and move toward it in loving thought and commitment with immense energy behind their intention. It is the difference between small individual flashlights on a stormy night and one huge lighthouse beam where the beam is clear and strong.

Just as one person's light will combine with other lights into a larger soul connection and a greater thought form, truly do the combined thoughts of many amalgamate into a huge single thought that can be brought to fruition more easily than the smaller thoughts of several single persons. So, mutually committed purposes and the power of multiple energies to support them is the essence of this Golden Age. That and peace are the framework.

Now draw in a breath of peace and think on something exquisitely beautiful. In the Golden Age if what you think of is God-made, be assured it will last. If what you think of is mechanical, be suspicious and turn your thoughts to that Source which cre-

ated all the universes, the planets and stars and life upon them.
Then think again about what is beautiful. Your answer is guided
by your soul's understanding, for it knows you were created by
a Force beyond your comprehension and yet not without your
sensing, your knowing.

This is why meditation is so vital. In the stillness as you seek
God, you grow quiet and become peaceful. In that act alone you
fulfill the simple truth which is the greatest of all the experiments
in all the universes. You become, for just a moment, a created
being of light without judgment or worry or fear. You become
peacefully wise. For just a moment you touch upon your true
identity which is love.

In meditation you let all the rest fall away and breathe this
love and peace in, and out, just as the Creator did in all the work
brought forth by "the word" -- the implemented thought behind
the universes. As you will learn, God breathed out life and is
breathing us back home again, and you of the 12th Universe are
moving from the farthest reaches back toward the center of light
and energy that sent you out.

This particular historical time in human consciousness is focused on that aspect of God that clarifies the difference between
concrete, material world science and the science of the soul,
which is a far greater thing. Thus each being on earth must
choose between the things of sensory perception (of the physical
senses and intellect) and the greater knowing from the intuitive
or soul aspect of self. Each must seek the science of the soul
first to achieve the needed balance in life.

Those who choose wisely to know the truth of life will assist
the planet in her, and their own, ascension to higher realms.
The remainder will insist that the material world is the only reality and will fall short of the challenge that is being presented to
them. For the planet must demonstrate love and wisdom for her
evaluation and graduation, and humanity must do the same.
Intellect cannot bring love and peace! That is not its purpose.
Your key to reaching that goal lies in bringing to balance the
soul's science or knowing the universal laws and bringing them

onto the physical body of earth to manifest. Many of your present scientists, especially, will be caught in this crunch of realities. But each person must make the soul choice if progress and ascension are to be assured.

Then send love and blessings to the technological and scientific communities on this planet, for they need your prayers and support during this time of challenge. Put another way this is the personality's Armegeddon: the questioning intelligence versus the intuitive knowing. And in this apparent war of intellect against heart, peace must be found through using both in a perfect state of balance ... but beginning with the intuitive. For it is from reverent awareness and inquiry that humanity grows in the imperishable quality of truth hidden from your view in the third dimensional world.

Remember, then, that it is only after you are grounded in true spiritual direction that you can become an effective group member ready to freely serve based upon suggestions from your soul. Only when you have integrated your personality, purified it, and let it become a channel for the soul's expression can you be blessed by any real measure of Christ Consciousness.

But when the personality of the little human self is finally infused with the soul knowing and commitment, life changes dramatically in the miracle of that accomplishment. From here the events of your life are guided by a greater power than your own decision making and you transcend the personal, becoming like a healthy cell in earth's precious body. When groups are formed by those who have willingly joined soul to soul, you will experience the transpersonal love which radiates in a brilliance that would blind you if you could see it. That is why I insist that you meet with others like yourself every week to meditate. You will not only enjoy the company of friends on the same path but have a truer knowing about the potent reception of the group energy.

High vibrational energy literally changes your mental and emotional subtle bodies so there is a direct, immediate gift to yourself. And from this higher vibration even your cells change the structure of life within you. Such is the power of large group connection to universal, unconditional love. Thus you are left with a feeling of Oneness that words cannot really express. The truth is that in the bonding of soul energy to soul energy you are taken into that heaven which once was your permanent residence, and which now is only briefly enjoyed. But by this steady commitment of daily and weekly meditation you will grow rapidly under our persistent barrage of love which especially comes to you through 1986.

The expression of this deep and indescribable bonding is called *fellowship* wherein the broad goals of humanity overshadow the desires of the little will of each person. Thus there comes unity within diversity, and the individual chaos of ego dies to the connected purpose and common vision. Truly the soul contact with self and others fills the body with a quality of light that refines and purifies all levels of consciousness, synthesizing the physical, emotional, mental, and spiritual aspects of your being. And by your joining in a network of light with others, you glow even brighter as individuals and as a group.

Do not be surprised if you actually feel lighter and if others say that you are looking younger somehow -- more peaceful, more contented. For these are the hallmarks of God and of the spiritual presence of that power within you.

This peace and a joyous heart are your rewards for the willingness to have that Infinite Presence enter and direct your life. Those who serve others receive joy and light and love beyond the earthly treasures you might enumerate as valuable, for these everlasting qualities take you across the bridge of illusion into the only true vision there is.

Your genuine, untarnished residence in light awaits your return, beloveds. As we of heaven do! So reach out in willingness to grow and serve that you may return to your own supreme mansion of consciousness.

To know what is happening will give you strength to persevere through everything with love in your heart. For all of the great experimentation has proven that combined love and wisdom last, for they alone bring peace.

Take your legacy, beloveds, and join me in whatever evaluation lies ahead. We of the Godhead love you. On that you can count. In that you must trust. See me no more in Jerusalem for that is not my essential identity, nor need it be yours.

Give up your past, your frozen memories of me, and let me appear to you in the fullness of my many talents and great knowledge. You are no longer to be encased in the bleak, black experience of your ignorance while your planet and solar system go forward in growth. You must catch up and join your family of advancing truth and life. YOU MUST ACCEPT A NEW BIRTHRIGHT OF COSMIC PROPORTIONS AND A NEW JESUS OF UNIVERSAL MAGNITUDE TO KNOW YOUR OWN POTENTIAL PLACE IN EVOLUTION.

"But who is this new Jesus you claim to be?" you may be asking. "Can there really be such a thing? Could Jesus be an even greater power and presence than before?"

I answer, "YES!" And I will share what you must know to free yourself from the past, for those who dwell only in the past tend to reinforce it in their actions and cannot bring the gentle rains of change to soften the soil and feed the tiny tendrils of life that seek further delight in growth above the ground.

If you ever had someone else try to explain something you said to another person, or if you have been interviewed by somebody for a newspaper article, radio or TV broadcast, you will know the feeling of frustration that occurs when another speaks for you. They may get a part of it right and then totally misunderstand another portion. Or they may misconstrue the entire theme you wish to impart thereby bringing forth information that is absolutely incorrect. With this background of your own experience, you can imagine what a difficult task it is for spiritual teachers, both living and dead, to avoid being misquoted and misunderstood in holy books.

This is why the major world religions of the past brought teachers to the world in physical bodies or had prophets come to share their understanding of the teachings for others to grasp. This was necessary since most human beings had no awareness of an inner connection to Spirit. In this way the message was directly given but the time lags between visits were long and those who wrote the teachings down had no way to update them.

In the Golden Age, however, we shift from this former pattern so that every soul may speak directly from its personality facet to the soul. Through the process of meditation and contemplation, in times of silence and solitude, direct inner messages and assistance can come forth.

That is why I call these chapters the New Teachings, for in this material I tell you that humanity can now reach self-mastery through connection with its own soul and the Creator beyond. Once you develop the connection that makes this possible, your prayer and meditation link gives you direct access to the truth of who you are and what your actions should be. And then you will become the creation that was intended from the beginning through your own ability. When this is accomplished we can guide you all in a more personal and immediate way than you presently enjoy, which is the ultimate meaning of Sonship. From your growth you will become that peaceful citizenry capable of expressing God's purpose on the planet and humanity's obligations as her Caretakers.

Therefore, trust this new process of contact with your soul by contemplation, prayer and meditation, and realize that it is available to all who will take the time to give it the importance it must hold in your daily lives. But I will say more about this later on. For now please accept that the holy books of all religions need to be understood in a higher state of awareness which you and you alone can create by your wish to have it so. Why not install your cosmic connection?

I say to you that people who limit me to a past understanding of who or what I am are dangerous to themselves, for life is ever evolving in Spirit, and growth is the only measure it knows. Even your Universe is expanding. And why not? If love blossoms and the new seeds fall into fertile soil, is this not a natural thing?

Therefore, put away the old rugged cross of crucifixion and replace it with one of growth and expansion. Let me explain so there is absolutely no misunderstanding.

When I came as the light of that first son of God -- The Christ -- it was necessary I take on a physical body in which to reside and prove to humanity by my love that there is no death to their true identity. My resurrection is the energy force that is in me now. I am divorced from the crucifixion. It is over and done, and that story is part of an old time of guilt for you which is no longer alive, unless you keep focusing on it and making it your own.

Take me down from the old rugged cross if you yourself would be free! See me alive and beautiful and forget the story of the crucifixion and all its guilt and pain. Focus only on the resurrection if you are grateful for my coming -- if you would call me elder brother to the human family. As a symbol, use a circle with a short cross within, or a rainbow or a glowing sun, anything which denotes life or growth or unity. Your symbol of the crucified body on a cross must end unless you realize it is your human personality that must die to your soul. Then and only then does this symbol serve you at all.

Then let us each choose to forgive ourselves for anything real or imagined that was in any way related to that earth event 2,000 years ago. Be absolutely certain that as a group, and as individuals, you accept forgiveness for anything about that incident. I free you, today, from any sense of shame or guilt you may hold; just let it go. The experience for you must be completed and freed of negative emotions if humanity is to go forward in the light of this new time, this Golden Age.

Leave the remembrance of pain and guilt behind in the glory of my love for you, even as I ask you to forgive me for coming in the way I came to teach, not with my army of angels and military might, but simply in the singleheartedness of devotion and the clothing of truth. Do not blame anyone for not understanding the teachings. Release any judgment of self or others if you would be happy again. Hear this, churches! And deliver only this message. Know today that the crucifixion aspect is hereby cleansed and forgiven and only the resurrection is real!

Each soul learns from experience. But, if the experience is never healed and brought forth to greater understanding, it rests like a festering wound in the soul, holding valuable space which needs releasing. Since no two things can occupy the same place in your consciousness, I beg that you dump out the old memory so we can create new ones. Join in this present healing by your willingness to forget the past. The Christian religion is replete with guilt and negativity and needs to be changed. These are my new teachings. Follow them if you would be made whole again. Follow them to know peace.

Let your soul vomit out the old pain and be filled with the balm of forgiveness, mine to yours and yours to mine. This love counteracts all negativity, my beloveds. Stand free in the light of now, allowing the past its decent burial. Leave the cemetery of your yesterday and focus only on a new you and your urgent responsibility in this time on earth. Cleansed and filled with the grace of greater knowing and a transformed reality, you are truly healed. So, release any last tears and regrets and take my hand in peace. We must go forward for we have much to do now, children of light ... corps of love.

To help you understand my own growth and spiritual expansion these past 2,000 years let us look at your own earth family's experience with birth and aging. Perhaps you have a scrapbook of photographs taken with a camera over many years? If so, pick any one person's photo, possibly your own, and see what you looked like as a baby or young infant in your early life. Like your own image of yourself at that age, imagine me also as a infant -- great as I was -- and realize that just as you grew and changed and acquired new ideas and experiences, you were different as the years passed. So, dear ones, I am 2,000 years different.

For heaven is not some static place where nothing happens. We are related to the Universe and all that it does. This is the law. Each is a part of the whole, from the tiny to the immense. There is no separation. This is critical to grasp! Urgent to remember! On your earth you are in a hologram of the greater universal pattern.

Therefore I ask you to believe the story of my departure from human tribulation back to God -- to understand its significance -- and then to enjoy the new estate I hold while everything around us advances and expands in light and love. If I was powerful 2,000 years ago, you can expect me to be even more so now, even as you in your work or in a favorite skill, sport or hobby become more perfected in your activities as you use them. So I am even greater than before in wisdom and love as are all spiritual beings who came to teach. We do not remain frozen in time and space! Nor are we suspended somewhere!

Relate to the me of this time and place, and move with all of heaven as we come together again to learn and grow wiser. Leave these old photographs behind, nostalgic as they may be, and stay only in the present moment. You have grown up; your soul is here and empowered to create harmony. What are you creating now? What will humanity do to attain peace -- that blessed and promised peace?

See God, me, and those others who gladly assist humanity, both in the daytime of sun and clouds and in the night time of moon and stars, loving you and Mother Earth. And let the poetry of your wisdom remind you that everything we do is but change, expansion, ever reaching toward the greater love awareness.

The Omniverse is like a weaver with busy fingers creating a tapestry of magnificent beauty and dramatic impact. We do this together, each pair of hands connected to a loving heart and mind gathering the secrets God would share. Wisdom lies at the heart of this tapestry, glittering in crystal clarity for all to see and know. As we share the joy of bringing forth this NEW NATIVITY SCENE, we acknowledge the birthing of a new time and a greater spiritual awareness from which all good things come.

Now the good things of Jesus-past are not lost, but only expanded into a more beautiful diadem of love and wisdom. In the same way, your own souls are stretching into more infinite territories, becoming the greater light and the true knowing. And we go together. For each gains as any one gains. We are the One.

We are the unbreakable, eternal web of life, of beauty, of joy and love. And in this joining together the harmonious waves of sound and light fill the Universe to overflowing and it stretches forth another movement of life to expand itself and create more light, more light, and more light. The process is unending until God calls us back into that cosmic parental presence. For by this magnificent, unspeakable power we are wombed and breathed forth in a gush of life that explores and returns, goes forth again and again to bring back the experiences and growth of all travelers.

Let us travel together, then, my brothers and sisters, with God's light as our beacon, God's love as our diet, and God's ultimate wisdom as our map. "Seek ye the kingdom of heaven," has been said many times in many ways by all of God's teachers. Will you not listen and unify yourself in this unending adventure in life without death?

I, The Christ, have been raised up higher still during these past 2,000 years as have all of the beings of light who know God as the only creator of souls. We have not stood still! Heed my call in the name of the many here in heaven and beyond who will fill your thoughts with the life-transforming light and wisdom that love rests upon.

Come, faithful ones. Come those who have delayed! Do not be afraid to smell the sweet perfume of eternity. In this very moment are you made clean and pure, brought forth in the flowering beauty of God's creation. Brush the sleep from your mind and drop the dust-encrusted yesteryear from the garment of your soul. Gleam with me awhile in the quiet moments of our inner unification. Are your present activities so important that you would not trade them for the everlasting peace that love brings?

Forgiveness is offered you again, beloveds, ere the Creator's call takes us one step closer to home. Do not linger in your earthly toys a moment longer but raise your consciousness in meditation to the infusing movement of love energy which insists firmly and eternally upon peace within, and peace without. Does not the scent of truth fill your being? Then breathe with God, with me and all who divinely love you.

Breathe out all personal negativity, especially that which has infested and bludgeoned Mother Earth, and let us bring her the balm of healing thoughts and actions she needs. Enfold her in your love even as she has cradled you upon her nurturing soil. Treat her with respect and caring for her goodness; return like for like. She, too, lives and grows and learns. If you do not love and nurture her your soul will weep one day in immense sorrow.

Let your eyes be opened to the truth of your calling now. Earth is to be the planet of love and wisdom. Take your citizenship, then, in this great planetary movement into cosmic vibrations and peaceful pastures. The shepherds of whom I spoke long ago are needed still to lessen the number of souls gone astray. Let us do our best to enclose those who have forgotten their own true beauty, true nature, so they will choose again and choose correctly. With just a little willingness -- for anyone can still leave the old life and the old ways behind, this very day -- you can select a pattern of love and wisdom that your soul yearns to experience and to share.

Come, then, all. As our Creator-of-the-Many-Universes calls us home once more we will share, in the inner sanctuary of that Great One's mind, the tales of our many visits, of our many journeys into the reality of who and what we are. Yes, dear ones, we are the weavers of the tale, the story-tellers to all who seek truth. We are the kiss of God.

Then step into the arms of love which heaven promises. In ecstacy and bliss beyond your fondest remembrance will we be received into that Source which is the All-in-All. There is only one commandment for us. Peace.

Peace, dear ones. Peace. Amen.

1994/1995 COMMENTS

Now let me say that in reviewing some of the outdated astronomical information given in this chapter about the universes, galaxies, solar systems and planets, and my role as your world teacher, please remember one thing. There is so much to existence that you have yet to discover and remember about yourselves, let alone the many other lifeforms in the galaxy and beyond, that it is quite an overwhelming task to comprehend the vastness of it all. An inordinate amount of life and activity exists out here in the many dimensions and dominions which you cannot presently fathom because of your mutant DNA condition—yet you have only to look at your planet's variety and beauty to see the flamboyant expression of color and life all around you. It is extraordinary!

In what you call the void, space, the heavens, or the many mansions, there are literally billions of galaxies in one Universe, and within those galaxies even more solar systems and even more planets. It is a network of light and consciousness and physical expressions in material worlds beyond the counting. And because there are so many different levels and kinds of creation, it is an unending and imaginative experience. That is why Archangel Michael is gathering his legions of light. There is yet to be another world, another dimension and dominion requiring experienced beings to serve in harmonious intention. Perhaps you will be among them?

From this information you may surmise that the human species is located in a fairly recent part of a birthing area of evolution, situated in a part of the galaxy where active gases, particles and elements can support rapid development of physical planets and various lifeforms of considerable variety. In this way your own solar system was once birthed and sustained in that great cosmic fire of creation, and your spiritual essence took on the cloak of flesh for a time to be responsible caregivers, stewards, and maintainers of the planet and its many lifeforms. Dominion is a word used in your holy books. You were given the responsibility of dominion on this planet although in recent years this has been difficult to maintain. Still, there is now great hope that light will soon reign here again and that humanity's dominion will be reclaimed and properly maintained. Earth is a gorgeous planet deserving of your wisdom, care, and love, is it not?

The other message I would like to have you remember is that there is a misunderstanding about who I, Jesus, am in the higher heavens. Just remember that I am now willing to announce to the world that I am an energy supported by the power of Archangel Michael, who is the being referred to earlier in this chapter, though named only as a Creator. Since he has come in person to call all beings of light back into the fold, I am now free to describe the close ties we have and the close ties you can have, also, if you chose them.

May you hear me well, then, dear ones. I cannot be in the presence of the Father/Mother Creator—no one can, but I do relate to the one called Archangel Michael, among the first-born of God, which is what I intended to explain in this chapter. Then know that I am one son of the living God who loves you—one who holds the vision for your resurrection and return to the full consciousness you deserve. But do not erroneously assume that I am the only son of God—there are many. Somewhere in your soul you know this story very well. You know who and what you are and why you are on Earth. That is why I came—to remind you to remember and to rejoin the divine plan that needs you. Please awaken, my beloved ones, and come with me to do the Father/Mother's work. In group consciousness we can experience the essence of soul love and apply the enormous wisdom that love assures in its application. Will you answer the call to reclaim eternal life and stand with me in the circle of unity's power?

Peace be with you forever. Amen.

Chapter V

Using Your Inner Guidance

In every Universe be herewith advised that forever and ever all of God's commandments are still required, particularly DO NOT KILL! Nothing has changed. But, humanity as a group has not practiced these directives. Since so many people have *not* heeded the old commandments to love God with all their hearts, and to love their brothers and sisters as themselves, let us review their meaning for the modern day.

LOVE GOD. This means you must believe there is a force, energy, or light being that has awesome powers beyond your comprehension and that, since you were created by him, you must let him lead your life experience according to a Divine plan which you may not truly understand. In a word, you must be willing to TRUST that there is a blueprint for your return to God, and follow it at all times. Do not trouble yourself with why you became separate from God! Know that, however it happened, all is forgiven and you have been freed from any guilt associated with past actions. However, this grace, or being freed of the negative effects of past deeds, can only be validated by a change in your attitude and behavior toward yourself and others. Unless *you* take action this gift of grace has no meaning!

LOVE YOUR BROTHERS AND SISTERS AS YOURSELF. This statement means that EACH of you must love yourself as a creation of the One Source. That is, your spiritual awareness must tell you that you are more than the mere physical body and the personality you call "me". Your awareness comes not from some egotistical love, but from a soulfelt nature which knows God lives within and must be expressed. By that acceptance of yourself you can then love your brothers and sisters in like fashion. But do not attempt to love another from your own perverted personality self. Without soul guidance the personality cannot love. It can only seek to possess, to control, or to use others for its own needs. Your greatest challenge today is to find out the many levels of yourself -- particularly that vital spiritual level -- and then do the inner exploration, the cleansing of the personality characteristics that lie unexplored in the unconscious record of all you have ever experienced. These hidden aspects frequently prevent your full cooperation with the soul, unfortunately.

You are required, therefore, to relinquish all within your human personality that stands in the way of truly knowing yourself as the light, an ever-brightening soul quality. This cleansing is more than just going to a psychologist, minister, or counselor and becoming "well-adjusted." This process requires partnering with your own inner teacher, who knows what you need. Your path is unique and your inner guide knows your particular lessons. Do what it requests. I do not say other human beings cannot assist you in that process for there are many healers on the earth. Select one who knows psychology means the study of the soul, not just the human personality.

My point is that YOU are required to learn of yourself from that part which has not forgotten it was created by God ... your soul. Your lower personality has not known and recognized God and must be brought under the soul's purpose. Any therapy or art of healing which does not begin with the point of view that you are a creation of God will *fail* you. You will be incomplete without your soul at work in your life. It is your key to happiness. No other relationship can satisfy, because you cannot hide from nor ignore who you really are if you want to be truly joyful.

When you agree that you are a soul created by a power beyond comprehension to your mere mortal personality, a power which carries you to wider love and joy, you will begin the healing process. You will begin to feel peace. When you are finally healed of the disbelief and limitation of who and what you truly are, your life will change. And you can then love your brothers and sisters as yourself, for they are like you in Spirit. Not in personality, certainly, but in Spirit. When you can love and honor the Father/Mother's creation in you, then and only then are you safe to say you love another. Do you comprehend?

Therefore, seek only therapists who have themselves been healed and who come to you from that inner acceptance of themselves as a creation of God. For then they can love you and model what I came to teach. How will you know them? Dear ones, by your sensitivity, by the guidance your soul will share. Let this inner teacher, intuition, or God guide, lead the way. When you finally decide to know yourself as the created soul you are, you will be led to all who will serve you in your full and rich development.

You came to earth to live from your soul's level of understanding, and when this occurs you will be the peace of God, and this planet will be transformed by the glow of your light. "Blessed are they who thirst" applies here. Thirst to become a full-time light of the world, and all else will be added. Are you willing to begin this quest? If so, my heart is open to assist you. You will have strong companions through the depths of that exploration.

To bring you absolute success in finding your soul purpose and expressing it, I will give you the perfect guidelines to carry out this divine exploration and encourage you to accept the responsibility for their use. For it is their use which will open the door to a changed life. Please listen exceedingly well as I review these guidelines as tools for God-awareness, for enlightenment.

ONE

To contact the living God within you there must be a daily time of listening established. I have called this experience of quiet listening, *meditation*. By my definition, prayer is requesting God to do certain things in your life and thanking God for that gift. *Meditation is listening,* however, and is a different process. There is no schedule or agenda after you acknowledge that you are of God's light, by whatever name you give it. Then call the light, or Christ Consciousness, to be with you, for each must ask to receive it. After surrounding yourself with God's light and love you simply sit quietly to hear, with the inner voice, what is being transmitted.

Many from western cultures are drawn to the Oriental religions because they know and stress how to still the mind. They know how to be quiet and listen. It is vital, dear ones, to acquire such habits, so I have asked you to sit quietly each day, preferably at the same time, in order to establish your own personal channel to your soul and then to God. Then since habit plays a large part in your life, use habit to establish what is good for you, but separate the time of asking God for what you want from the time you *listen* to what God would say. These are two different things. I have used the word meditate to mean *listening to God.* Contemplation may also be a useful word here. "Be still and know I am God ... " is the way this was previously given in the Bible.

That which is called meditation, contemplation, or being still within, is as old an activity as human life itself. In fact, it began as a gift to those with individualized souls so they could stay in touch with the First Cause while they were living in the material world of physicalness. Meditation, therefore, is the primary way a human being can find peace of mind and connection to love, to light and to the spiritual sources which are always available to the individual seeking holy guidance ... the true knowing of life's blueprint and direction.

Meditation begins with the simple act of stopping the everyday activities and sitting quietly, with a salutation or prayer of reverence and thoughtfulness to God in mind and heart. This, combined with quieting of the mind by the natural act of deep breathing until a relaxed state is reached, brings one to the place where God can be known. For the nature of God cannot penetrate into the busy mind ... it comes only to the peaceful mind, willing heart and relaxed body. All religions speak of this, the Christian Bible included.

By greeting God in love and respect, by allowing relaxation to be deepened by taking ten to fifteen deep breaths and letting go of the busy details of human life, you shift into a place which is refreshing and peaceful. If the mind insists on trying to divert your attention, you simply put your attention on your breath as it comes in and goes out, for it is the breath that connects your life thread to the Creator's nature while you are here in the physicalness of flesh.

Breathe. Breathe deeply and release all thoughts of everything except God and the immense cosmos in which life exists in a myriad of forms and experiments. BREATHE. This simple act can be done anywhere, anytime, under any circumstance. There is nothing mysterious about it. You do it all the time unconsciously. In doing the act of breathing with your attention upon it, however, you permit your own soul access to your mind and heart, allowing certainty and clarity to enter your experience.

Breath was the gift of God upon your birth into the body. It is yours to use until it is given back at that moment you call death. Your whole existence is based on the act of breathing. Then use it daily -- and consciously -- to take you home to the Parent-of-us-All. In this way do you reestablish the connection of your mind with the Source who has always loved you, always will love you, and who has given you this simple procedure for tuning into that unconditional love you long for at the core of your very being. This love is the only true reality.

Just as you have your home telephone connected in order that you may call others on the earth, or they may call you, you may connect to the Source, during this quiet time of peaceful meditation, to know the highest and best solution to any life circumstance. This solution will always be in your, and the planet's, best interest. Be assured that this innate gift was provided for each soul's individuality millions of years ago here on earth.

Know also, and without question, that your free will choice to accept God is your lifeline to truth, your helper in every situation. You have not been left comfortless, dear ones, but it is something which you must wish to have and for which you must ask. Is that not simple?

If you were starving for food or thirsting for water, what would you do? Let us hope you would ask for help if you could not obtain the things by yourself. By your asking, our help is provided. As director of this life you lead on earth you may ask or not as you wish. Be assured once more -- and with the deepest of conviction -- that any word spoken of to God with fervor and clarity will be heard.

In prayer, for instance, if you give a heart's longing your daily attention and focus for a period of 21-30 days you can be sure that it will eventually manifest, unless you refuse to do your part in achieving what action needs to be taken at your end, or unless your soul's pattern would be adversely affected by the fulfillment of your request. Neither can you ask harm against another in your own best interest, unless of course you wish to connect with the black forces which will quickly assist you in that goal for a price -- your soul.

There are many on earth who by their direct agreement or a lazy capitulation of their inner wisdom have, unfortunately, done just that. Yet even such a detour can be forgiven and the soul returned to peace and light through the earnest reverence for God and the will to have love in place of power. For this is the age old theme with which humanity struggles. The possession of power draws many souls to the mistaken belief that this is the most important aspect of life. But the petty personality's need for power is a substitute for God's power and can never bring satisfaction even if it is temporarily attained. But many there are who must learn this lesson the painful way.

The only true, safe power is of God. When you invite this into your life, you will discover the security for which you have longed and the power will be given you to do the desire of a loving soul. God's power through you as a channel of light and peace is the greatest experience possible for a human being. With this pure motive your life will become a heavenly balance of love and wisdom -- the hallmark intended for your species. Give thanks this is the truth and let your gratitude be expressed in a joyful heart and contented soul.

In nearly every major religion of your world, and in the smaller sects, as well, there have been meditation or contemplation practices used somewhere. Therefore, if you belong to a particular church, find out who practices meditation and learn it yourself. Begin to focus more and more upon this activity, which takes you into silence and direct connection to the God within you.

If your church does not focus upon meditation, ask it to do that. Perhaps you can change its focus to meet your own needs. And if it will not assist you in obtaining your heart's desire, explore other institutions which do. As I have said previously, simply group together with other meditators and hold that activity as your personal avenue to God.

The point here is not to destroy the churches per se, but to advise them that they must meet your spiritual need to know God directly. If they cannot accept this mission for their members they will become archaic, of this you can be sure. For this is a Golden Age, a moment in spiritual evolution which requires change and willingness to surrender your selfish goals for that of God's planetary blueprint. And you can only know God's design as you become still and listen to the hymn of loving direction which is even now forthcoming. Peace, peace, peace. Surely your heart knows this celestial message!

Then take the tool of meditation to learn the specifics of how peace is to be accomplished, beginning in your own daily life. Revere God's message and, then as you live it, this true path will bring you across the bridge of higher consciousness to your soul's homeland and to its perfect relationship with our Creator.

Please turn to the sunshine of this new time and leave the foggy day of confusion behind. You have a right to live under the warmth and vitality of God's personal direction upon this earth as well as in the eternal, everlasting life which follows. You need not settle for less when you now know the truth!

I can only fervently advise you to become a contemplative person and a consistent meditator, for the very fabric of earth's existence depends upon having a majority of human beings turn to God each day for the guidance, direction, and spiritual revitalization of love and peace. For when you are surrounded by earthly negativity how can you be refreshed and spiritually fed every day? Meditation works! Please do this in remembrance of God.

Let me repeat this to reinforce its importance. There are many styles or forms of meditation -- but a simple one is using the breath to still the mind as you relax into inner peace and let go of earthly attachments. You will receive guidance from your soul, or the many spiritual guides, teachers or masters of the light who serve mankind on earth, more easily through relaxation of mind and body. You will be drawn to the highest relationship possible for you by asking within for inner guidance. At the least you can begin at once to sit still, loving God with all your heart, and breathing deeply until your cares and concerns fall away.

This is a natural process, as ancient as life itself, and is *foolproof* provided you always follow this method. Begin your meditation by acknowledging that you are of the Christ Consciousness and by asking that the pure light and love of God be with you. If you are ever contacted mentally by a non-physical being (even myself), challenge it by asking, "Are you of the Christ Consciousness?" Every non-physical entity or vibration must answer this question truthfully. On this you can rely. BUT YOU MUST ASK! Beings of the light will answer this question joyfully in the affirmative. In the rare event that a negative being should attempt to contact you and you challenge it with the question "Are you of the Christ Consciousness?" there will either be silence or a clever argument which avoids a "Yes" answer. In such a case, simply insist that this energy leave you, and it will be done. Those who love God with pure spiritual intention and commitment are seldom bothered by negative influences. However, anyone who still harbors fear, anger, lust, or the need for power over others could attract those qualities to themselves. If for any reason you are ever discomforted during your meditation time, simply invoke the Christ Consciousness by calling on Jesus or the Archangel Michael to attend you. Rest assured that if your meditation is intended as a stairstep to God, it will be so.

Always listen to what comes to you during or after this time of quietude. Once the daily practice is established as a focal point of each day, the power of God will enter your life to the degree you request and accept it. Not overnight, but in due time as you remain constant in your commitment, your life will change for the better if you allow it to be guided by the forces of God. Not only will your own life change, but also the entire planetary consciousness will be improved. For by improvement in the small part you play, and in the spreading of that personal peace to others, they will also be ignited and your joint participation can truly make a difference.

Enjoy your meditation, prayer and contemplation time. It is God-given. And may your example of peace and love spur many others to this activity now recommended to you on earth as both a personal and planetary healing tool.

All great saints and sages who have listened in the stillness have had mystical experiences, which is to say, they have known God directly. It is this experience you may have also.

In truth this process is your stairway to the lighted halls of soul consciousness. Please join us there, dear ones. We await you.

Meditate daily for 20-30 minutes. Do this in remembrance of God who waits for your acceptance of who and what you are. Let this be your proof or demonstration that you are willing to be led. In this time when you sit quietly, you are actually establishing a strong light within yourself and then building a beam of light between your physical body and your soul. After the year or so that it usually takes to establish soul communication you can sit quietly and be guided from the soul level (or your "higher self") that is in contact with me and other world spiritual teachers through mental telepathy.

As you become purified in your lower personality and choose to listen to your soul's direction, you will be cleansed of your subconscious memories of pain, anger, false beliefs and stifling limitations. From this cleansing, great peace will follow. For as you are purged of the hell you carry inwardly, your human personality is freer to know and express that spiritual peace quality beyond your present comprehension.

Yes, each human being without a connection to God is chained by those hellish negative thoughts given by parents and all the society members who have placed their own opinions into the baby's memory banks. Even spiritual people have misinformation in their subconscious memories. And it is not until that memory in the subconscious -- or hidden, emotional record beneath conscious awareness -- is stirred and cleansed with light that healing takes place. You must be willing to give up those false beliefs, negative barriers and limitations -- whatever they are -- and *surrender* them in order to spiritually change your daily existence.

TWO
The next thing I recommend each of you do is join together with other human beings of goodwill who also practice the quietude of meditation. This way you can join your vibrations of love and peace with theirs. Then on a weekly basis be sure to meet and meditate together for 20-30 minutes, allowing all separation to fall away. Let the love and dedication to God join you in a glow of light that we in the higher dimensions can literally see. For we do see! And we do know! Your light shines as a tiny pinpoint or marker in the darkened area of your planet even as a city street light gleams away the night.

Believe me when I say that you can pool your separate energies during this weekly meditation. This combined energy is extremely powerful and useful for healing the planet, for healing specific people who are named, and for purposes you cannot yet imagine. Therefore, be assured that wherever two or more people are gathered in mutual intention, we can join you and amplify your light and energy immensely. For when you received a separate soul millions of years ago, the angelic realms were told to guard and guide you as you found your way into full awareness. Thus, you are served with love and a knowing far beyond that of your limited personalities.

The more people who join together in meditation, of course, the greater the amplification of energy and light, which is why large groups are extremely valuable in creating an energy focus of immense power. When all focus to project the same image ... as of peace or love, or for healing ... a huge concentrated light and the rainbow colors rise to be magnetized and returned from us with even further amplification. Obviously the more people and the greater their focus, the greater its impact will be when we add the power of heaven. This power, or union of light, dispels darkness. So let all in your group agree that they are there to be useful and ask that the light of God be added to assist the planet for peaceful purposes.

Leaders can take turns in a prayer or affirmation at the beginning of a meditation so that the opportunity for all to learn leadership is provided. Shy ones can ask for help if they need it, but should not, because of human personality fears, give away their turn at calling forth the love of God. You are each as God created you. Accept nothing less even if you have to work up to full demonstration gradually. Be willing to take the tiny step toward certainty.

I wish you to realize, also, that not only do you give love through this time of mutual meditation but you receive as well. For your own light and energy are increased and magnified and your soul's contact with you is advanced. Thus do you grow to higher opportunity and awareness and join those who await you in the gentle silence of home.

Form a group of three people or more if you cannot find one already started, or join with even one other person to feel the joy that comes from this willingness and commitment. For by your light and love are the imbalances of negativity brought under control.

When you combine with God through your soul, and with any teacher who has joined with our Creator's identity and energy, you begin a process of inner healing that frees you from the old ways which attract back to you undesirable life experiences. For what you think and feel are real things, with a life of their own. As they travel from your mind and body into the unseen ethers of space, they magnetically call an identical energy forth to join them. There, like attracts like, whether positive or negative. *The quality you send out is what you receive!* Until you realize you are causing these particular vibrations, and that they will return a negative response, you are a prisoner of pain and suffering and will blame God for your problems. But this thinking is not valid.

When you ask to give up your negativity and bring God's light into your life, major changes will occur from that small initial willingness to have heaven rather than your own confusion. Life will indeed become miraculous: individuals and groups will prosper. Therefore, to begin a more beautiful life, ask God for help. And, if you are already under God's direction, ask always *to be open to receive that which has already been given you.*

Say to yourself, "God, why am I here on the planet? What is it you would have me do today that serves my own growth and my love and service to others?" As you sit silently in communication with your soul, focusing your attention inwardly with love, you will link yourself one step at a time to its love energies which will serve your spiritual path in love and peace. Call upon the light to surround you and protect and guide you in all things. Any sincere prayer which asks for this is sufficient. Light and love are your keys to a glorious, inner kingdom. Use them ethically and offer your life to God's service, individually and in groups.

Love is wholeness in which God's power can flow through the cleansed human personality and manifest itself in the everyday world as peace, as light, and as joy. The willingness to know yourself and to know God is all that is required. As you meditate and receive God into your life, you will be changed. Harmony will become your hallmark! And, therefore, earth's as well.

I want to explain how this happens and why. It develops naturally out of your love of God and your willingness to cleanse yourself of negative thoughts (which is to say, "Be born again").

At the time of the so-called fall, all were given separate souls in order to learn the lesson of love and devotion and wisdom as an extension of God. A communication line from the Holy Spirit within to God's higher mind was then connected to each soul so it could still be in spiritual communication. Thus your soul is connected to God and when your personality is cleansed it can reach the soul and beyond. This process of God to soul and soul to personality brings enlightenment.

Some souls receive better than others because of their willingness and prior experience in doing so. Some are already self-masters, but many others are still seeking that mastery. Due to the ever increasing soul development of those on earth, then, doubt not that other people today can see and hear aspects of the living Universe that you may not have reached! But it is God's plan for everyone to see and hear as humankind grows and evolves in love and service -- to see, hear and sense beyond the physical world. Surely you realize this potential in yourself. Aren't you capable of far more than you have already done?

So, just as some sports players are more skilled, and some doctors are more truly healers than others, so it is true of communication with God and the forces of light. Some souls do this better than others. Yet all souls are capable of, and encouraged to, become champions in this area of their lives. But like anything you value, there must be sincerity and true investment to make it happen. I promise you that we in the higher realms are already speaking with many earth souls about God's plan for the planet and its upcoming changes, and we are also assisting human personalities with their daily activities in creating the heaven on earth which is soon to come. In fact, I speak today with a soul who, as my scribe, records my thoughts for you!

The critical thing to remember here is that there are as many levels of skill or *quality* in spiritual knowing, as there are in anything else. I repeat that word *quality* and will take this idea further. One day when you are all rejoined with God, the entire creation will have full spiritual powers of knowing beyond the physical senses as once you did formerly. This is the return of powerful, forgotten abilities, dear ones, and is natural! In the meantime, many have some or part of these abilities, frequently referred to on your earth by the word psychic.

I remind you that in its true definition, psychic means knowing from the soul. It does not tell you what level of soul development a psychic has, however. In this respect you must be cautious in your exploration of those who claim to be psychic. Be sure they are spiritually committed to God and humankind! From this spiritual seed only good will grow and blossom.

The truest information is intuitive knowing -- soul channeling when it is highly developed -- and it is for this you should strive. Never believe what others say without your own inner consultation, and never totally surrender your own authority to their suggestions about life situations, problems, and the like. But use what is offered in a thoughtful, soulful manner. Even these words of mine should bear the test of your own heart, beloveds.

You should be developing your own soul expression for direction and understanding, although you can learn much from some of the great soul channels now on the earth. Again I say to you, however, that even if you ask another for soul channeling on your behalf, it is from God you must seek assistance through your own daily meditation and evaluation of your dreams, for these are your personal avenues of truth, and you must develop them as you would practice any desired prowess.

Therefore, become the recipient of your own inner guidance by surrendering any disbelief about the possibility of such things and ask in reverent sincerity to open your own higher knowing in a safe and protected way. If your true intention in having this expansion is to love God more deeply, and your brothers and sisters as yourself, heaven will assuredly reach down to assist and empower this development!

If you are willing to know yourself, truly, many present earth activities are available to those who would grow and develop in this way. Listen within and you will be led to those earth beings like yourself who can best teach you and learn from you, as well, for in all things we are both learners and teachers to each other. Even the angels learn from humanity as they assist mankind in its spiritual evolution.

We are sending much support to earth at this time so that no one who truly wishes to grow in love and self-knowledge can fail to achieve it. Trust that you can actually know us of the heavenly realms in very real ways as we bridge the gap between your disbelief and God's reality. Simply speak your word and back it with your intention. This recipe for loving recognition of the truth is foolproof, indeed, for it was created by God. Be glad that it is so.

Match God's gift with your own soul's joyful fervor and see what happens to you in this ever unfolding adventure in the Universe. The Creator has many mansions. Claim yours now by meditating your personal lifeline into existence. And give gratitude to our Creator that there is a plan and you are allowed to knowingly participate in it. What a gift!

Notice how often I have suggested, and will encourage again, that you turn within at least one quiet time per day in meditation so that you may be guided to the voice for God within your own beingness. If I am repetitive it is because of the critical nature of the historic hour you face and because of my deep and abiding love for mankind. It is like watching a child play with matches near an open gasoline tank. I am deeply troubled. I cannot fail to speak, for your earthly warmongers play with the matches that can only bring devastation and remorse. We of the higher realms are concerned for that beautiful land you call earth and for

God's creation gone astray. That is why we come to you again to try to connect you with your God-self, or inner knower, so that you will not only appreciate the seriousness and value of this recommendation but put it into practice.

I have said, dear ones, that you must forge the connection between God and yourself by your own *free will*. This action of a daily meditation time actually forges, with an invisible energy you cannot see, a communication device of marvelous substance and beauty. Like an inter-stellar radio or television device, after you have built it by constant and serious devotion, much information will be available to you from a variety of higher sources. These minds cannot reach you until this communication system has been established by your commitment and perseverance.

In doing this, some may come to see beautiful light energies around living things. But most on earth are unaware of them and cannot presently see the light, the colors, and the power that has created the Universe. Once connected to the higher dimensions some will receive our thoughts telepathically, or even hear clairaudiently, as well as just sensing or knowing things.

Your scientists are just now understanding that all life is joined as a web of energy particles, waves and other not-yet-discovered-by-you forces and entities. Soon you will understand many of the unknown universal laws that have so far been misunderstood or undiscovered.

For instance, we of the spiritual realms are currently showering your planet with higher and higher love vibrations and frequencies to assist you in achieving soul advancement. You might think of it as being fueled by a miraculous substance that allows you vaster understanding, a more open view of the cosmos, and the healing joy that comes when Divine love pours upon you like balm on a burn. Some are aware of this love energy but many are not. Even if these vibrations are felt, they are not generally seen and are therefore denied.

As you meditate you will be aided by these tremendous boosts in your energy quality which will help you raise your identity from one of a mere earthling to one of a more cosmic nature. This energy change is another step transmuting the lower nature of man to that of a heavenly one. In truth, the opportunity is now made for the Child of Humanity to rise into that supreme position as the Child of God. This was my mission, and is my mission! To bring my brothers and sisters home to the Creator once more. And I have much help here with me from all religions of all times for this task. We now request your earthly help.

Through meditation you can raise your energy vibrations and come home to us. Will you make this choice and ask us in? We are not allowed to establish mental communication with any soul who denies us access. For those who do choose God, let me outline the type of commitment that is required and the results you may expect as the outcome of that spiritual choice.

As you begin building the communication system from your human personality to your soul, or your higher self, through daily meditation and a time of sitting quietly, the light will be constructed in actual physical ways which psychic eyes can observe. But the system cannot be built overnight. It is a gradual thing for most people unless they are already highly committed and have just been trembling on the brink of this further spiritual step. As this bridge is forged out of the energy of your commitment, there will gradually be a change in your life which shifts the way you know things. Within a year it is certain that you will feel more peaceful and receive insights for the finest form of daily living. So you must be consistent and patient in your devotion and practice.

If you meditate daily and join with friends of the same intention -- or if you seek out meditation groups of good repute -- you can do much to speed your spiritual progress and strengthen the built-in communication system, which has been dormant in unused portions of your physical brain. One day soon your doctors and scientists will learn that the brain's pineal and pituitary glands work as a gigantic crystal along with that large portion of the brain which is currently not used by humanity. Then the process as well as the capacity for mental telepathy will be understood. Take no heed of those who say "I can't meditate" or "I can't sit still that long" or any number of other personality-defined excuses. I have heard humans say "It sounds stupid to me" or "I have no time."

I assure you these limited perceptions are foolish and irrelevant. The truth is that for any normal person some practice of stillness is possible and necessary. How else can you still the buzzing racket of your everyday mind to reach God ... to reach those of us at the fourth, fifth, sixth or higher levels of consciousness above your own?

Only a few humans have become so connected to Spirit that they have *become* the meditation -- as I did -- so these are rare indeed, but all can learn the simple process I have shared. Be still, then, no matter what you call it, and quiet your rambling thoughts every day. By this practice do you grow and all will truly benefit as each of you begins to demonstrate a greater inner harmony and peace. Is it not obvious by now that your intellect has failed to do this?

MEDITATION IS CONNECTION TO THE ORIGINAL SOURCE ... TO GOD'S FREQUENCY. It is much like your TV or radio receivers which must be tuned in for proper reception. What we of the higher realms are offering to do is align or fine-tune each being to the frequency of the original creation. God is there, at a presently distant point in your awareness, and so we must act as transmitting stations for you to receive these clearer thought vibrations.

God's vibration, through myself and other beings known as "the rays," is being focused to you now. The Central Being's energies are sent through us and directed toward planet earth. So the supportive energies are here for you, just as radio or TV waves are constantly available if you have the right equipment to translate them into sound and image. Unfortunately, most human beings are walking around out of a-tune-ment. They feel out of sorts, confused, and non-peaceful.

Now if someone were to walk up to them and tune them into the correct frequency, like a TV receiver, all of earth's population could be on the same thought vibration, but free will prohibits our doing that for you. Free will, the gift of God, requires that you ask for assistance, and that is why so many people doubt and are unaware. Once attuned, however, a being has the bright light of clarity because the channel frequency is in proper focus. Then a person is "on the beam" and life is beautiful. There is no longer desire to harm anyone. The person seeks to do only good. He or she is peaceful.

Meditation is a method of fine-tuning humanity, for each who chooses it. In this deliberate choice to sit silently the frequencies unite and awareness of that great source, The Beginning, becomes possible. What you call the Christ Consciousness is lovelight, even when clothed in flesh, still retaining the full awareness of, and commitment to, God.

My statement to you, therefore, is merely this: all of these teachings, as each being enters the Golden Age, are to help every individual become finely tuned, or to reach a-tune-ment to that God-self which lies within. For each of you contains the spark, or possibility, of knowing God, the first and only giver of energy and light to support all life. To be in touch with this Source is to live eternally, or if you wish to rephrase it ... to have life everlasting.

God gave you everything you need to function on earth and earn self-mastery. Dreams, prayers, and meditation assist in this process. For a few even Divine revelation is possible. Do not doubt. Proceed as if all things are possible and await the miraculous changes that will surely come.

Once you have connected your lower personality to the original and higher part of you -- the God part -- some of you will be able to receive mental telepathic communication from Spirit as your power is intensified and you focus your ability and commitment. As the inner voice of God becomes stronger and stronger in your life, it will bring you peace and joy unspeakable. To be used of God in this way is the only mark of an enlightened person as we proceed into the Golden Age.

Until now your churches and schools have filled you full of facts, many of which are false, not because they wish to deceive but simply because they, and the societal values they represent, do not yet understand who you are and what education really is. Education is the spiritual connection with truth from the highest source and its consequent flow through each soul's communication system down to its earth personality for implementation. We place no special blame on educators. We do, however, require that they and all society grasp that the true purpose of education is a spiritual process of unfoldment in which each person and the whole of humanity gain.

The Golden Age absolutely requires that humanity move to a new, more loving nature and commitment to God and peace above all else. It does NOT mean you will automatically advance spiritually.

I have noticed that many so-called Christians think they can claim love and forgiveness for themselves through the grace of Jesus or other religious teachers and then become inactive, self-satisfied, even self-righteously complacent do-nothings. This is *not* so. My name definitely does not guarantee which place in the Father's mansions you will attain. It means only that you have chosen to perceive love instead of fear, hatred and guilt, and that you are willing to express this love in an ever-expanding way.

You must be willing to learn and to follow God's instructions. You must be able to model the highest form of love you can. Most of all, you must truly adore God, love yourself as the heavenly realms love you, and then love all of life as yourself. Be love. Model love. Become the Christ. "Christ" means light. Be as strong and bright a light as you can if you would advance in this current opportunity to demonstrate what you came to learn. The opposite of light is darkness ... or death.

Because of misunderstandings which your religions have created regarding death I hasten to assure you that the experience you call death does not advance you to an eternally quiet, boring existence, as it is most often described in the name of the Christian religion. Heaven is not some continuing vacation land! We do not just play harps and wait for something to happen. We are vitally alive and involved for the Creator in many places with many assignments. It is a stimulating opportunity wherein you may continually advance and be used for higher and higher purposes. Think you that I am not serving the one you call God in greater and greater purpose? If you believe that all the dead are asleep until some far distant judgment day you absolutely have the wrong picture and incorrect understanding of life and spiritual purpose. Therefore, I say that your deeds on earth do count, do assist in your future placement in the heavenly realms once you accept Spirit into your life.

Believe, then, in a *constantly expanding Universe* with opportunity for all to learn and love, and do all you can to express love and give service on earth. This loving expansion makes heaven on earth possible, does it not? As we of the light help raise humanity and the planet into the greater heavenly realms beyond time, the light spirals everywhere. Are not the "many mansions" of the night sky shimmering and stretching from horizon to horizon? Yet you have only a microscopic view of the Universe because planet earth exists as a tiny suburb in the outskirts of the Milky Way. In the center of this throbbing galaxy lies the spiritual seat of power to which your small solar system gives allegiance, yet you know it not. But by trusting and following the Creator's will, you earth children will have God's purpose unfold to you now in this present time, in its own way. Trust, dear ones. Trust. There is a plan and its hour is here. The event cannot be delayed.

Finally, I wish to amplify two more words, *dreams* and *prophecy,* as they are also gifts to God's children far, far from home.

DREAMS
Human beings have always had the power to learn and receive guidance through dreams. I smile when I hear uninformed humans say, "I never dream." Say instead that you have

not chosen to remember your dreams and that will be the truth. For in all things you have free will and you must deliberately intend to remember dreams, just as you must request and desire anything you really want in life.

All humans dream nightly for a variety of reasons even if they don't choose to recall them. First and foremost dreams are given for inspiration and remembrance of your true estate in consciousness. They are a kind of interdimensional communication from your guides and teachers, or angels, to encourage and support your life's progress. Dreams are also symbols of self-understanding which can bring relief and release from pain, anxiety, and grief -- from all earthly negative emotions as you experience these, day by day.

When you have struggled in vain for answers to urgent problems or challenges, dreams can swiftly provide an answer that has eluded your conscious mind -- that resistor of what cannot be seen by the five physical senses. In this way, dreams can assist your solution to problems which usually have a specific and perfect answer for all involved. They are given to those who ask and will truly implement higher guidance. Is heavenly insight not worth the trouble of encouraging and recording? For the dream can slip away in a yawn or the darkness of your bedroom before you can write it down, unless you persist with new habits of recording them and working with them later. You receive mail every day. Why not receive your nightly messages also and respond to them with the seriousness that dreams deserve?

So begin to ask for dreams, men as well as women, even if it comes easier for some females of your species. Your goal is for each person, regardless of their physical sex, to have the balance of both male and female characteristics within them. For intellect alone is cold and unfeeling and rampantly endangers life as it blasts its bombs and tramples cruelly across Mother Earth. Spirit needs both the love and the wisdom aspects for perfect balance. The sun and the moon -- intellect and nurturance -- must be combined if your souls would find true peace. From this pure androgyny is peace born and spread throughout the ethers.

Thus a male will combine the highest masculine and feminine qualities within himself for expression in life and a female must do this also. Your world struggles now in this growth and understanding! It is not just the female's task to express love and build a balanced wisdom factor, but a male requirement, as well. For balance within self is the key. All must achieve balance, irrespective of the physical body being used, to attain spiritual self-mastery.

Dreaming is, then, both practical and inspirational and is one of the tools given you when God granted you a separate soul and you left the original Mind-of-All, that unified home of all souls. As such, this gift from God should be used by all human creation as a way of cleaning out negative emotions, of being guided in daily affairs, of learning the deeper truths about themselves and of growing spiritually.

Since dreams come from another dimension they are presented in symbolic format to prevent distortion by your conscious mind. And in fact, the process of sleep is not only to allow your physical body to rest and rejuvenate, but was created so the emotions could be cleansed and restored to harmony, too. These purposes of sleep and the understanding that your awareness can really leave its human flesh for excursions into higher portions of its consciousness in heaven, and with God, is not a widely held belief by your doctors. But it is one which would assist them in their understanding of the importance of rest, relaxation and de-stressing. For only when you choose to change the busy mental activity of your intellect can you escape the confines of earthly boundaries to learn and play in God's world. The time is coming when this will be clearer to all concerned, however, and health can be practiced in a more profound and holistic way.

Because dreams are interpreted at a feeling level and thereby represent emotional guideposts, they bring greater peace and allow the elimination of the barriers to love's presence. In this dramatized capsule of guidance, dreams deliver a pictorial short-hand to help develop health. Since dreams exist in all cultures, you may be sure they are a way of bringing your human personality the awareness of itself in relation to Spirit.

Thus, if you feel confused about dreams and how to interpret them, look into your local community resources for those who have an interest in dreams and dreaming. Or simply begin the process of exploring your dreams by asking for inner guidance to help you. It is your willingness that establishes the avenue through which you know yourself and become more whole.

Dreams, like symbolic movies, reveal your place, your purpose, and your progress in life. Use them, for they were given in love by that Great One who holds you in memory as once you were and who has saved your original kingdom in the holographic and electrifying flash of your creation. Let these capsules of truth help free you from the bondage of earth and the path you tread here. Like meditation, it is a time of listening and receiving. Be grateful you are not alone on your journey and that an eternity of caring surrounds you.

PROPHECY

The highest form of superconscious, or spiritual, contact is a vision of profound impact which smashes through the darkness of your awareness with such clarity that you will remember it lifelong. The feeling and power of visions are so intense, so real, that you are temporarily lifted from the limitation of physical senses and raised into audience with a higher form of Spirit which is never forgotten. Anyone who has had such an experience holds it like a warm treasure in the heart. Visions are rare for most humans but will come more and more frequently in this new time.

Also, it is important that you realize your meditations will bring more dreamlike states in which you are guided by us so your awareness can begin to blend heaven into earth's new reality -- *the fourth dimension.* Therefore, even if you do not receive a major vision, be prepared to receive what you call precognitive dreams, or announcements of future events about which you had no prior knowledge in your everyday conscious mind. If warnings and messages of assistance are required because of sudden earth movements, catastrophy, or man-made war and devastation, you can be informed almost immediately within your own consciousness.

Precognition, or knowing things in advance of their occurrence, will become more and more common for many of you. Again, accept this gift with gratitude for its intention is self-preparation. Knowing a thing *prior* to the happening is a gift of your soul. You may recall in the various holy books of your world that prophecy was of paramount importance and the prophets were always harbingers of the events announced before their coming. And, I might add, generally not believed by the majority of humankind, shrunk as they were into the physical body and unable to perceive the light energy or power source of their own existence.

Realize that in the New Age the knowing of things generally considered unseen, and unseeable, will change, as heaven and earth blend together once more in the higher vibration of existence. Knowing, from your soul level, things which lie out of the range of the five physical senses will be more and more usual. It will be very natural for many to receive truth from what you refer to as psychic levels. There are a variety of ways to be psychic that are spiritually acceptable, the highest of which is communion with your soul and then to spiritual teachers like myself, through your soul's focus to us.

In this coming time, therefore, there will be some prophets in all lands, describing events and circumstances which the physical body and the intellect cannot see or know, as they are in communication with us in your heavenly realms. There will be a variance in the quality of information received because it must filter through the particular human personality qualities in order to reach earth's dimension. If you wish to receive the pure thoughts that will be given you, please remember to cleanse yourself of as many negative personality aspects as you can, for only in this way will you be able to receive them with the highest quality possible.

As you meditate in weekly meetings with others like yourself who seek only love, this will provide a sanctuary for truth to dwell in more perfectly. By this process of mutual growth and sharing, much will be revealed before its time with reliability and accuracy.

Do not be surprised if more appreciation of life and all that gives lasting meaning flows into your daily life henceforth. Perhaps you will hear celestial music or have poetry begin its joyful rhyme amidst your daily thought. The animals and the birds -- all life -- will feel the gentleness of your increasing love vibration and will respond in kind. If the hummingbird circles your head and then lingers awhile in the whirling gyrations of wings to greet and bless you, let your heart be filled with joy and send a message of love back to this feathered one who acknowledged your light. And kill no thing that can be avoided. Remember God's commandment ... DO NOT KILL ... and extend this as far as you can.

If you must kill a fish or fowl, or a plant to eat for food, thank and bless it so that its existence will have been honored. Would you not want the same? Treat your own body lovingly and it will repay you with good health.

Please honor God's creation of all life, from the tiniest blade of grass to an exploding nova. In honoring the cosmos you honor yourself, because life births out of energy into matter and back again. These earth rituals of life beginning and then trans- muting into a different energy state are everywhere present around you with obvious reason. God is all, and God is in all. Therefore, salute yourself and all living things for the fascinating panorama you display in the Universe. And, dear ones, you have only had a hint of what it is all about. So much is still ahead to be savored and appreciated, if you can but savor and appreciate what is before you here on earth and in your own solar system.

So to you light bearers of earth, we thank you for your work and service to God and assure you, each one, that your names and deeds are known to us as you would know your own child. Never fear for your safety or your protection. We are with you always, especially through this present time of transformation, after which you will be reserved a new place, a greater opportunity to know heaven once again on a more intimate scale.

Remember that this earth was intended to be the peaceful showplace, the jewel of your own solar system, and the most beauteous lady in this quadrant of the galaxy. She will be brought forth in glory regardless of how many souls fail to honor their spiritual father and also this earthly mother who feeds their bodies with her love and her generous soil.

Having so shared, let us review the behavior befitting humankind on this planet.

Do not doubt your responsibility or your power. As a cocreator in training, there is much you can do as one person and in groups to bring peace. For *peace* is the issue. Think peaceful thoughts, then. Meditate and pray *daily* at least 20-30 minutes without fail. Behave peacefully. Join your peaceful heart and mind with those like yourself at least once weekly in meditation for peace.

Reach out to those who are lost, afraid, or uncommitted to peace, to love and to God. But realize they have the free will to reject your overtures and may not choose to spiritually advance. About this there is nothing we can do, for God himself granted this gift of choice. Love, but release them. Those who deny God's truth will go their own way and these souls will be separated into a more suitable learning experience elsewhere.

This is the message I bring and this is your role as an initiate of self-mastery. Do everything *you* can to establish peace on earth. It was for this you journeyed here. Remember your identity and place this advice in true perspective. You are CARETAKERS of earth. You are disciples. What is a disciple? A dedicated server of mankind -- a person bridging two realities, heaven and earth. A disciple is a mystic who experiences God's presence in heart and mind and exemplifies higher truth on earth so struggling humanity can be touched, be healed.

In this compassionate purity life is exquisitely simple, and the personality is not entrapped in the false glamours of living on earth. Rather there is immense clarity and ease of purpose through apparent obstacles and dark valleys of illusion.

As a disciple you choose to become beacons from a Divine reality to a floundering, endangered planetary citizenry longing for love and peace. Like the solid rock that gives security amidst a flood, your lighthouse of peace will overcome fear and help solve the human problems of the earthly environment which must be met -- the misery and unhappiness caused by unconsciousness. Above all, the spiritual journey as disciple requires that you live and demonstrate what you profess to the best of your ability.

You were created by love to love, and with wisdom to be wise. Reverence for all life is your major theme and the measuring stick for your behaviour. In light and energy you grew, as the Creator's intent for your immortality sang its song throughout the Universe and birthed you as a cosmic petal on love's flower. You are beloved beyond measure on the skeins of eternity where your love and wisdom now display themselves before a parent's delight and the eyes of your galactic family.

We are with you now and far beyond this time and place, but know always that you are *guided from within.*

Peace in the name of the One who parented everything. May your appreciation and gratitude for your life -- all life -- be shown by your thoughts and deeds. Begin the day in reverence; end the day in thanksgiving.

Show appreciation for all you are and all you can yet become as we go together now in happy homecoming. Blessed is life; blessed are we! And in that certainty we rest in love and joy forever.

Amen, God's child. Amen!

1994/1995 comments are contained in Chapters X and XI.

Chapter VI

Guidelines for the Religions

I came 2,000 years ago to guide you into this present opportunity for spiritual ascension, as have many other great teachers of the past.

Did you listen to us and take action? Do you follow God's inner voice for love and peace?

If not, I will now clarify that the present day religion is still for this purpose, to connect you to God through your human personality's communication with its soul, and then to connect your soul to God's higher realms. Therefore, every organized institution held in *my name* is herewith ordered to examine its rituals and to change them if they do not include a time of quiet meditation. The membership should be allowed and encouraged to sit quietly for twenty minutes as part of the service, to hear what God would say to each one. A message may be given and the use of music is uplifting, but the critical part of the time should be spent in quietude with the soul.

Yes, you all still have the same commandments while you remain in the third dimensional body -- the commandments to love and not kill or harm -- for you live in a zone of temptation and negativity. This third dimensional zone requires you to cross the veil between what you see with your mere physical senses and what you know exists from your soul level. And for this a bridge is necessary. Meditation, prayer and contemplation form that bridge. Churches must implement and encourage this practice, dear ones. Otherwise, many who seek to build the bridge to God in meditation will be forced to go outside of the present church organizations.

As your World Teacher and the love/wisdom ray for planet earth, I recommend daily prayer and meditation to remind you of your connection to God. For I came to demonstrate humanity's immortal soul nature. That which you call death is only an upgrading of your present physical body into a form of glowing light that is eternal and ongoing. By my resurrection you were shown the model or pattern that you yourself acquire at the time you presume you die.

I repeat to you that you cannot die! However -- and this is critical -- what you think and the way you act do have an effect on both your earth life and your after-earth-life!

The greatest gift any religion can give its members and participants is to place them in touch with their own inner teacher so their awareness of death, as a transition process, becomes certain. The way religions teach about this transition from matter back to energy and the rituals they have about it vary greatly, but the idea or theme should be the same.

Since soul essence lives forever, your first requirement as a human being is belief in God, belief in the nature of your soul, and your certainty of a beforelife and an afterlife. Since you are all one in God if you accept that identity, it matters not which world religion you follow if it takes you to God with clarity and certainty that death is not the end. Let us have unity about our love for God within the diversity of the various groups and not separate ourselves as superior or more beloved than others. Do not be self-righteous! It is an easy trap.

God loves all human beings and does not judge them. You have judged yourself, and therefore others; I recommend you relinquish judgment and accept love and forgiveness for everything real or imagined that has been done by you and others. The focus of my appearance was to bring love and institute forgiveness, to bring simplicity!

Therefore, I am angry (and I use this word advisedly) that so-called Christian religions held in my name are filled with pomp and grandeur that distinguishes the priests and ministers as those who know God -- from the congregation as those who do not and must be taught. This subservience is erroneous as a pattern for love. For love accepts and is in partnership with all others. Temporary assistance may be given, but no one person is more entitled to or worthy of God's love than any other person. These theological differences are a human limitation and prevent upward spiritual progress.

When I came to you 2,000 years ago, I said to you, "*You* are the light of the world." I did not expect churches with glorious robes and artifacts of gold to be established in my name. I did not expect people to seize power in the name of God and to perpetrate their individual needs for glorification through the use of my name. I did not expect Jew and Gentile to be separated or Christians pitted against followers of Buddha, Krishna or Mohammed. No, I did not. But look what has happened.

This planet's formula for spiritual growth has been undermined by those evil, egotistical personalities whose need for power has overcome them and short-circuited the opportunity for humanity's spiritual return to God. Still the plan will unfold as these structures and rigidities of spiritual limitation are released or destroyed.

I ask every soul to consider whether its minister, priest, rabbi, guru or teacher is in direct connection with God and is intentionally bringing each of its charges into direct guidance from God. If the religion, or group, in which you practice your belief and love of God is not bringing to you the opportunity for full spiritual development and soul growth, through direct revelation and inner knowing, then you should leave that group and find another!

You need not cling to ritualistic practices, but may begin your own connections to God directly through your soul. No longer should financial support be given to those organizations that do not bring you a personal connection and experience. If your churches and your temples do not bring you into the fruition of your soul growth, then they do not serve you and must be abandoned. I repeat -- must be abandoned.

The truth is that all sons and daughters of all colors, religions and nations are welcomed in God's family if they choose it. But each individual soul has a unique path which gives different opportunities and expanding levels of growth both on earth and in the heavenly realms beyond. Because your depth of love and service create the type of assignment or activity here and in the many mansions of the Universe, you have been advised to practice love and to give caring to others. For it is upon this record that you receive, by magnetic attraction, the next experience. Spiritual progression has always been a part of God's plan for humanity's evolution because there is much to learn and demonstrate before you are fully healed of negativity and ready for the potential opportunity that awaits.

Look into the night sky and see the Universe with its sparkling stars and planets, comets and other objects you do not even know yet. Are they, too, not alive? Do they not also serve God? Surely you cannot imagine that earth life is all there is. That would be amusing. Open your minds if you've ever held such a thought. You are not ignorant peasants of yesteryear any longer. Your technology has brought you to the brink of a so-called space age. God is there, everywhere present. Do not doubt. YOUR RELIGIOUS TEACHINGS MUST INCLUDE THIS EXPANDING AWARENESS OF LIFE BEYOND YOUR OWN TINY PLANET.

A religion must inspire humanity to know more and use what it learns with love. Always love. This is the never ending commandment to every religion. For love is an actual energy or substance of which the Universe is made and held in place. Without it we would all perish. It is not some unimportant ingredient of life without first priority. Love is your primary obligation on this planet, and if you deny yourself love, you will become stunted, probably ill. But it is always your choice, by God's gift.

Those of us in the heavenly realms, which even now beckon you onward, work as a team to develop humanity's abilities and attitudes. No one who wishes to grow will be overlooked.

Your every desire to know and serve God will bring you higher and higher in the universal scheme of things. Then you will understand my mission, and your own, more fully. For now just accept that this is so and that death is merely the end of a single drama with many soul activities remaining. This tapestry of becoming a worthy companion to God, and of divesting your personality of its limitations, is the true teaching of any belief system, philosophy, or church. Without imagination, love and joy something is missing in spiritual teachings. Look within your belief structure to see what goals you hold and how you express them.

I promise you that any church which deifies me instead of acknowledging God is behaving erroneously and should stop immediately. You pray and meditate in *God's house;* however, God can be experienced anywhere.

Those who have experienced God's nature themselves frequently bring forth a great creative work of music, art, or literature which draws us nearer to God and to the vivifying expression of love. The beauty and aesthetic uplifting of these soulful, intuitive things may be more meaningful than a ritualistic church meeting, just as the simple beauty of nature crowns your hearts and souls with joy. Open your eyes! All around you are these witnesses of God's love to humanity. This abundance is freely given for your use and enjoyment.

Sit by a stream (if you can find one that is unpolluted). Listen to birds singing (where the trees have not been sickened by your smog-filled cities). Examine a tiny flower for its exquisite expression of symmetry and color. Amidst this variety, feel the presence of God's unending love for you. Allow your heart to expand and reach out to the animal life, things of the sea and water. Is it not difficult to kill the lambs and cattle for your food? Are you not the caretakers of the earth and all upon it? Yes. God's original design called for all lifeforms on the planet to be interdependent and symbiotic. Even today there should be a cooperative, mutually beneficial relationship between humanity and the animal, plant, and mineral kingdoms.

Cannot fruits, grains, fresh vegetables, dairy products, eggs, and such be served more often? You will not starve without red meat every day, dear ones. The persistent eating of large amounts of animal flesh will have more and more unhealthy results in the human body as your planet raises its vibration. Small portions of fish or fowl, which do not require multiple digestive processes that clog your system and bring on early disease, are recommended. A diet balanced with fresh, living food, consumed daily, is the most nourishing. There is a cost for unhealthful eating; remember this suggestion and begin to change your diet if you wish to accommodate the higher cellular vibration of the fourth dimension. Eat to have a healthy life, not to gorge. Be judicious in your habits and grateful for your abundance, but do not make eating the center of your life.

Since all souls must learn the lesson of compassion for living things, some human beings cannot bear to slaughter animals nor to eat their flesh. They have learned this lesson of compassion for the living animals that are in their care. One day all of humanity must resume responsibility as caretakers of the earth. This, as in all things, is a free will decision bearing cause and effect in every individual's life. As a rule, higher levels of meditation and mental telepathy with us in Spirit are difficult to reach by those without compassion.

I remind you that cause and effect must be experienced by those who overimbibe on habit-forming substances at all levels of their being. Alcohol and drugs can destroy the spiritual fabric of your mind and emotions as well as bring misfortune to the body. Do not risk this potentially disastrous effect of drinking and drugs. The Golden Age will require disciplined minds and clear emotions, attitudes of non-violence. Use nothing in your body which puts you out of control of your peaceful behavior. Use nothing foreign as a substitute for a peaceful mind and loving heart.

The churches of the world have much to do, and it is not just going to Sunday meetings to praise Jesus, I assure you. Let your coming together in love serve God, serve humanity, and serve peace. Let us devote our time to peace above all things for the planet is in a serious and threatened condition. It is ENDANGERED. Do all you can to speak peace and model peace. Teach its ways by your own behavior. This is the purpose of any religion -- to strengthen the soul's practice of love and peace. So be peaceful with one another, in or out of the church, and serve those in need. As you learn on earth to practice the teachings of our Creator, you will earn the higher opportunity that awaits you at the time you call death.

The purpose of any church, ashram, temple, cathedral, or place of prayer and meditation is to teach the love of God above all things. It is not to deify one world teacher or any combination of them. It is to appreciate and understand their teachings so much that you *practice* them. That you live them! This mutually loving behavior brings and sustains peace. If you wish to honor me, for instance, it is your loving behavior that will demonstrate your affection, not your cowlike or solemn affectation in the use of my name. Your prostrations which are not followed with everyday application are useless.

If you love me for my example, follow it. Spread love and peace. That is all you need do. Love for me is shown by your behavior, not by grandiose buildings and expensive organizations. These often detract from love's true mission. If you love me or any world teacher, honor us by the actions of your daily life. Prepare the earth for its coming cleansing by establishing peace and love in government, as well as business and industry. Conduct your business as if a world teacher were in your store or conference room. Love and cooperation are vital everywhere; believe it. Many a soul has lost its way in the greed of commerce.

A major value in churches, synagogues, ashrams, temples and such lies in the cooperative effort to have love and peace on the planet. Without the love of God, the love of humanity for one another and the establishment of world peace, many humans will suffer. All who refuse their responsibility in living and promoting peace will not be selected for the thousand years of peace and the Second Coming.

Is my message to those in the religious occupations on this planet clear? Your sole responsibility is to bring the children of God home again. Do this by getting everyone in touch with their inner teacher, the Holy Spirit, and the soul who knows its life purpose and blueprint designed by God. Encourage, inspire, and feed the souls who seek guidance, ever turning them back to the Father/Mother, turning them within.

Theology is usually useless and argument over scriptures is wasteful energy. Simply take the theme of loving and live it. Put your energies into the fabric, the work of the world, where it will bear fruit. Anything less is a poor response to God's message.

When you give the love of your hearts to those who wish to know God more intimately, you will fulfill your purpose. When you assure people that they will return to God at the time of death, you tell them truly. When you advise them to guide their lives by the message of love that dwells inside, not just in scriptures, you will expand them and make them self-sufficient. These activities may not fill your coffers, but they will fill your own soul's progress with a reputation to be valued and rewarded by all of us who see your actions, know your intentions. Is your life lived for any other purpose?

My brothers and sisters, it is not appropriate that you deny this new spiritual information that I bring now simply because meditation was not called by that name in the Bible. Prayer and contemplation were mentioned, as was "Be still and know." Realize that no past religion should interfere with God's truth and plan for an ever evolving soul progress. My teachings of today do not change the need for love and peace. However, they must be held in a current context in order to be fully expressed.

What I have to say to those of the so-called Christian faith may seem difficult, but I promise you that this is the new gospel for the Golden Age disciple. Heed my words. It is REQUIRED that you expand your present limitations in thinking about me and our Creator if you are to achieve self-mastery.

If you cleave only to the *exact wording* of a holy book which was released as a guide for past times rather than practicing the basic concepts expressed therein, you will not be growing in the way God wishes. Your interpretation of all holy books must be expanded to recognize the higher vibrations now being transmitted to the planet earth in this, her time of greatest need. Some insist the Bible is a final work or that the Koran is absolute truth and there will be no more prophets. To these ideas I say a resounding "NO." Life is growth and therefore change. This New Age is the age of transition when you must take the prior teachings to a higher level of understanding based on present world knowledge.

Please listen carefully to what I say and grasp it firmly in your mind. Even if your prior training resists furiously, hear me through. It will be your key to expanding your growth in the coming years. Keep the simple truth of yesteryear, but allow it to flow upward as you further exemplify it into a higher interpretation and experience.

The One God has sent many teachers to earth over eons of time, leaving on the planet many world religions which seem today to separate mankind into various camps and groups. THIS SEPARATION WAS NEVER THE CREATOR'S INTENTION. The teachers were to pull human forgetfulness back into true knowing of the oneness, not to create divisions and further boxes.

Your challenge today is to see the universal message that runs through all world religions and to amalgamate that theme, to go beyond your present divisions and separateness. That is why I came, to combine all men into the brotherhood of One. How you failed to understand me! I am heavy laden because of the way in which yet another church was formed, one that may have taken you away from listening to the master within you. There can never be any one code of teaching which will not need to be updated, aside from its one basic message of peace, love and forgiveness. The reason I explain this to you is so that you understand my present message in its totality.

God is assisting mankind's return home in an evolving progress one step at a time, like a circling spiral ever moving upward to sanctuaried levels of greater awareness and unity, bliss and joy. As you become wiser in each higher understanding of the basic truth which appears and reappears in different guise, your soul becomes more purified and able to demonstrate by its behavior that it has truly learned that one truth.

Change is difficult for the human personality, however, and it will balk at having to rearrange the information drummed into it through habit and misqualified data. How long ago was it, dear ones, that human beings thought the world was flat? Or that the solar system revolved around the earth instead of the earth around the sun? You could not fly until recently, but the knowledge of how to do it has always been there. You are discoverers, are you not? How slowly you take your steps to God's waiting arms. Yet the plan is sure and, like a river, offers a continuous flow of deepening ideas and spiritual comprehension for those who will partake.

Let me repeat this for its urgency. *There can be only one basic truth, brought to you over and over again in higher sequence of understanding and application!* With each new flow of God's energy you can go to an increased level of knowing who God really is and how you are relevant to God's plan. You grow by incorporating new applications of that energy -- and I ask you to accept this new level of understanding which I now bring to assist humanity's accelerated return to the fourth dimension, one step nearer to God. For there are more rungs on Jacob's Ladder than you have climbed.

If you cling to every phrase of the Bible and argue its interpretations, you miss the point of God's message. Simply accept its basic tenet that you have a Creator, a powerful force who has a plan for your return home in love and forgiveness. Accept this promise. Live it. Enjoy the full measure of its healing. Following this plan is your function here.

Again I reiterate this idea so you will not misunderstand my message. The truth is that there is a God who loves you beyond your mortal mind's ability to grasp. Your origin lies far beyond this time and place. Don't deny or forget that! Your world currently is developing the technological devices to allow you to see the truth; so it is now possible to explain this in more scientific terms.

Yes, since my coming 2,000 years ago you have learned to take a gigantic scientific step. Now you must match it with the spiritual growth it requires. Your scientists must connect to their inner teachers of God to see their relationship from a new vantage point else you will harm the planet and leak misery into the Universe beyond. You are still children in your demonstration of love and peacefulness, but some have become scientific monsters without conscience or respect for God's firmament. This discrepancy in some human behavior must stop.

I told you that "In my Father's house are many mansions ... " and this is absolutely true. But what does it really mean? The limited scientific background of humans on this planet 2,000 years ago could not grasp what your mind can grasp now. Surely that is obvious. Yet, you are presently children playing with such horrible tools of destruction that the angels lament and other lifeforms watch you from their space craft with justified concern. Some of them are even here on your planet to guide and assist you from behind the scenes. These are truths you will know more fully in a few years for your governments cannot continue to hide the truth out of fear.

That is why I come to speak to you again. You are off course, humanity. You are drifting further and further away from God's noble plan for earth. Stop this insanity and listen to reason and love. Cleanse your emotional attitude. Give up negativity, war and violent thoughts.

If ever you believed any words of the biblical Jesus, felt my love, or trusted my leadership, I ask you to abide with me still. Reserve respect for me as your wise, older brother. Take my hand but do not kiss the hem of my garment. Open your heart

and mind to comprehend our beloved adventure in its true context; once cleansed of negative emotions, you can rise into the
stars and regions deserved by you as a child of the Universe.
Remember I came to help cleanse humanity of negative emotion,
but my grace does not mean you have nothing to do. Since your
group endeavor cannot progress until humanity's emotions are
cleansed all have a pressing task of inner sorting and release of
false beliefs and psychological limitations.

I came to teach you love, for the many mansions of life already formed by God cannot abide the evilness and sickness
your technologists would bring out into space. There is a ban, a
quarantine on earth, until all people -- of their own free will --
return to the Creator. Your surrender is not to me but to
something powerful, loving and awesome. And you must surrender your little will in order to follow the greater knowing. Do
you not remember the far-flung mansions, Precious Ones -- the
filament and the starry diadems of light twinkling away darkness
and fear in realms of glory beyond what you call time?

You are presently a three dimensional physical body with
soul consciousness at the fourth level. My role as World Teacher was, and is, to prepare you for the fourth dimensional level of
soul love, of higher responsiblity as energy living in matter.
Your preparation time is over. Stand ready to affirm or deny
your spiritual ascension, no matter your earthly religious path.
We must go forward now or lose the accelerated opportunity.
Beloved of God, I promised long ago to return and not to leave
you comfortless. I am here with you now in thought to announce this Golden Age and encourage your efforts of self-
discovery and expansion.

Yes, I modeled for you a resurrected body, one of light and
beauty. You can have the same. To achieve this state for yourself, all has been made ready. Heed heaven's call and these
instructions, then, for when you accept a loving identity that
cannot die, by your own choice you will join us in heaven's
plan. Now it is time to express love to all your brothers and
sisters, not only of this earth but also beyond.

You are not alone in this huge Universe. Many lifeforms of varying sizes and shapes abound. Though you are only one blink in the vastness of eternity, you are important in the Creator's mind. Prepare yourself for this cosmic initiation by agreeing to turn within and take hold of the lifeline which will be provided through meditation, prayer and contemplation. Individual and group meditation is the tool for this upcoming age. It comes now so that every soul has the opportunity for the inner truth and the inner certainty. Please use it.

The New Teachings are not based only upon past religious documents; I do not say this to you lightly, for the past religious teachings have been useful. They have been a necessary part of a Divine plan of recollection and remembrance to bring you back to the heart of God, to bring you back to the eternal flow of God's mind and the oneness of all living things. Nonetheless, I say to you today that in their place will come the *inner teacher* within each soul, which will again be reunited with the Creator and will become the funnel and the channel of love to bring you home again.

The church structures as you know them are suspect. I repeat, the church structures and organizations and institutions as you know them now are suspect. God's church is the same church that I spoke of 2,000 years ago in Jerusalem and what every true teacher has spoken to you about in every time period before and since. God's qualities are within you. Be still and listen to their message.

As each soul awakens and returns to God through its daily meditation and through its weekly experience of sharing in groups in a prayerful way, the planet can yet be healed and a resurrection of humankind achieved. Those who can expand their belief will advance under my tutelage but not if you worship me as a dead thing of the past, as the Godlike figure your organized churches have made me. Remember I live and have grown, as well.

My love is the Creator's love. My service is an expression of that. Let yours be the same. Hold fast to the voice for Godhood within you and not to earthly rituals and substitutes. Believe your heart. Only listen to the words of priests, rabbis, preachers or teachers who model peace and treat you as an advancing creation of the Almighty. Remember that if they had all been true believers, the salacious religious organizations of pomp and grandeur would not have been started and could not endure. Are their buildings and power used for God's purposes or their own egotistical needs?

There is and has been mischief in your midst. There are those grasping for power in the Creator's name and in mine. Do you not dare to see this truth? You must see if you would evolve spiritually. I said you must be born again of the Spirit. That means you must acknowledge God. Cleanse your negative emotions and follow the guidance to an ongoing, higher understanding. This is the last opportunity for that to occur. I invite you to become disciples for a Golden Age, a new time. All are welcome and forgiven past ignorance, if that is their choice. Let us start over. You are already the Christ Consciousness, dear ones; you've simply forgotten. The Christ is the full circle of light which exists in the hearts of all who love our Parent.

We are moving from an age of structure and form into the Golden Age of Aquarius, the age of inner knowing. It is the gift of God to all beings. Once again you can be connected directly into the knowing of God's mind through your soul. You will have both physical and spiritual mentors. But if the people on the earth who call themselves your teachers and ministers are not tuned into that higher nature themselves, you must seek elsewhere. Let me be clear that there are teachers of light upon this planet to whom you will be drawn, but their purpose in relating to you is not to formulate an institution to carry forth their own power and glory. Their only teaching function on the planet is to free you from such bondage and to return to you the power of God within you so that you may recognize it and use it in the name of the One God. Anything less than this understanding will create for them karmic, unbalanced effects which will hold back their own spiritual development and advancement.

Let every man and woman who calls himself or herself by the name of minister, priest, rabbi, swami, lama, guru or any other teacher in the name of God, receive this notification. *Henceforth your only purpose is to find your own inner soul connection and assist everyone else to do the same.* The purpose of any church organization, institution or clerical body is not just to foster or continue itself, but rather to free the people to turn within their own soul's church, their own house of God, into their own lordly connections with the higher one known as the Creator. This will create the neglected demonstration of peace on earth. If church bodies or spiritual institutions are not formulated on this principle then undue suffering will come, cannot be withheld, and must be experienced.

Brothers and sisters of the light on this planet earth -- brothers and sisters of the Love Corps -- this is your time for that love to be manifested. I came as a teacher, *not* to establish institutions that take you away from the inner knowing, but to bring you a pattern of personal commitment, personal remembrance and personal inner prayer and meditation to reconnect you with the mind of God. There is no other purpose in my speaking to you at this time. Churches and temples and ashrams and other spiritual organizations are for the expression of heartfelt love -- places where love and peace can be manifested outwardly once they have been experienced inwardly.

If you choose of your free will to have the inner knower, the voice of God, then truly I say to you -- *you* are the teachers and ministers of God's only church which is everywhere present through direct experience. Therefore, by your choice and willingness you are free to leave any ritualistic organized body which does not assist and support this plan -- no matter what name it bears, who founded it, or what reputation it may hold in the world today. You must fall away from any organization that would prevent your inner knowing of God, your own intuition and soul certainty.

This is my advice that I gave 2,000 years ago: "Seek ye the kingdom of heaven within." I repeat that statement to you now with every fiber of my love and devotion to you. I say unto you again, my beloveds, "Seek ye first the kingdom of heaven within." Listen quietly to the small, still voice of the holy power which was given you by our loving Creator. Remember your eternal identity as beings of light, love and goodwill, truth and wisdom, and be joyful as you recall once more your true identity as the children of God.

I say to you that the Parent which created your Spirit placed you here with an opportunity to live in flesh while still remembering your origins, to become peace on earth. Now you are returning through that flesh body's experience back to the higher, invisible realms of the greater body I demonstrated in the resurrection. This is your pattern; it is your gift from God which can never be taken from you but which must be chosen and selected by your own free will. I beseech you, once again, as your brother in Christ (Christ is the Light of God -- Christ is the remembrance of who you really are) to enter the New Age as a teacher of light and a listener to the inner truth. For this is your identity forever and ever. Do not let it be buried or disguised by any religious dogma, institution, or organization presently on this earth.

Peace is our God-expression. Love is our path.

Once again, I urge every minister, guru, priest, rabbi, teacher or member of any institution that calls itself spiritual to heed this warning. Take your members into their own inner soul space. Help them find the God within. This is your function with them, that *they may each find their inner connection to God.* You have no other purpose here. If you are not fulfilling that function, but are acquiring and piling up a storehouse of monetary holdings that you are not sharing among the poor people of the world, change right now! If you are constituting a body of power in which you hold the little human lives as unimportant, then I warn you that you will pay the consequence for continued negative behavior.

This is the critical time of choice and opportunity for forgiveness of any real or imagined crime against God, humanity, or

Mother Earth before the close of earth's school term. Take it. A vital time phase is coming to a close. Those who have made or will make a commitment to the Love Corps will go forth like a band of physical angels to create the heaven on earth that has always been desired here and which has been denied these past seven million years by the darkness of ignorance and evil.

Those on your earth whose souls are open to the remembrance and demonstration of God's love will know the glory of the Creator in the physical world and in the evolutionary process we are all following into higher realms. You will all be glorified in Spirit. Your hearts will know love and joy and your minds will be peaceful and able to perceive the highest teachings as you journey into the stars. You must understand that no spiritual entity who has not reached a high level of love and compassion and caring for all of life can be allowed to go into the stars. It is forbidden to send the evil of this planet out to greet your brothers and sisters of the light from other planetary systems. Limitations are therefore placed upon this earth by God's universal laws. No one who is not of loving spirit will be allowed to go very far beyond this planet with violent warlike intention.

The choice is upon you. Remember who you are. Look at the religion in which you participate and ask yourself if it teaches you to go within and then know God above all things. If it does not, do you belong there?

To those of you who have been agnostic or atheistic because of the hypocritical teaching of the churches, I say that you may not be allowed into the kingdom of heaven simply as a reaction against what is unsatisfactory. YOU must now choose to go within yourself and to make contact there in meditation with the higher nature of your own being, and with God's commandments. To do less places you in jeopardy. Therefore, as of this day, let it be known that all on planet earth are invited home through the inner teacher of their own souls and the invisible spiritual teachers of that Creative Force which sent life out. Return now in peace. Return to that Force and that Source which breathed us all into existence.

Do not merely read about God's message. Live it. Then you can call yourself a minister. Then you will bring peace to earth.

Officially educated or not, any soul who is drawn to the sharing of love and demonstration of peace is automatically in God's Love Corps if this is desired. What an opportunity; what a joy! Will you come forward as a volunteer now? The Love Corps needs you -- each and every one.

And so we ask and await your reply, dear ones.

My personal blessings, and those of all your spiritual teachers, touch your soul this very day. It is so -- and in that act comes joy everlasting.

In the Creator's name, then, we leave on the wings of truth but our soul call lives on in your heart now. What has been joined in peace lasts forever.

Amen, amen and amen.

1994/1995 COMMENTS

I remind you that doing the 18-Breath Ascension Meditation, daily, will greatly assist in utilizing these incoming energies for the healing of your brain-chakra-DNA mutancy—and your return to full consciousness as safely and quickly as possible. It has not been my intention that you should suffer, and now that we are more bodily empowered by Archangel Michael's intervention in the solar system and galaxy, the wise will insist that their churches and ministers meet this urgent meditation requirement or they must turn elsewhere for instruction.

These meditations and processes will help you: 1) cleanse and heal your aura, 2) align and expand your chakras, and 3) rebuild the full 12-helix DNA cellular circuitry. They are especially needed to ease the body's burden of opening new chakras in both the torso and within the skull area so your body can be reconnected to the Creator's incoming energy. Because your thymus gland has degenerated and your pineal gland is inactive, ascension without death is difficult. It is this situation we seek to help you reverse as you achieve health and life everlasting.

Godspeed and Amen, beloveds.

Chapter VII
Guidelines for Scientists, The Military, and Governments

The basis or foundation of science is reverence, a term little used in your earth's technological societies today: reverence for God and all of life! For to live a life of appreciation for God and all living things -- to actually adore or worship the Source from which it all came -- seems difficult for those having *free will*. Yet to fully love and admire your Creator should be a daily hour by hour practice, not something reserved for a once-a-week Sunday church meeting and then abandoned the rest of the time or never thought of at all in the currently popular intellectual climates that foster the seeds of disdain. This lack of reverence has sent many civilizations and even entire universes to their destruction and so it is your nemesis, your enemy, the satanic aspect within yourself to be overcome in your 12th Universe.

All twelve universes were created by the one Central Being and then assisted by other immense beings of light and by wise and loving energies unknown to most of you on earth, but selected for their specific talents by the One-Giver-of-Life. This great plan has generally been captained, if you will, by the twelve sons, or rays, of God who were created from that awesome power your vocabulary cannot describe and your imagination cannot formulate. Under these superlative twelve rays a gigantic congregation of light workers was selected to manifest the blueprint of God's lifeforms into matter -- and of course those souls without the light who do not have reverence and respect for what is planned are never chosen for further opportunity in these spiritual/scientific implementations.

If you would be a true scientist and an understanding human being, it is critical that you recognize that God is expressed through rays to your planet and you will need to know which rays you are most influenced by, which you will be drawn towards in particular.

All of these rays come from the Creator and can only express to you on third dimensional earth as light broken into the color spectrum you see in the rainbow. Thus, you know them as the seven rainbow colors but actually they are facets of God used to *influence certain qualities* of your beingness. This may be difficult to understand but if you can accept that color in your world has more than just aesthetic value, even your medical profession can use color for healing purposes as did past civilizations on earth. Thus blue is like a gentle sedative and brings peace and relaxation -- good when overstimulation has occurred. Red has the opposite use. You have many books about this but they are not believed by most doctors on your planet, regrettably.

In addition to your seven colors of the rainbow the five higher colors, or rays -- those with more luminosity -- are scarcely known at all to you but that which you call silvery, as in moonlight, will be appearing more and more in this time, and is the energy to bring you an emphasis on peace and preservation of life. Silver can come as moonglow or as a blend with your other seven colors to provide different nuances and emphasis to the colors you now know. In the Golden Age there will be great emphasis on colors, or the rays, since they are aspects of God.

In addition to the twelve rays there is yet another energy force called the Black Ray, a fallen son of our Parent which has existed the last 38 million years and to which the non-reverent are drawn by attitudes of self-aggrandizement and need for personality glorification. (Black is the absence of light but understand I do not refer to skin color as the same thing. Do not use this concept to support prejudice against black people in your earth reality!)

This Black Ray of defiance and lovelessness has been at home on your planet, earth, for some seven million years, where it tries to control the minds, attitudes and actions of anyone in positions of power or authority, having abandoned its own powerful station in the Godhood. Most certainly it strives to claim all scientists, for through them the great discoveries for military might and war machinery are gained.

I hope you can grasp that the separation, or "the fall" which is spoken about in many religions, occurred because of this exact issue of reverence, love and commitment to the Source-of-All-Life. For when your light bodies/souls teamed up to perform a task of great importance to this planet eight million years ago as CARETAKERS OF THE EARTH, under the direction of the rays of God, you implemented a masterful blueprint for habitation of life in peace and love. There was a million-year period of great glory and beauty as this immense family of God -- a scientific community as you would understand it -- introduced the plants and animal lifeforms and performed the continuing role of caretakers, caregivers, in your dominion of responsibility.

It was an indescribably beautiful time and one of satisfaction for all concerned. Would you imagine for a moment the thrill of bringing God's life plasma onto a magnificently created orb glistening in space, evolving from gelatinous state to solidity, so it could receive its planting time of life?

Yes, it was a million years of adventure, beauty, learning, and glory as the result of perfect cooperation and sharing in this monumental but exciting task. And yet the Black Ray very nearly destroyed this creation. On earth today you still see the dramatic effect of its negative power.

Touch a rose, but not too closely, for the thorns will prick your finger. Why thorns? Is this the work of a loving God or a satanic imitator? You see the honey bee and taste the sweetness of its gift to you, but whose aborted attempts at creation brought out the wasp, the hornet, and yellow jackets, as you call them?

This type of hurtful and non-loving creation is not in God's design plans I assure you, nor are the weeds against which you must toil to bring forth gardens and fields of crops to feed yourselves. Even the separated teeth in your jaws are a response to the murderous desire to eat flesh, for you had them not eons gone by. But by now the idea of teeth to consume flesh is so ingrained in your racial, unconscious memory that any other idea seems almost impossible to comprehend.

Therefore, reverence, love, and cooperation with the highest force of all is vital if you are to advance spiritually and have another opportunity to be useful at high levels of scientific endeavor. Many souls on this earth today have forgotten that they are the caretakers of the earth and without a change of heart will never again be given the power and responsibility in the New Age to cause a similar mishap of evil and cruelty -- which is always the result of a non-worshipful soul.

For thorns on roses are small matters compared to the decimation of entire universes and hundreds of thousands of planetary bodies, a few similar to earth, which the fallen ones have caused. However, we are gratified to tell you that the power of that Black Ray has been greatly curtailed and will likely be removed from earth before the end of this century by the power of your loving thoughts and sincere respect for all life. You can hasten that moment through the power of positive belief, of silent reverie, or meditation, during which the forces of light will be with you in thought and guidance. Spiritual contemplation is vital!

Now I must speak of an issue very painful for me to address. You may not find it an easy message to receive but it must be confronted and shared if earth's purpose, and humanity's, are to be achieved. Yes, I came long ago physically and I am come again in telepathic conversation to shepherd your thoughts toward peace and non-violence. For your bodies, your souls, your planet and space itself are all in jeopardy because of some earthlings' perverted intentions with weaponry and actions of war, hatred, and violence.

I come to point out these current deplorable attitudes and to help overcome the evil thoughts and actions used against others. You are hereby advised and warned that if humanity continues its sickening development of space age weaponry, you will have returned to you exactly what you give out. So if your fear, hatred, and violence are expressed to others in the Universe, they will return to you in a measure of intense suffering and pain. Why? Because what is given must return. I tell you, then -- invent with love! Invent with the intention to HELP HUMANITY and NEVER TO HARM it. I remind you that there are moral laws required of every soul and you are most particularly required to obey these laws and not misuse their applications against anyone, anywhere! And the scientific community is now advised that it cannot just bring evil into existence and disavow any responsibility for its use by what you call government and/or the military.

Of course you excuse yourself by saying that it isn't your fault if some principle is misapplied by the government. All you do is seek to unlock secrets of the Universe. You can't help what happens then. Ah, men and women of inquiry, don't you see that it is you who hold the power of decision making regarding the use of those inventions? For how could a government and its military personnel take bombs or killer satellites or particle beams to employ against other lifeforms if you refused to release them for that purpose? Really, if scientists worked with God and insisted that government did the same, you would see an immediate change in the kind of world you live in. This is so, for without your discoveries the military would be limited.

All governments would be limited in their horrendous misuse of scientific principles if you stood by each other in a vast federation of love's purpose: purpose that crosses the borders of what you call nations. If life is sacred, as God has proclaimed it is, who are you to ignore the commandment DO NOT KILL? And added to that is my own warning that those who create the blueprints for killing must accept full responsibility for that action. This is true whether you are hired with research funds by direct government aid or by funds of so-called non-military organizations. And it is true whether you are in or out of uniform! The responsibility cannot be shifted with a shrug of the shoulders and the thought that someone else bears that responsibility for your invention or application of inventiveness. Be you now advised that if you continue in that madness you will bear responsibility for its result.

Science is the sharing of the Creator's mind by direct revelation. If you delve into the principles upon which the many universes exist, you are delving into the mind of God, whatever you may call it. And it is clearly not the intention of this information to be used destructively. You must know that in some small corner of your heart or you are satanic in nature. Your obligation to God must be expanded if humanity's progress is to be assured.

You are not all of God's handiwork, people of earth. You are a blink in the vast network of life that stretches far beyond the light of your own Milky Way galaxy. I remind you that you are suburban dwellers of an enormous, magnificent light and life creation. Treat all of it with the dignity, love and respect due it and you will be permitted to advance into the higher dimensions where life truly resides. You are not alone in this vast consciousness called space. And each act you perform, each thought you express, is carried along the network of light you are unable to see. What you send out returns but also affects others along the way!

Thus space is not empty, nor is it to be abused. It is not a dumping ground or an area you can claim as yours. All belongs to God and you are merely custodians of it, even as you were given dominion, or custodianship, of the planet earth long eons ago. And what have you done with that responsibility? Are you so proud of its condition and the kind of life you've created here that you wish to share it with other lifeforms?

Since space is not empty but part of a far-flung web of life so vast you would have to fall to the ground before it in awe, numbed by its breathtaking power and blinding light, you must awaken to your role regarding its use. The concomitant responsibilities that go with membership in this unending family of creation has been told you many times. It is sacred. Life is sacred. Why, like a foolish child disobeying a wise parent, do you ignore the truth?

You volunteered as *caretakers of the earth* and have been evaluated as unsuited to further tasks until that one is satisfactorily completed. Make earth the pure heaven it was intended and then you may be worthy to carry its value forward to other consciousnesses. Meanwhile, clean up your minds and hearts and the very ground you walk on. Then, and only then, will you be fit companions to other lifeforms who already exist and have been watching your violent nature with the suspicion it deserves for many years. Yes, I refer to that which you label the UFO's or "flying saucers."

Mentally superior beings have always monitored your life behaviors -- in a constant surveillance of what earth people are doing -- especially in the ever growing insanity of your space race and invention of advanced weaponry. Since the atomic bomb they have been particularly positioned around the earth to assure protection to space and the lifeforms in it, but they have watched for thousands of years. For their own seed is here germinating.

Unless you heed God's warnings and come to a state of love on earth, with the help of those here in the heavenly realms, you are considered detrimental to life and will be treated accordingly if there are further transgressions made. This is not joyfully said but the point of warning must be given.

We, your teachers of light and love, are come again to warn you, then, and suggest some specific actions that are now required if you intend to save your bodies, your souls, your beautiful planet, and the space beyond your tiny speck of life.

This is our message. Listen and heed.

YOU MAY NOT VIOLATE THE SPACE LYING BEYOND THE 250-MILE STRIP OF YOUR OWN BOUNDARIES WITH WEAPONRY. I repeat. YOU MAY NOT TAKE WEAPONS INTO THE SPACE BEYOND YOUR OWN 250-MILE ATMOSPHERE WITHOUT THE CREATOR'S PERMISSION.

The reason for this is simple. If your intention is not loving, you are morally diseased and unfit to do so. In a sense you are contagious, as your violent thoughts and actions demonstrate to the greater family beyond your borders. Therefore, consider yourself under QUARANTINE until further notice. This is why I come now to speak with you. Open your minds and hearts to the love of God; change your behavior; live in peace!

There are presently madmen in many countries working on weapons. Underground hydrogen explosions in both Russia and the United States are likely, and there are a myriad of other experiments with killer satellites, particle beams, and other offensive weapons currently in use already. These will not be tolerated any longer! HYDROGEN IS AN ELEMENTAL BUILDING BLOCK OF THE UNIVERSE AND MUST NOT BE HARMFULLY EMPLOYED IN ANY WAY AT ANY TIME. HYDROGEN EXPLOSIONS COULD AFFECT THE ENTIRE UNIVERSE.

You must also cease offensive space launchings until you become morally acceptable life-mates to the other beings who watch you now. We of the spiritual realms will be powerless to aid you if you continue in this madness. You will have taken the matter out of our hands and space will be defended against your insanity. Believe this. It is so. Any grace I brought nearly 2,000 years ago cannot save you from the cause and effect principle after this warning because of the present and potential damage you are causing.

CEASE PLANNING, CONSTRUCTING, OR EMPLOYING ANY SPACE WEAPONRY IMMEDIATELY! You cannot hide behind statements like "The government is doing it" or "It's the military." All humanity is responsible in one way or another. For who draws the salaries that feed the so-called economy? Does not the profit made from war spread from one nation to another? Are there many alive who are not, even in some small way, assisted by the profits of *war?*

No, you cannot hide behind the evil of war on your planet and say you have no relationship to it. *You must turn your*

attention to peace and find a way to make peace profitable.
When peace, not war, is profitable and desirable there will be a
great practice of love and sharing which your God has taught
you. Those who promote war and those who make no effort on
the behalf of peace on this planet are not accepting the guardian-
ship role which has been given to humanity. YOU ARE THE
CARETAKERS OF THE EARTH AND ALL LIFE UPON IT.
This is your destiny and your purpose. Please turn your attention only to this issue and let war cease.

Know that you are at a *critical* moment in earth's history and
evolution. We in heaven have planned long for the second coming of peace and love among her people upon the landscape of
Mother Earth. Why aren't you cooperating? Have you gone
mad?

You must stop believing that there is evil in every human
heart and that one nation is out to destroy all others. Without a
belief in peace you will behave with suspicion, hatred, and ven-
geance. Stop now and remember love. Love and forgiveness
are your only true helpmates in achieving planetary peace. At
least one nation must put the weapons and armaments down for
all time. Truly some country must turn the other cheek. Which
one dares to begin such an unheard of thing? Whose name will
be written on the skeins of time as that country to disavow war?
Yes, there may be several small nations who say they have done
this already. But which of the giants has the heart and courage
for such a task? Who among you so-called Christian countries
will put my teachings into practice as the wayshower?

My heart is saddened by the silence, the uneasy glances, and
the looking away from this truth. Will your eyes not meet ours
with a promise for peace?

Where is the love? If not love, where is the respect or simple
courtesy? Where are the hearts who can say and mean, "We are
One planet, brothers and sisters all." If not the love and respect
for each other, where is the love for your Creator, for the beauty
and bounty of this earthly paradise you were given to care for?
The so-called primitives whom you self-righteously seek to civi-

lize were closer to God's mission than you with your massive technology turned against humanity's good. Have they assaulted space and the invisible life beyond your own boundaries? What does being civilized mean? How do you describe earth today? Is it a civilized planet to be emulated?

To understand the commandment of God regarding love at the political level is a most difficult enterprise and the one failure which has brought humanity to the brink of destruction unless immediate action and change is instituted. Let me repeat -- you have failed as a planet to practice love by any formalized, consistent application and will be so judged by your own actions. Although there is an organization called the United Nations which has done some good toward world peace, its very structure, which allows a nation's veto power, automatically cancels the potentiality of God's laws to be fulfilled. In its way it is like your personal human free will which also votes for its own protection and separation. Because you are frightened men and women you only have frightened nations, separate from one another. What lies within each one of you, individually, is projected into the larger global connection you think of as earth.

You have forgotten what peace is.

Long ago when you lived in a Spirit form there was only one government in heaven -- that government was God which is love. When you fell away from constancy of that one love mind and separated into the physical body form now used on this earth, your challenge, your responsibility, was to rejoin that former belief and evolve back to that which you had experienced before. In this emergence, you would have chosen God above all things and would therefore be a useful member of a vast and marvelous Universe strewn with planetary bodies, star systems and a myriad of lifeforms. We smile at your concept of heaven as a quiet harp-playing existence. There is peace here, and there is music, but it is not at all dull or boring, that I promise. Great activity and adventure exist for those who are able to share their heart love and apply God's wisdom and direction.

Because you have forgotten what peace is, many spiritual teachers have come to earth with repetitive regularity to remind you to challenge your soul's recollection, to reinstate you in the Father/Mother's flock. Yet through willful disobedience and stubborn resistance to love, this beautiful planet earth is now in jeopardy from the very ones she has fed and persistently nurtured.

Dear ones, my heart saddens to tell you this truth but you must know why this world is in its present condition so that you are not asked to experience the future happenings without full knowledge of why these events occur. Listen well and believe. I would not lie to you where your souls are concerned.

Although you -- the person called Mary or John -- have not personally been on this planet before, I say unto you that your soul has had experiences here, and elsewhere, and has for eons of time been inching its way back to the beloved mind which created it. I, The Christ, found my way back and undertook a mission to help your soul remember its destination. I still give support to your expedition, to your own journey from Spirit to matter and back home again, and I now aid your awakening from materiality into the etheric heavenly realm.

Truly I say that as a planet intended for love you of earth are failing, as most nations are failing, and it is because you are not individually peaceful. I come to remind you that you have arrived at a learning time in which a choice for or against God must be made. In God's plan for rescue you have been brought to this closing chapter on peace. Will you choose it or not? This is your free will choice. If all or most of you choose it, the planet will not have to be cleansed and will rise as a beacon of light in the Universe as a wayshower to other lifeforms. If only a minority learn this required lesson, then only the minority will be allowed soul progress as examples for others to observe and emulate.

As your loving brother, I came years ago to share that message and prepare you to cleanse your soul of false beliefs. I come again now to remind you that time is running short. The concept of peace awaits personal and planetary application.

What choice has any loving individual to make at this time, then, when the madness of nuclear weapons can destroy the planet and extend destruction to the other lifeforms in space? Only one.

Mobilize. Mobilize your meditation and prayers and spiritual intention. Mobilize your efforts through political action. Use your money and time and total being to bring about what you want at a national and international level.

If you live in a democracy insist that the president and your legislators offer the world a pattern for peace. Insist that they lay down their weapons and seek no more to defend or attack. Only your belief that you can be harmed allows such things as weapons in the first place. It is your soul's growth that is vital and which alone takes you higher and higher into the spiritual realm where I, and many others, reside.

If you are willing to die for peace through war then you are free to live in peace without going to war. Being free means you are willing to assert: "Dear Mr. President: We must set the pattern for world peace by being willing to show the other nations that we are spiritually prepared to live God's laws. We, a nation founded under God, are truly willing to lay our weapons down knowing that in the final analysis our model will touch the hearts of many. We trust the plan of God for this nation and this world. The acceleration of weapons has risen to unacceptable heights and must stop."

But dare you say such a thing and mean it? Does terror not grasp your mind and begin its multiple arguments that this would be stupid? When you know what love is you can truly make such a statement and mean it. Anything less is a lack of trust in God's plan for the planet. For that plan is peace! Peace! Peace! The earth was destined to become a teacher of love and peace for the Universe. Mark me well. This is a destiny about which you have no choice. Your only choice is whether you can let go of fear long enough to change your own behavior and the governmental view of life -- and then seek love and peace as an ultimate reality.

In America the money proclaims "In God we trust"; perhaps you memorized it as a child. If this is true, let your government so speak. Let the heavens hear your commitment.

Please be advised that you are being watched on the universal television system in far-flung areas of a Universe beyond your imagination to understand. That is why the space vehicles you call UFO's have been monitoring earthly activities. Since you have taken violence into space, and more of it is being planned, they are greatly concerned about the developing destructive technology and weaponry here. We of the spiritual realms must tell you that if you do not stop the madness which threatens space, these space brothers may be called upon to intervene -- to keep the planet from your path of annihilation.

Be convinced that other solar system lifeforms will not allow the spread of this insanity into their areas, for although you cannot see them because they reside in the fourth dimension and beyond, they do exist. It is just your limited third dimensional reality that prevents your perception of the higher vibrational life bodies.

Know, without a doubt, that you are being observed, dear ones, and if any nation on this earth makes further serious moves of violence or threat into the ether beyond earth's boundaries, you will likely be contained in some fashion.

We -- your spiritual teachers -- now pass this information on to you so you can never say later, "No one ever told me."

Do you not know that your governments have been advised by your space brothers to stop making aggressive actions in space? Your war-drugged governments are inviting intervention. Find out the facts. Require your leaders to tell the truth. Meanwhile, for the light workers of humanity known to me and other world teachers in the spiritual realms, be comforted to know that through your daily and group meditations you will be personally informed of what is occurring so you will always be exactly where you should be for your soul's purpose. This is why I say you must meditate and build your own communication network to your soul.

Once connected with your soul you will be led to the higher truth and granted our guidance whatever happens in the coming months. Meditate *daily* and join with others at least once a week to increase the consciousness and power of your knowing. This mutual support and sharing is already part of earth life in physical ways. Let it also expand into the mental level, as well. Through the meditation process you can send love from your heart to this beautiful earth and to all those negative forces which seek power, war and violence. Remember that a great mental force created heaven and earth and the far universes. Use your own mental love energies to assist us now in reclaiming your planet for God. PLEASE DO THIS IN REMEMBRANCE OF YOUR CREATOR.

Because it is possible that your own governments will create a nuclear war or other disaster on the planet, do all in your power to be peace yourself and to carry this attitude with you wherever you go. By daily meditation you increase your glowing light and love which is the very thing this earth needs. If you become actively involved in working in peace organizations and impressing governments with your beliefs, do it with the power of certainty and peace. Anger may give initial impetus to a cause, but it creates division and separateness if maintained.

Remember my own example and that of many earth teachers, also. Fortunately, thought is your most powerful tool for any purpose. Imbue your life with its positive strength. By a steady personal application and group amplification, you can accomplish far more than those who become filled with desperation. Be calmly centered in the certainty that your soul is feeding you daily, thought by thought, with love and clarity of action. This will help you radiate the light of God in times of conflict.

There is one possible activity that could draw humanity together and take the focus of war away. That would be changes of the earth herself in what could be called natural disasters -- earthquakes, pole shifts, or weather severities bringing famine or pestilence. If such should occur, your warriors would be likely diverted from space weaponry projects to care for one another in a common cause for humanity. Through caring for others the sparks of love's remembrance could be fanned to benefit humanity. So if there are natural earth changes, welcome them as a gift to draw closer together as One.

I have mentioned the intervention from the space lifeforms which would affect mankind immensely and provide positive avenues for change. What will happen depends very much on the plans and activities of your governments. So keep the love of your heart open to radiate great light and insist that your governments take actions for the people's goal of peace. If half of every nation's population were absolutely focused on peace, life on this planet would change. Join this movement. Peace is a powerful belief! And for you on earth now it is a necessity.

The timeline established by God's realm for the population to practice peace is nearly over. Time is critical; every moment is precious. Each human heart is vital to success.

To all government officials, elected or autocratically empowered, and to all military leaders on this planet -- from generals down to the lowest private in any military force -- I speak bluntly. War is the opposite of peace. It is not based on love but rather on the deliberate destruction of other human lives. These battles of one nation against another are inherently wrong because all of humanity is created equal by God. If you deliberately plan a war, and attack others, you are creating for your soul a terrible effect which you will have to repay at a later time. I therefore caution you *not* to kill or destroy human life.

The armies on this planet should be spiritual armies of love and peace, for only that attitude can prevent further scientific madness and technological disaster. You have armed yourselves with horrendous weaponry to commit violent acts rather than to build bridges of peace and cooperation. Let it be known that scientific inventions which are brought forth to create carnage on humanity will cost much soul disintegration and lack of spiritual progression. These evils must always be balanced out at a later time so if you participate in such activities be forewarned it is not without self-penalty.

Scientists and warmakers, hear me. Any intention to create attack is viewed by both spiritual realms and those lifeforms you think of as UFO's as adversarial. Beware you do not enter space on anything but an unarmed, peaceful mission, certainly not with created weaponry which will violate God's inter-federation boundaries and agreements. If you had ever meditated upon life's purpose and your role in it you would know these things. Wake up from your spiritual amnesia!

War is not a toy to be tossed around in the mind like a game. It is the epitome of soul evil. Cleanse your heart and mind of such ideas before it is too late! And ask the Creator-of-All to teach you your true purpose here on earth. Perhaps it will mean a change of occupation. Certainly it will mean a new attitude and a heart open in love. For only the loving will be allowed beyond your space boundaries, I assure you. You are ignorant and willful babes who try to play God with terrible repercussions for all of mankind. Do not do these unconscious things or think these unhumanitarian thoughts. You defile mankind and God's intention.

I, The Christ, who came to teach you love and forgiveness say this to you now. If governmental and military personnel will lay down this negative pattern of thinking and simply sit in prayer and meditation asking forgiveness and a new opportunity, there is yet time to cleanse many souls and reach the positive love energy of God's magnificent peace. Call on any great beings of the spiritual world whose words touch your own heart. Ask them to tell you the truth about your actions. Establish contact with the good and cease the path which now you tread full of vanity and without compassion for humankind. Ask. See what happens. For no prayer of sincere heart is left unanswered. You shall receive guidance and assistance.

Oh, I hear the reply come forward, "But our intention is to protect ourselves." And I say to you that you cannot protect yourself against evil by returning evil action. Have you not heard my message? Did I not say to turn the other cheek?

Why would I say this? Why would I tell you not to defend yourself?

Because the need to defend means you do not understand that there is nothing to defend. All is God. Your only permanent object is a soul. You have nothing else but idols; your house, your money, your automobiles or airplanes or buildings are impermanent. I tell you they are illusions. And if you put great store in them you cannot believe in God. Be willing to give your illusions away and your lives will change. Be willing to use them in God's service and they will have value.

Hear me. Ask within what your path should be. If you love God and humanity and seek only to grow and serve, your little life will find its perfect niche. And through your joyful connection with the heavenly realms you will be supported every step of the way up the mountain.

There is a plan beyond your finite minds which you deny and resist, my brothers and sisters. Surrender to the fact that you cannot know its design unless you seek to establish contact with that which created it -- with God.

Kings, presidents, leaders -- elected or autocratic officials -- legislators, governors, mayors, and all others in both small communities and great nations, ask to be guided before you vote or take action on any issue. Commune with that soul part of yourself which knows what you should do for the greatest good.

Let no leaders or judges make decisions on law without consulting *God's* law. And let the judges and lawyers seek always to bring peace to their clients, not attack and bitterness. Resolve is the greatest tool of government on earth. Mutual harmony is the sign of success. To deliberately push battles into the camps of right and wrong is not a creative or desirable attitude. Mediation is.

Let the government and the law, at all levels, offer only the tool of cooperation and reconnection. For wherever separation is fostered there is loss to the soul for pursuing disunity rather than wholeness. This is true for all. Work, therefore, with diligence, to create earth laws in reflection of God's purpose through you. Seek conciliation which brings peace. Then your life purpose will have been fulfilled as a person, as a family member, and as part of a community, nation and planet. To fully live is to love and allow God's purpose its fulfillment. God's will is peace in all things. Then create peace not conflict.

Many of us in the higher spiritual realms have experienced your trials and challenges in our own way and learned what they were for and how to balance them for God's purpose and love. That is why we are able and willing to assist you in your own time of tribulation and inner choice. We have a map for you. We know the way.

Accept, if you will, that we are physically present in many dimensions, including your physical earth, and that we can speak to you by mental telepathy once your higher meditative connections have been established. Only a few can see us appear in the physical now but one day the soul sight will return and the veil of blindness will be removed forever. Be assured that in the process of meditation you will gain the true knowing and understanding and that you may possibly experience hearing with the inner ear or seeing with the inner sight. These gifts from the unused portions of your pineal gland and the human brain are stimulated by the meditative process -- by the practice of an awakened love.

All persons who seek God will succeed through this meditation in which you sit quietly and still your mind. Once quiet and at peace, your soul's higher vibrations can penetrate your usually busy minds and speak to you in support of personal and universal peace. Like the invisible power source which comes through your radio or TV reception, which you accept as perfectly natural, your soul can come insightfully to your receptive brain once your set is tuned in. There has never been a greater opportunity to grow in love and service, never a more fruitful opportunity for expansion in your soul's journey into higher consciousness, the true space.

We call upon all of the scientific, military or governmental leadership of this planet to hear these remarks in the recesses of their hearts and souls. No matter your past course if you change now. The very air you breathe is particularly potent in these next months to assist you in giving up negative thoughts and actions. The sunshine has more love. The moon glows more fully with a cleansing power to release the hidden miseries and confusions in your subconscious memory. Take advantage of this support and use it wisely. Choose the Love Corps now!

Do to all humanity only that which you would have done unto yourself!

The scientists of this world should realize that spiritual power is the basis of what you call science. For who is a greater physicist than I, The Christ? Who among you on earth has used God's ability to come from energy into matter and return back again? I tell you that true science is using the universal laws with purity of intention. You can play at magic and destruction but they are not science.

This was the model I brought before and that I request you follow now. Use purity of intention to explore the many mysteries beyond your ken. I tell you that if you come from the Spirit, these and greater things shall you do. Without love your discoveries can lead only to misery and suffering for all. Finally, I invite you to join me, and all of the heavenly forces, in this Golden Age when much will be revealed to those of the open heart who love God above all else. Many universal laws will be given the *peaceful* scientists. Many mysteries will be explained.

Remember that the unloving may not go forth into the stars because they would be too dangerous there to themselves and others. But those of light and goodwill can.

Make your choice; make it in love.

Humanity's path is strewn with the evil names of history. Be careful how you select your place. Consider how your name will appear in the annals of remembrance. Consider also why there are thorns on a rose or watch the wasps, hornets, yellow jackets and flies swarm around you giving you little to enjoy.

Remember why this is so -- an attempted form of creation which has failed because there was no reverence in its pattern and image. The test of our Father/Mother's work is always beauty and the gift of love. For love creates only love, and any demonstration less than that is not of God.

No loving consciousness would create a thing of beauty and arm it with barbs, but, since "the fall," much has happened to change this once perfect Garden of Eden. Do you not think the myths of half-man, half-beast have basis in fact? They show the type of creation which the fallen angels created on this earth by their perverted and unloving thoughts. And your genetic engineers, as you call them, are back at work today, remembering in their souls a time when they truly played at being God eons ago. Will you empower them again to bring forth evil and tamper with the DNA structures? If you do, it is your responsibility to bear the effects of that cause.

No one is to change any lifeform for any reason without God's express permission to do so unless it is for the good of all -- which any reasoning and loving person should be able to fathom. All life is a hologram and part of a web in relation to all other aspects of life. Therefore, to change any part of the formula will upset an entire ecological system in which each thing has a relationship in the support of life for all. Your science should only be used to ennoble the race you call man, to improve all life upon the planet, and to respect all other lifeforms in the Universe.

Without absolute love and an attitude of service, no planet or its lifeforms are to be touched or changed in any way. If, in deep meditation and willingness, you listen to your soul and to the higher realms beyond it, ideas may be extended to you to further humanity's progress and to make improvements. You will be told as needed. Otherwise, if you choose to tamper with God's plan for a loving environment and peace for every form of life, there will be a major lesson of remorse to learn in your soul's education.

Murder, or the deliberate taking of another life without cause, happens in many ways and is forbidden. Beware you do not fall further still into the belief that you may do as you wish with God's plan for this planet and for all life hereon. We are in the process of helping you upgrade your lower wisdom and love factor to a higher one. Be patient as we work to assist in undoing the miscreations of your soul's past errors, and let the planet unfold natually in full cycle back to truth, to God. In this time of near-instant manifestation you must proceed with love for all as your theme, as your code of ethics.

Through interference with a near-perfect plan of creation and development here on this beautiful being called earth, you are now separated from God. Intend to do only what God would have you do and those of us who know that plan from this higher level of consciousness will guide your soul's interest in scientific exploration and creative expression. Be guided from Spirit to truly express the best of who and what you are.

With the thoughts of many here who would support your life's mission in the light of true discovery and understanding, we say, "Peace be with you." For peace is your key, your passport, to solar secrets and the Universe's mysteries. Take this key, use it with purity of intention, and you will learn much.

I thank all those who have already joined the Love Corps and who have chosen the path of peace. I commend your names upon the heavenly records of all time and no time, and I encourage all others to be so remembered.

In seeking your maker with a love-filled heart you will have guaranteed yourself a place of beauty and wonder forever!

The Creator -- and humanity -- await *your* choice.

May you choose what you would want another to do for, and to, you.

Let God's blessings surround you and fill your yearning soul's quest for peace.

Amen, amen and amen.

1994/1995 COMMENTS

I repeat the cautions I gave earlier in Chapter 1 regarding peaceful excursions into space and the cessation of hydrogen and nuclear explosions above, and most especially below, ground. Since it is the scientists, military personnel, and governmental leaders of many nations who plan, execute, and finance these dangerous and immoral acts, it is they who must accept the ethical responsibility for such thoughts and deeds.

In democratic nations, however, it is you—the citizenry—who must realize that it is your tax payments that support such ignoble plans and actions, so you must take the voting power and responsibility in directing where your monies should go and how they should be spent. Become a truly democratic citizen by applying spiritual wisdom in government.

For the past 60 years on Earth, you have allowed secret government agencies and military programs to flourish—to invent horrendous weaponry and continue to create an atmosphere of violence and war that will be carried out into space unless you intervene. Then please intervene for peace at once!

Since the 1940's, these secret military programs have interacted with an alien presence, so called, and allowed them to perform objectionable experiments on human beings in order to gain greater technical and scientific war secrets. This lust for power and control still continues, though we have interceded with those beings you call the "grays" so that they will be going elsewhere for good. But many governments, official and unofficial, have deceived the people beyond belief and there is great evil afoot! Surely you realize this is unpleasant but true.

Because this is the case, we encourage you to take advantage of these current spiritual energies and apply them courageously to the questions of what your governments have already done—and are planning to do, especially in space. Then be about your Mother/Father's work, using this new era of group consciousness as your tool, beloveds. You are urgently needed! For some people, ascension lies in the balance.

In the Creator's name, we are eternally successful. Amen.

Chapter VIII

Guidelines for Parents and Teachers

Let me now clarify the way in which God's teachings are to be presented by parents and teachers (and the entire society) to all of humanity, but especially to the old and beautiful souls now being born on this earth again. Beginning in the last decade children who are old souls came with an eagerness to express God's love, to grow in light and understanding, and to populate the planet preparatory for the thousand years of peace.

Please ask yourself as parent or teacher, "Why am I being a parent or teacher? Why have I chosen this method or way of expressing myself and interacting with others?" (And every human is a teacher merely by your presence upon the planet. Be careful what you model and exemplify, then, for actions speak a universal language.) Your soul answer regarding parenting and teaching will have different replies than those made by your lower personality, which may be interested in parenting to please families or because it is what people always do or because teaching is simply a way to earn a living. The soul's answer lies beyond these reasons for its need is to experience God's love and return it to all living creatures. There is also a deep desire to learn and grow.

Then what are the particular ways all humans should do this work? As a parent -- above all -- be ready for the unusual! At this time in spiritual evolution be flexible and know you will magnetize a soul which needs to be approved and supported for its ability to see beyond earthly definitions.

Take these suggestions to heart, and as you apply them there will be great personal joy and delight as you practice God's loving exuberance. Although there is responsibility in this, let it not become the somber dutifulness that has choked off the message I brought before. Do these things cheerfully. Important tasks done well can give both responsibility and joy. Remember this. Lighten up in your outlook. The new children will teach you this joy from their personal experience with the invisible realms which I once came to share. Heaven is a joyful state of learning and sharing and loving! To think it less than this is to misunderstand it totally.

These new babes will have the capacity to personify heaven on earth if you will cooperate and share their vitality and clarity. It will be anything but boring, dull or dreary! And even if you do not have a personal infant to raise, or teach, you will be involved with this new age energy and love, which will delight your own soul's journey. The purpose and promise of this Golden Age is to fill the earth with beings of a nurturing, loving nature whose devotion to God sends out a blaze of light vibrations dancing like rainbows and sunlight, embracing the entire globe.

Understand that some of these small Golden Age beings, with great soul knowledge and awareness, started arriving a decade or so ago. Others enter now and more will be coming. Many of them will outshine your own ability to see and hear the spiritual beings like myself. They may have mental capabilities you lack. Mind over matter will become a new reality. Therefore, your first step is to accept that although you are the bigger in body you may not be the spiritually wiser. For the personalities of some parents this will be a great blow to human pride. But the parents' souls will rejoice for the experience of psychospiritual abilities will be a major part of New Age life.

As a parent or teacher do NOT let your pride get in the way if you see the little ones talking to invisible angels or hearing inner heavenly voices. I assure you that as a child you had more of that ability than you have now, and the reason you lost it was that the adults around you had forgotten these abilities themselves because of parental, societal and educational displeasure

or ridicule of some kind. Many children in your own generations heard and saw the angelic realms but were forced to abandon this ability because they could not face a loss of respect and
love from family, friends, or teachers who denied this reality.

You must acknowledge the children's abilities to both the
children and others and do not ridicule or deny their connection
with the heavenly realms which are very real to them and which
will become more real to you both if you allow and encourage
this communication. In fact, if you are willing to grow from
your interactions with the children you will learn as much or
more than you teach.

My greatest suggestion for all humanity, especially you as
parents and teachers, is to say something like "Until now ... " or
"We have believed until now ... " For instance, if teaching
science to a child say that "Up until now we have believed that
the speed of light of 186,000 miles per second is the fastest travel possible. Look within and see if this sounds right to you." In
other words, give present knowledge the *tentative* nature it
deserves, for in fact this is not a correct way of looking at the
speed of light, and the wise ones beyond the veil will be working with the incarnated ones to correct much erroneous material
that passes on earth as accurate.

Not only are they willing to teach the little ones, they are willing -- by the process of mental telepathy -- to teach *you* more of
the truth of this Universe and your place in it, as well. However, to pierce the veil, you must believe it is possible, you must
become very quiet and still in order to hear the truth, and you
must be grateful for the Divine plan that God has given humankind.

Meditation will help.

Once, eons ago, you lived only in God's mind and all things
were known to you. After the descent into materiality, you were
no longer connected in the same way. You became, in a very
real sense, lost in space without your communication device.
Fortunately, we who love you seek to restore your connectedness back to God, so that the division between heaven and earth

is joined and you can once again be part of that Great One's love and knowledge.

Know, then, that humanity's fall -- or detour out of communication and direct awareness of all that is known to the Creator -- is being healed for you if you wish to have it restored. This is the truth, but you must be willing of your own free will to accept and joyously participate in this restoration. Like a broken television or radio set, let yourself be repaired to receive the heavenly channels that await you once more. Or at least attune yourself exactly in a clear state of reception.

I, The Christ, am not the only channel of God's truth. There are many others. But for those who believe and have faith in me, I assure you that I am no farther away, once you restore your communication system, than a mental phone call. One day soon many more will actually see me than do now, especially the children.

You were told in the Bible that you needed to become like a little child. I meant by this that you must have no limitations in your thinking. No barriers that say, "Oh, that's not possible." And like a child, you must be accepting of a loving Father/ Mother's role in your life. Not a Parent who would be unworthy of trust or would abuse you, but one whose affection and concern are eternal and assured. TRUST IS THE BASIS OF LOVE.

It is not I, dear ones, who has created the plan. However, it is I, and others in heaven, who have totally accepted and participated in it. Your task is the same. For the sake of the Golden Age children, you should encourage them to experience contact with what you may not yet see and hear yourself. This will mean surrendering the past ideas you were taught and to be ever present in the moment. For spiritual evolution is accelerating to bring you home again. Build your own communication lines through meditation and encourage every person you know to do the same.

Children are open, curious and willing to love, to learn. Then be like a child so you can be taught. You will feel the peace and harmony and love your soul yearns for! And by this step forward you can open the door to vistas beyond the time and space of your past knowing and flower anew in the fertile ground of heaven.

Teachers, of course, are faced with an almost superhuman challenge in the present educational system since their textbooks are partially distorted, incomplete, or untrue. School organizations and boards have established curricula that society requires as manuals of truth. There are study guides or agreements about what is true on earth; however, these generally limit the heart and mind. As a teacher do not give present information as the final truth or you fail in your soul's task as an opener of human consciousness.

Tell the children that until now these are the ideas humankind has believed, but always ask them to go deeply within to see if they feel these ideas are true. Be willing to allow freedom of expression and new ideas. "What if ... " is a playful tag to place in your teachings. "This is what we've always thought, but what if there is more to know? What would it be?"

The primary attitude is not to be dogmatic out of your own need for security. Be willing to know more yourself. If science is your field, be open to new discoveries and applications, be willing to receive previously unseen connections of truth. In your meditations ask to be made a gifted teacher of these new beings and ask to continually deepen the truth of whatever subject(s) you teach. You will absolutely be assisted if your motive is love and peace your goal.

By mental telepathy a few of you may even talk with the great teachers of the past to see how they would update their earth teachings given that opportunity. Or at the least each can write down new ideas that come -- little "aha's" that are creative jewels given by the soul to stimulate or clarify a greater knowing. In a word, grow! Be open to the expanded Universe that will whisper its secrets to those minds willing to receive. By your model the children will feel safe in turning within.

Listen to these babes, make it safe to be different and ahead of the times. Many social and educational beliefs must fall. Welcome change; accept a greater understanding. The small ones will need your encouragement, your support, and your love. Many will be masters of truth, heralds of this upcoming Golden Age, who need your unique nurturing. I ask you to attend them very generously. Give so that you may also receive.

Until now your schools have filled students full of your facts, many of which are false. This is not because educators wish to deceive necessarily, but simply because they -- as part of humanity -- do not yet understand who human beings are or what education really is. Education is bringing out truth from the highest inner source, not parroting textbooks, though the rudiments of certain subjects may be useful. Education is allowing truth to flow out through the communication you have built to God's sources. We place no blame on educators, but challenge their self-evaluation. We do recommend that they begin to understand their true purpose, however, and direct the glorious new souls being born on planet earth to tune within to know the truth of all things.

Many of these small baby bodies you will meet, which are arriving even now, are of a higher vibration in energy than most parents who give them physical means of birth. And they may be more spiritually capable than most of their teachers on the planet. Therefore, your first step as a parent or teacher is to acknowledge that their capability makes *you* no less. In fact, it offers you the greatest opportunity of your life in loving and allowing them greater latitude in higher communication with us in heavenly realms. They may well have eyes that see beyond what you see and ears that hear beyond what you hear. Do not be defensive. Instead, be curious and have them share their experiences. Encourage openness.

Give these wee ones a loving structure to mature in but do not limit their soul or higher abilities and, above all, do not make fun or deny the existence of what they have that you do not. You will learn much by saying "Tell me who is there" if they report a vision. Or by asking what they heard beyond your own auditory range. Become actively interested and supportive lest they lose the gift that you lost as a child through doubt or denial ... or because you were scolded by adults blind to the higher worlds. All children are closer to God when they arrive than are adults who live in cultural conditioning which forces much of their true nature underground.

I beseech you as a parent or teacher, then, to understand that each generation will arrive in higher vibration than the one preceding. Be glad of this. Use your knowledge to aid and assist the small in body but great in truth. Help them accept and share all that they are. Of all the gifts you can give them, give loving permission to be who they truly are. Know also that one day you, too, will have these powers again provided you commit to God now and agree to use the power for good, in service to humanity. For your soul's tests, or initiations, have to do with your willingness to use power for the noble, ethical purpose required by those who will become not only a heavenly creation, but a child of the Universe, of life far beyond your present grasp. Your destiny lies in the birth of stars, the expansion of worlds unseen.

Taking one step at a time we grow in love and responsibility. This growth leads us naturally, automatically, to our next pinnacle ... and our next. I promised you our Parent has many mansions. Do you not sense them? Aren't there more possibilities than you can yet imagine? Seek only the *highest* level of consciousness for your own mansion.

To the teachers, then, as disseminators of society's truth, fall the responsibility of responding to *constant* change and discovery. Old information must be immediately updated. And all of this change depends on your willingness to stay current with the knowledge explosion. This accelerating flow of information regarding the laws called science, particularly, will require radical understanding of new universal principles previously misunderstood or undiscovered. For the Universe will share her secrets with humanity more and more now as the Golden Age begins and you reach the fourth dimension of conscious life.

This is why all education must be accompanied with the sense of responsibility and love in the use of these new inventions and technological advancements. And every curriculum that exists must have this quest for nobility built into it so that these scientific discoveries serve humanity in a *positive* manner. You have only to look at your present world to realize that somewhere society has failed to teach that the heart must precede human curiosity. And love must precede any intended use of God's principles.

I do not say this is the school system's total responsibility. Rather, all of society must play a part in creating this nobility of purpose in humankind's historical tapestry. Nonetheless, I urge every teacher and educator of whatever grade and subject to take the initiative in preparing a curriculum which speaks of humankind's ethical nature and responsibility to fellow members. And I repeat that rapidly changing information will make the updating of knowledge a gargantuan, never-ending task.

Let a part of your role as teacher, then, be the sharing of the very latest knowledge as it is discovered. This knowledge may even be discovered before your eyes in the classroom where the New Age souls reach within their memory banks to disclose truths not presently in print, not currently known. This experience will become increasingly familiar to you as the years pass, dear ones, so pray that you be given the openmindedness to take your place as a leader among school faculties and as a guide for those not so spiritually aware. Become a torchbearer for this exciting new time and reap the immense spiritual benefits this position will afford. You are needed to play your part in this critical time. Turn to us so you will not falter. We stand beside you always to assist as we are called upon!

It is our promise that those of you who teach from a spiritual -- and I do not mean a *religious* -- point of view will be infinitely rewarded. From the children you encourage in their powerful expression of God-knowing there will come joy and your own self-expansion through that sharing. For the child of your yes-teryears lives in you still, anxious also to flower in God's eternal growth. God is not static. You are not static. Change is ever present and necessary. So aim always for that which has al-ready been given you. As a teacher you also will be taught.

Our Father/Mother is, indeed, magnanimous and generous to all, but you must be willing to receive the truth. Therefore, open up to obtain your overflowing portion ... and attune to the heav-ens in a way that guides you into an ever deepening understand-ing and acceptance of what you have already received. Open your mind and heart to obtain your own abundance.

In your teaching you are blessed for you join the work that I, The Christ, and many other spiritual teachers came to do. Let us be partners, then, in God's plan for bringing the human family back to the heavenly dimension that is its destiny. Do not let the fear that you might be accused of putting religion into the schools hamper your usefulness in spreading the truth. There are many ways these lessons of looking within can be taught without the use of the word "God." Words such as *light* or *source* and *oneness* can mean many things, as can words such as *intuition*, the *inner knower*, or the *truth bringer*. The Creator does not care what name is used. Use whatever vocabulary al-lows you to obey the regulations of the public schools, working always to change them for the better. Be creative and unafraid.

A few of you will truly change the organizational structure, content and usefulness of education! But whatever your part, large or small, play it with love and dedication and you cannot fail. By listening within, you will always be guided to the high-est good and finest choices. Teach the little ones, too, that quiet times are essential and will provide them with strength, certainty and inner knowing.

Parents have the greatest opportunity to teach and model the New Age awareness to children because of proximity. Teaching your children who they truly are and giving them the encourage-ment to take leadership where their soul would have them go is a vital task in this time.

Mothers, you are not just producing babies. You are bringing forth the lifeform that a soul needs for purposes of growth, love and service. Talk to the soul of the babe while it is yet in the womb and discuss with it what purpose it wishes to express upon the planet. Fathers, you should join in this process, also, for the birthing of a great soul requires the partnership and devotion of both the male and female principle since within the soul there should be a balance of both.

As a family team, give the structure of love and inquiry to the child and watch this blossom expand beneath the tent of heaven's purpose. A couple can find no greater satisfaction than in bringing life to such a soul. Remember always, however, that the child is not your property or possession. It belongs to God and to all that exists beyond your tiny experience. Do not limit the being as you share a code of spiritual responsibility and joyous love.

If you model that love and devotion are possible in a family, the child will learn by your example what humanity is capable of. Therefore, before the pregnancy you must cleanse yourself of as much doubt and limitation as possible and as a couple pray together that you will rise fully to this great occasion of child rearing. Then listen to what your soul and higher guidance advise you to do in this process of providing a physical body for another soul to use on its earthly journey.

Birth brings a soul its greatest trauma for it is cut off from its usual place in the light, the joy and peace. It often becomes sad or depressed at the surroundings it finds on earth. Therefore, use as natural a childbearing process as possible and do not roughly handle the baby during its entry. Provide a tone of caring long before it enters life and continue that attitude as richly as you can throughout the years you have offered to be responsible for this soul's visitation. In the beginning be especially comforting and gentle; then later give a structure of loving responsibility for the child's welfare. *This does not mean letting the child's personality do as it wishes*, for this human personality has to cooperate with its soul through willingness and understanding. It must also learn to respect the rights of others.

The same is true of every adult personality on earth, not just the children. When an adult is asked to surrender to God it does not mean to become a vegetable without purpose or goals. It means that the little human personality becomes viable and useful to the soul without the fears and anxieties, guilts, and uncertainties that plague an individual's habits -- habits created by those early conditionings and personality tendencies.

Humanity's goal is to produce as few of these negative conditionings and limited beliefs in each child as possible. For these barriers and misqualified thoughts will have to be sorted out and released later in order for the soul to focus its full expression and delight into the body which is its physical form here on earth. To create an open space for the soul to practice truth and love is the main purpose of the physical body experience. For this reason I have suggested that the fewer false beliefs you fill a child with the less cleansing she/he will have to do later.

Telling a child the basic belief that God is a loving and unlimited source is obviously far more important than saying we are worms in the dust and God will get us for our sins. Such comments are false and limiting. I continue to be saddened and appalled at the ideas your churches program into the minds of children and adults to frighten them, dishearten them; these ideas describe a God whose nature is fearsome and capricious, at best. Who could *love* such a God?

I say to you that our Creator is not like this fearsome, heavy-handed figure taught by many religions today. Therefore, teach your children the truth and do not let such nonsense fill their subconscious minds with this evil! For it has sabotaged the love and forgiveness message that I brought 2,000 years ago. I am grieved that my meaning could have been so abused and twisted by the ignoble goals of church officials -- grieved that the masses should believe God held them in such low esteem.

Let me say for all humanity that our Creator knows nothing but love. Therefore, the unloving conditions on the earth did not come from the Creator but from humankind. My role was to clarify this truth and help you understand that your own thoughts and actions were the bringers of your experience, even when it seemed you were not responsible. You are not victims! You are doing it to yourselves. This lesson is what you must teach the children. As co-creators you are responsible for most of life's experiences. Learn this lesson well. Then you can teach it with feeling. I assure you that *your thought* has created the experiences you've had and our effort is dedicated to cleanse your mental and emotional nature so that your thoughts are only of love and peace which will return to you.

Remember that my resurrection demonstrated the power of my mind over life and death. Use its power in your own life for your own resurrection. For the children, then, please teach them they are lovable, that the way they think will create their view of life and reality. Tell them God is not some arbitrary old man sitting on a cloud dumping these evil events onto mankind.

When human beings truly know God, they will realize that the choices which they make -- created by their own thinking -- will come to pass sooner or later. If people are suffering and experiencing difficult times because of persistent negativity of thought, it is *not* God's doing. This difficulty is self-created. Humanity's creation! When children grow up knowing this truth, there will be a greater opportunity for peace.

When you and they can be so cleansed of the human personality's fear and the desires for power and control over other people, of the violence and hatred and war, then the circumstances in your times and upon the planet will change. That is why I say unto you that the time has come when all must choose God! For the higher realms have programmed a heavenly chapter to come now in earth's history, and this chapter requires positive thinkers. This is your opportunity to believe, live and teach positive thinking.

Do not falter as a parent or teacher in telling the children who they really are. Then they can take advantage of this moment in spiritual evolution and ride the love stream into higher experience. Never mind the forecasts of what may happen on the planet so long as you are tuned in daily to your higher self. Just follow in peace. Accept that you will experience only what your soul requires to enter the Golden Age.

I hear some adult men and women say, "I would not bring a child into this awful place of war and violence." But I suggest to you that if a soul is eager to come and find a family that can teach him/her truly, you should not reject parenthood out of fear. Fear has no place in the New Age. This is the point of my message. Trust that you will bring into the world a child who needs exactly what you can offer. Trust that the soul really wants to be here for its own reasons which you are not necessarily privy to. Trust, trust, trust. That is the greatest commandment I can bring you now. Do not be afraid. For love is more powerful than all the fear that exists anywhere in the Universe.

Teach your children to love and trust God ... and not to judge themselves and others. Then they will be safe during whatever experience arises, as will you. Loving, focused thoughts will carry you through any difficulty! That was my message to you long ago and that is still God's goal for you.

I believe one of my greatest teaching roles on earth was to show that God's presence does not just descend upon humanity as some *external* force, but lives within each person as well. I hoped humanity could see that God is an intuitive experience, very personal and totally achievable, and that I was an example of a profound *internal* experience. My life was a statement that no matter what others said and did (governments, religions, or uninformed people) they could not defeat or change the power of my internal awareness of God. Give this message to the children.

Anyone who fails to see that I never veered far from the course I had set, in spite of life's events, misses the fundamental understanding of Spirit. For that inner power of God's nature expressing through a cleansed personality lets nothing overcome it. Nothing! Even though circumstances are difficult.

My purpose was to show you that even though I was arrest-
ed, persecuted, and in the final analysis abandoned by even my
dearest friends and disciples, I knew something more profound
than the external physical experience. I knew God. My mind
was filled with that truth above all things. Can you sense the
importance of this teaching? Trust is the cornerstone of love.
Teach it to the children!

I knew God loved me. I realized I was worthy of that love,
as you are. And I accepted that nothing of the world -- nothing
outside of my mind and thoughts -- could control my will and attitude. This is your present task, too. Tell the children that God
is planted within them as surely as a seed carries the blueprint of
a flower or tree. That seed may seem to have disappeared in the
greater body of growth surrounding it, but in fact it is the God
seed that created an entire system of life, Universe upon Universe. You and the children are the seed of God. Within you is
the outpouring of a vision which can be denied or ignored but
never destroyed.

I came to remind you of your identity, dear friends. I came to
say that you and the children are a marvelous creation of mind in
matter and that you can do almost anything you set your minds
to. For this internal God-self is the director of your experience
if you would choose it. That is why I have asked you to sit
quietly each day in meditation, so you can touch the core of your
true reality in your contact with the Almighty. All children are to
be taught kindness and love by your example. Later you can
meditate or sit quietly together as they are ready for it.

Tell them God is everywhere present. As a parent or teacher,
you, also, are a spark of the Creator, the light of this world. In
concert with others you are the mind of God present here on this
earth. Accept that responsibility. I say again you are not victims
of a malevolent God, not the stepchildren of some angry, raving
parent. You have the same potential qualities of love within you
that were the Creator's tools in creating the cosmos and the vast
regions of space you can scarcely observe or comprehend ...
and you have your own *mind* and your own *word* with which to

create. Your use of them determines future spiritual placement. Teach love to your children and students, then, for that is what you and they are. Anything else is an illusion and a cry for help.

Because parents and teachers are themselves repositories of culturally transmitted belief in violence and war, it is the task of every loving and sincere human being to examine this group consciousness and sort out all of its negative aspects. Do so until you can forget the thought and feeling of all violence in yourself. As you are cleansed and healed personally, you will be fit to teach children of the New Age. Let this cleansing be your credential to teach, then. And in your universities the course of study must include this aspect of responsibility. Does the world just need more teachers of mathematics and science or does it need teachers who live peace from their inner core of being?

Change must come among the teachers of teachers, too, as teaching standards are revised to stress the necessity for peace. And those who set standards for teacher accreditation must find ways to bring only the most perfected beings into daily contact with groups of children and young adults. This is not an easy task but it must be done. However, it makes no sense to do these things if parents allow children to spend hour upon hour viewing TV, videos, movies, and the like, which fill the conscious and subconscious minds with horror and the constant teaching of violence and hatred.

I must insist to all parents that TV is not an adequate baby-sitter, as you call it. Most programs are not fit company for adults, let alone children. Be selective, then, in what you give other people permission to put into a child's subconscious memory storage. You are hereupon charged with the responsibility of filling the "at home" hours of your children's minds with only the finest of conversation, entertainment, and life activities. Anything less than this will cancel much of a school's efforts to nurture each young one's innate feelings of love and peace.

As I speak to parents and teachers regarding their unique opportunity to help children of the Golden Age rise to greater

heights of love, I remind you to continue the cooperation between parents and home, teachers and school, and family and
church if these forward that great endeavor of peace. A word of
caution to Sunday School teachers regarding a teaching method
often used to threaten children by saying, "God will punish you
if you are bad." What must be taught is human responsibility.
Therefore, teach that God's law is love and all actions should
bear that touch. WHEN HUMANS ACT UNLOVINGLY TO
THEMSELVES OR OTHERS THERE WILL BE PAIN AS A
REMINDER THAT LOVE IS NOT PRESENT.

The message every child must learn is that God does not
punish. God creates and shares love energy and asks each of us
to do our very best at living love on a daily basis. You punish
yourselves by non-loving behavior, dear ones. Once this is
clear your life on planet earth will make greater sense. Your
misuse of the law of love and also the law of cause and effect
harms you. What you cause or create returns to you. It is so
simple! And this teaching you must practice so you can model it
and explain it to others.

Therefore, a great mental and emotional cleansing on the part
of each human, individually, must occur followed by a projec-
tion of that loving, peaceful intention into the wider cultural conglomeration called society; for these broad cultural chains often
shackle the human who would live in peace. Is there one among
you whose life is not limited and imprisoned by the governmental attitudes operating in powerful expressions of violence and
war? Attitudes that seem resistant to your need for love and
peace?

Yet I must ask you how these governments achieved their
power. Did not the majority give tacit approval to be so gov-
erned? And who has not benefited economically from these
decisions that war must be a way of life?

One person joined by another, in a growing decision for
PEACE, will form an indestructible belief pattern of such magnitude that the broader body of power and execution of policy will
reflect it. Nothing short of this will save the planet. So become

the peace, teach peace, and join together in a mighty demand for peace at every level of local, national, and international government. There must not be any possibility of veto allowed on this issue if humanity is to be saved. Commit to peace, therefore, and settle for nothing less. It is a passport to life in your present physical body; it is the recipe for Mother Earth's well-being, and it is your only key into spiritual realms. Is this clear? One by one an agreement for peace is chosen and implemented, and for those who raise and teach children, it is the only and the absolutely *necessary* curriculum.

Where in your schools today do the concepts of love and peace appear in the curriculum? And where in everyday practice does the organization of a school put these human attributes into application? Ponder these well.

Join together, then, those of you who parent and those who teach. These delineations of responsibility on planet earth will change somewhat as the higher vibratory energies now permeate your experiences. As you teach you will learn ... and every learner will teach. Merely be alert to the opportunity to do the best you can both individually and in all cooperative ventures. As this current age of form and structure departs, carrying with it the narrow compartments of your minds, the world becomes more free flowing and unencumbered of its former physical definitions and boundaried content.

Welcome the advent of this age of ether, or etheric energy, which is much lighter and finer in its vibration and therefore relatively unstructured in its nature. It is with even finer levels of this substance that the Creator makes solid objects by mere mind intention which is what you have known and done before and is what you do now on a lesser scale. This is why you have a body to show the effects of your thinking. It is your verification of belief. From this new higher energy vibration we of the heavens now send you are able to receive the result of your own thought more quickly, thereby achieving a faster manifestation of it. That is why I say to change your negative thoughts immediately! You will soon think a thought and see its result in your own body or life experience quite speedily. Have you not noticed even now that if your mind wanders off-center you do something to your physical body almost instantaneously? Especially in your western cultures you see that quick manifestation in bodily diseases of heart trouble, where love energy is blocked, or in cancer where the cells become destructive agents to the entire body.

These awarenesses of a different feeling in the very air you breathe and the way your life experiences have taken on a rapid tempo in their happenings are guideposts of the changes at hand. Help the children understand this. Do not be alarmed by these almost instant manifestations for they are natural occurrences and will increase steadily until the Golden Age is more firmly grounded. It is as though you were riding up in a very slow elevator, and with each floor you pass the energy gets lighter and lighter and lighter ... but gradually so. Thus, as the days and months pass, you will notice change, but it will not be one that totally shocks you with its abruptness *if you are meditating*. Because you must understand this age of nearly instant manifestation in order to teach it, I am sharing the truth to assist you in your efforts.

This finer or lighter vibratory energy is given by us as a greater opportunity for creative abilities in your world of matter. We are in advance of you; we have learned to manufacture things instantly by using only our thoughts -- a skill you once had and are retrieving through our gradual increase in the quality and type of energy now available. Regretfully some of this energy is being improperly used by many of your earth scientists and military forces in the creation of weapons -- an insult to all life! That is why your great day of warning is here. God's love energy is not to be employed in such a fashion. And since the Creator has determined the planet will be raised up into the fourth dimension of consciousness very soon, only those with the love attitude toward God and humanity will be allowed access to that new realm. Does this not make sense? If you could inaugurate a more easily used energy, which a mind can form into anything it wishes almost at once, would you let those of evil hearts who would destroy life be given that gift?

No, clearly you would not if you desired to keep the Universe and all life safe from destruction. It is really very simple. Those who love will get a further chapter of spiritual advancement, and those who have icy hearts will receive remediation. You would not promote a child to a higher reading level if the child had not learned the basic phonetic sounds, would you? Advancement depends upon personal qualities of love and love is your prerequisite and passport to this advancement sequence.

If you will acknowledge the presence of God living inside of you, with all the power in your mind and love in your heart, then the human race can evolve into its next dimension of learning. Or if some will lag behind at least *you* will go forward. I came to show you that you will live beyond the grave of matter. I demonstrated that all the physical efforts to destroy my true essence failed. The same is true for you if you understand it.

Remember to share with the children that the Jesus of yore did not die in his inner seed of being, and neither can you, except by the misuse of power. If there is a death for you, spiritually, it will be caused by *your refusal* to practice this truth -- by your stubborn rejection to use God's power lovingly -- by your unwillingness to grow in light. BY YOUR LIMITED ATTITUDES YOU CAN BECOME SPIRITUALLY RETARDED. That is why the daily meditation is vital. Through it you touch your internal presence of God and ride the vastness of this gift into holy adventure.

In you lies a spark of the eternal rainbow and the completed circle. In this circle of Oneness lies the light of mankind's evolution and development. If you would teach or parent, let your heart express only rainbows and unity.

My resurrection was possible because of the love power of my mind over external circumstances, over the belief that death exists. By remembering this example yourself, you are empowered -- individually and in groups -- to demonstrate this in your own lives. Let nothing or no one crucify your mind and your certainty in the reality of things that you may not presently see. God exists. And God is in you. Believe!

Your own resurrection is upon you. Take my hand and step forward to greet it. All who choose to remember the promise are welcomed.

Heaven stands ready to promote your willingness as a Love Corps member, as a light bearer, and a worker for truth in this Golden Age. Singing our new song to that ancient melody of love, we go forward together in joyous security. What else could a soul created in beauty ever desire? Peace, dear ones, for you are as God created you and in this promise you may totally trust.

Please tell the children for me that they are precious drops of silvery gold delights shining in sunny countenance on the surface of the planet earth who is mother to all lifeforms upon her. And they also have a cosmic Parent who is traveling now on beams of sunlight to make you all a wider homeland to which they, and you, will happily journey one day soon. Tell them they are children of eternal light and exquisite joy whether they travel upon Mother Earth's soil or into the far horizons of the cosmos itself.

As you hold the children close for me, remind them that their name is love and that love is their permanent passport for starlight voyages yet to come. Please kiss them with a rainbow's joy as once on earth I touched the faces of those I loved and embraced them with the light of God. And as all of those in the heavenly dimensions reach to hold and support you, family of mine, take a kiss and an embrace to cheer yourself too, for all the times you were not held and appreciated and adored for the nature of your true self. For it is love you each need as life food above all else. For this purpose humanity was born. Then accept this pure and certain gift heaven brings, and let us all rest together gently enfolded in peace that has the taste and feel of spring.

For a new day comes into your hearts and Spirit will lead you even deeper into the mysteries and abundance of the Father/ Mother's blessings. This alone is education!

Take heart, my brothers and sisters -- family of man, family of God -- in the certainty that we are truly One although temporarily separated.

May celestial rhapsodies accompany your innocent dreams and meditations during this night of your long sleep, until you awaken in a dawning of reunited hearts and minds -- until you awaken into the unsullied purity of *peace*.

You have our love, dear ones, forever.

In the Creator's name, amen.

1994/1995 COMMENTS

Because so many things I have shared will affect the way you parent and teach Earth humans, let me remind you that love and respect are your tools for preparing the children for the future they have chosen here. Your foremost task then, is to allow them their soul purpose and to raise them in an environment that is based on strong ethical principles such as compassion and concern for all living things.

I encourage you to accept that you may, through meditation and application of divine principles, raise your own consciousness so that you can teach from a higher level of awareness and wisdom. This will one day be a societal requisite for parents and teachers, as it is on most other galactic human planets and star systems. As you may have read in <u>You Are Becoming a Galactic Human</u>, other human parents are required to be well-trained in this most important task of child rearing. In the same way, those who counsel and teach must meet extremely high standards before they are allowed the privilege of guiding children in the tenets of cosmic life.

Today, also, you are to realize that Earth children are becoming more telepathic and may be able to use abilities previously termed "psychic" as a normal development of their higher consciousness—talents you may not yet have.

Again, you must prepare the children for their roles as caregivers and stewards of Earth. They must be taught that their relationship with all of life is a holistic bonding that must be respected and maintained. The human tendency to abuse the planet and greedily use up natural resources must be reversed.

You parents and teachers need to accept that a probable meeting with similar appearing humans from other galactic locations will likely occur in your children's lifetime (and yours!). So you must release your own fear and limited perceptions about the existence of other forms of life. *We will appear to you, spiritually, prior to such meetings, however, for there are both familiar galactic humans — and other conscious lifeforms that are not of the human species which will look quite different in certain respects — perhaps as shown on "Star Trek" programs — much of which we have channeled to Earth.*

Because humanity's present mutant genetic condition encourages ignorance and many negative aspects of lower consciousness, I commend these infants and children into your heart and souls for safekeeping at the very highest level of your own increasing consciousness. Only in such a safe and caring place will they find freedom of expression until you have all come home to us very soon. Even as I have called you to awaken, I am joined by Archangel Michael and other great beings and essences who are also calling all light beings back into the shepherd's fold, the Father/Mother's protection.

Then teach only love, beloveds, for as I often say, "Love is what you are!" Then do I ask you, as our Love Corps emissaries and earthly ambassadors, to serve the light and teach only love and wisdom to the precious souls you call children and adolescents. Those brought up amidst drugs and the violence of media and TV programs are in great risk, not only for their own souls, but as future parents and teachers of the next generation's round of higher consciousness. They must be helped, dear ones. They must be helped! Please do your very, very best for them which will give everyone great joy!

God's love and wisdom be yours, forever. Amen.

Chapter IX

Enduring Endeavors

There are no endings in Spirit. And these last remarks are not in any way final, because I am still growing and learning, even as you are, for all life expands in the endless creation of God's nature.

Since growth is the only evidence that life exists, you constantly choose spiritual life or death by your willingness to transform your limited consciousness into the grace of a broader reality. To assist with that greater transformation in humanity's reality, I hope the offerings of truth I have brought will support your desire to become more peaceful, loving and joyful as you go toward your heritage with certainty and true companionship.

I hope that by identifying these errors of past thinking and showing you the promise of a new day, we now hold a common understanding from my heart to yours. Then let me highlight once more what I wish you to know and share with others, since I promised to tell you what the Love Corps and light workers of the planet must do in the time remaining. Beloveds, listen to these responsibilities once again and proceed into the world filled with both light and certainty in your step, your hearts, your minds.

a. Live every day, use every thought as if it were your last. Leave no kind action or peaceful thought unexpressed.

b. Meditate daily and listen unceasingly so that, through the holy power granted to your soul by our Creator, you will know the actions you should take each day. In your jargon, stay tuned in! That way you will never be afraid or wonder what is going to happen. You will be told, as the elect of higher consciousness, what you are to accomplish and with whom you will be working. A weekly meditation with others is also *necessary* -- for these groups of light workers sitting together will make the task of your continuous communication easier and more supportive. Moreover your own body will begin to glow from this increased energy amplification. It aids your own enlightenment or return to God identity.

c. Join with others to influence your national and international governments to embody the ideal of peace in all that they do and intend. Spiritual people often ignore the everyday responsibilities of citizenship but this must change. It will take every loving person on the planet to swell the voice that speaks to government. Do all you legally can to demand peace at every level of life.

I affirm that if you will do these things and do them willingly, with dedication and determination, you will likely be among the Golden Age dwellers on the planet earth during the thousand years following the earth's cleansing. This will be a time of great opportunity and joy, and I pray all will hear the call of their inner voice as it tugs their hearts reminding them to answer their Creator's call, if they have not already done so. Do this in remembrance of God and of all the religious teachers of this earth, and we will one day stand together in the great festivity and joy that is yet coming for those of pure mind and heart as demonstrated through everyday action and behavior. Christians, please give up your complacency and self-righteousness that Jesus is your savior and you need do nothing more. Right actions balance out past negativity and regrettable deeds and teach you usefulness and service much needed in the galaxy.

I tell you I can save no one who will not change! Moreover, I can save no one who clings to past memories of me as if they were today's truth. Only your own thoughts and actions can save you.

The Jesus you knew in biblical times has grown into a more powerful and important teacher than before -- even though the message brought to you then is the same as now. LOVE GOD!

You must acknowledge that a force greater than all your bombs put together has an energy system to rotate your planet daily in a cradle of rhythm and harmony. Honor the Force which brings you into contact with both sun and moon and the starlit heavens of your own 12th Universe.

It is time to say it again so there can be no misunderstanding. The majority on earth are spiritually lazy and have allowed a few minds to conceive of evil beyond description. Further, you have allowed a small number of maniacs to guide your destiny and to bring you to the possibility of nuclear destruction from which your physical body will not survive.

You are committing cultural suicide by your own indifference to the few who take power and rush blindly into technological doom. TECHNOLOGICAL DOOM!

Can you not perceive this from your TV news programs, the radio and your newspapers? Have you no sense of what you are allowing to happen?

Now let me be a true brother to you and a World Teacher who would have no one lost. Peace is a choice. War is a choice. Your human consciousness is choosing the path of physical demolition, and unless you begin at once to cooperate, I cannot save your body -- nor will God -- for you have free will to create your own world and live out what you have created. GOD HAS LITTLE TO DO WITH THE CONDITIONS ON YOUR PLANET. YOU HAVE BROUGHT THEM TO YOU BY YOUR OWN THOUGHTS, ACTIONS, AND DESIRES.

You live in a world of matter where the events happen through your own past and present volition. Therefore, by your FREE WILL look to see what you would have. And if you do not like the present train of events that bring me from the Creator to clarify your position, then it is you who must change them.

I will do all I can to assist, for there is a small core of spiritual light bearers already on earth trying desperately to turn the tide of darkness and to reach those uncommitted souls who tranquilize their way into emotional denial. Using a vast array of escape activities such as alcohol, drugs, food, TV and other pursuits to ignore the present danger and the responsibility to do something about it, the mass of humanity still lies asleep. It must be awakened!

I brought you grace 2,000 years ago. That is, I guaranteed that if you were willing to return to the Spirit of The Christ, which is eternal truth ... and if you would set a personal example, not of self-righteousness, but of unconditional love and caring ... then I could assist. And help I will if you agree to do your part.

Because of the plans our Creator intends for this planet, we have only a short time to create a more peaceful and harmonious earth. For the black blanket of egocentricity and irresponsibility chokes the earth upon which you walk. Wake up and come into the light where you belong and where your Creator would have you be. State your preference and live its tenets. The balance of energies is so critical at this time that the immense rescue team we are using to send out huge amounts of light will fail if you do not respond.

Now, some have already made the changes I ask. And it is to you, my light bearers, that we pass the wand of power and encouragement. You are the leaders of a New Age and a new civilization. Proclaim the truth of love most surely, but be the love as a model for those who cannot understand. This is your true calling. To be the light. To be the love. To stand, as once I did, in spreading the word of love to the minds of all children, men and women.

Since no stone will be left unturned by those of us in the heavenly realms to awaken all of humanity in this critical moment, we need every soul to remember its true nature and take command of this planet in the name of peace. We need a Love Corps marching in peaceful measure. We need earthly angels to practice the truth of mind and heart. We need a savior -- and the savior is you collectively. Together you are the savior and this is your most opportune hour. Behave like the savior NOW for the stage is set and the cast is called. Your planetary play is in the third act where the forces of good and evil have been long battling, and for the moment it looks as if the good force is not doing well. Yet help can come to reverse the situation if you will but create it by meditation and follow it with heartfelt action.

Mother Earth, your heroine, awaits humanity's support as her hero in this drama, and her hero is all of you collectively. The problem has been humankind, and the answer is humankind. You are both villain and hero. End this duality and speak your last lines. It is the hero's role to take the final bow and to receive approbation in a garland of spiritual appreciation, acclaim, and applause.

We, your audience of heavenly hosts, will walk forward with you as your last act in the drama is called, sending mighty streams of energy to back your motives. Who will walk with me and with all the magnificent ones of heaven as hero and heroine go forward to greater love? It must be your soul who leads the way for it is the soul's mission to gain. It matters not your size, age, color, or condition. All are needed -- children and adults. Peace is for all. Love has never met a stranger.

Before the curtain comes down, let us march into the light with heads high, hearts infused with love, and peace our only goal. Earth will herself be rescued and kept alive no matter what happens, but those beings of hatred and war will not remain here spiritually to see the planet's future adventures.

I, that one called Jesus in the olden times, am with you ever anew in your present situation and in your present plight. How many times I have carried you and your burdens, as have other unseen assistants who lighten your load with love. But this is a spiritual showdown, a time of separating those who love God and those who do not. In the last act of the play, which role, which part, do YOU choose? For choose you must. Even by refusing to say yes or no is your choice announced.

As I have explained, you must meditate regularly on an individual basis and then join the power of your will and love with others in a quiet time at least on a weekly basis. In this way additional light can be given to fill the very genetic structure of your body and carry you higher and higher in the vibrational consciousness called love and wisdom.

Joining with others in small groups increases the light of your aura, or energy field, but in addition you will have a sense of community, a community which may not be composed of your blood relatives or usual circle of friends. You may even find that your new spiritual family becomes very dear to you in a short time, because these beings match your soul vibration and the bonding which you can feel with them may exceed that of the usual love relationship you are used to having with family and friends. There will be exceptions, of course, but I urge you to recognize that generally this will be a natural progression as you join these high, loving energies together in meditation. If you can do this with your family and friends, all the better. But fail not to allow this shift of love to others who have previously been strangers. Why?

The explanation for this is simple. Like attracts like. This is a law of the Universe. As you raise your energies through daily meditation, and by sharing this greater awareness with others, you will reach higher and higher realms of soul communication and possibly mental telepathy with those like myself who await your increased ability to form the communication link, the system of contact with goodness wherever it resides.

The Golden Age of which I have spoken is that time when the usual solidity of things on earth must change. What has been invisible for thousands of years in Spirit, or as heaven, will become increasingly real to you. Your usual physical senses will be expanded and will flow into awareness of things unseen, things you previously could not imagine or reach.

This ability to flow ever deeper into spiritual awareness may seem strange to you at first, but I assure you, beloveds, that it is necessary and will quickly become your usual way of behaving in this world. Remember I said that you should be in this world but not of it? This was my meaning. You are here as a physical body but you need not be weighted down by its mere physical senses. You will be gaining the higher senses of knowing, hearing and seeing what humankind has lost during the past eons of descent into lower and lower vibrations in the material world. To know directly from the cosmic realms is the greatest experience of all and many will achieve this sensitive, intuitive state.

Some will learn again from masters of love in formerly invisible realms -- places you will now be allowed to contact in the New Age if you demonstrate love and serve the one supreme Creator. What a gift! What a joy!

Please realize that these invisible realms of love, truth and light will be reserved only for those light workers who choose it and earn it. Those who do not make the daily investment in meditation and weekly sharing with others will not gain the increased level of opportunity and spiritual improvement it brings. Committing to these two simple deeds will bring the greater gain. That is why commitment is urgent. Without daily contact, the new communication pathways cannot be built and the personality will be left in darkness when others will be leaping forward in their ability to intuit and know the will of God by soul guidance.

Be assured that the time and commitment you make will bring you great rewards, for there is truly a plan in heaven for humanity's growth and spiritual evolution. It allows the serious spiritual student to develop more quickly now and to reach heights of love and inner peace that would have been impossible even two or three decades ago. This is our gift to those of humanity's ranks who recognize their goal and move onward, fueled with this increased energy vibration and light.

You are coming into this Golden Age of the thousand years of peace, my dear ones; therefore, get your birthright in order by creating the only passport required -- your demonstration that you are light and light is what you choose. Your meditation times will build this communication link of light and higher energy vibration, which can never fail you once the link is forged.

Join us, then, for a supreme moment in human development. Contact your own internal spiritual teacher and your soul, who can then act like a gigantic switchboard to keep you in touch with the unseen beings like myself. Remember that you must build this communication system from earth to us. We can provide the plan, but you must choose and carry it into fruition. This is the only way you can be "saved" or born into the kingdom of God. Follow me in certainty about this. Build your spiritual bridge to us who wait in love and who desire to assist your becoming the resurrected ones that my earthly visit 2,000 years ago described and dramatized. Become what God envisioned for you.

When enough of you light workers have joined together to unify the positive love force on the planet, much will be possible in the realm of mind where all creation begins. Here, where the energy blueprint of manifestation is formed, one and one equal a sum greater than two ... and when two or more are gathered in conviction and agreement, that creative power increases by an exponential magnitude your mathematics cannot really express. By thought alone, by pure intention and feeling does creation cast its pattern onto the etheric life web which holds space together. And here, in that tiny web of refined subatomic structures, which your instruments yet fail to totally expose, does infinity sweetly coax a finite reality into form.

I once asked my disciples and apostles to follow me, so they could learn and share this same truth with a very unsophisticated humanity. They were few, yet the impact of their teaching about the nature of God and the love principles upon which the universes are built have not gone unnoticed or unheeded in spite of their own limited understanding of my purpose. Only through love could even they grasp a hint of how life began and how it continually expands beyond itself, ever growing and flowing in pure joy.

Today's churches must change. They have deified me instead of encouraging each child of God to go into his/her own inner soul sanctuary and bring forth God's empowering energy which could then be joined in concert with others of like intention. Today I advise you that any church official who does not drop meaningless ritual and lead its members to quiet times with their souls must face the effect of this behavior.

Then each of you must meditate daily in the inner recesses of your being to forge the tools of communication to which *all* are entitled, not just a select few. By meditating you can live God's commandments more easily, especially LOVE GOD ... LOVE GOD WITH ALL YOUR HEART, MIND, AND SOUL ... AND YOUR BROTHERS AND SISTERS AS YOURSELF.

Therefore, by the power of God and many compatriot world teachers who join me in this New Age effort, I call forth the holy God power within you to hear this message and bring you into the Golden Age as a bright and shining example of the new life all can have through willingness to accept the love we offer. God smiles on our mutual opportunity and committed endeavor.

When the light workers begin this mutual journey into a new time and a new spiritual experience, discipline is required. This is the test of your soul, then, to strike a bargain and keep it. Remarks such as "I don't have time" or "I'm too busy " are merely the workings of your egotistical personality, which keeps you in a place of separation from the Creator, from heaven. I assure you that if you meet us halfway your destiny as light workers in the Golden Age ahead is affirmed. But I cannot save you from your lower self, that little limited part which prevents your greater good. Through your disciplined mind you must take time to experience a quiet meditation period daily. This private time added to quiet times once a week, joined with others in a group situation, will reinforce and further fuel your spiritual progress and growth in the light.

I have told you that you are a child of God and that your recognition of this fact automatically makes you a member of God's Love Corps, a chosen light worker. It matters not what religion you have held, if any; it is only your willingness to be useful, to serve ... and your willingness to learn ... that count now. These are the only two criteria of the Love Corp volunteer's commitment. If you are willing to *learn* and to *serve,* then I welcome you into that far-flung body of noble souls who desire your

Mother Earth cleansed of the negative thought patterns of death, destruction, and harm to other lifeforms perpetuated by humanity. This is earth's time of transformation so light workers you must be unless you would become spiritually retarded.

This is the time when the Creator has required there must be *peace*. That word is my commandment, and also yours. Without peace the earth will be in pain and chaos. I do not seek to frighten you or make you fearful for your body. (Those who believe in God, and the lesson of resurrection which I brought to humanity 2,000 years ago, will understand that the loss of your body is not the vital issue anyway. The condition of your *soul* is!) Yet the present situation is critical.

Let there be no mistake about what I am saying. In times past, when mankind perpetrated destructive acts, the planet had to be cleansed in order that a fresh start could occur. And it is this experience you are about to face. There has been so much hatred, so much war and recent invasion of space that another cleansing time will occur on the earth before the end of the 20th century, unless humanity does a rapid reverse to peace and only peace.

You must realize then, that the time known as the Tribulation is upon you and upon the planet now and that this is a last, urgent call to all of you, my brothers and sisters, to wake up, accept your soul responsibilities, demonstrate peaceful thoughts and reactions. Each one must go forth into the world shining in the splendor provided to you by God before man was. You are the light of the world, remember?

When you have been weak, helpless, and impoverished, you have allowed the military and governmental agencies to carry the germs of war and the seeds of hatred into possible world annihilation. In this last great upheaval of the results of humanity's evil to itself, called "karma" or cause and effect, be sure you stay in daily contact with your soul. You are the *saviors of mankind,* and it is only through your efforts at this hour that earth can be saved.

Many hearts have prayed to me and other spiritual teachers of all religions saying, "But I have done nothing evil. Why would this happen to me?" The answer is very simple. ALL HAVE ERRED IN THE PAST BY *NEGATIVE* THOUGHTS. None has had *only* loving ideas. But those souls willing to serve and spread the light now will be advanced to a higher level of consciousness than those who are not willing to help. Then, if earth changes are required, only those who are of the higher consciousness will be brought back for the thousand years of peace. When the beloveds of God are returned to this new time and place in man's spiritual evolution, and peace on earth is established, can you not see the result of this? A clean sky, a blossoming planet who is loved and nurtured, minerals and plants and animals protected, and human lives joined together in love, not possessed by power and viciousness.

You cannot know how much we all desire your awakening from the thoughts of violence which you have committed in your mind, one to another, and how we wish to dispel these aggressive thoughts that have accumulated in the band of invisible light around your spinning spaceship earth. I tell you it is now choked, and your life continuance is *endangered!* Yet anyone who chooses to awaken can still do so with the least possible pain and suffering.

Know that I am joined in this project by the teachers of all times and places -- Krishna, Buddha, Moses and other prophets of the Old Testament, Mohammed, and thousands of others from around our Universe who stand together to provide the support that the planet needs.

You must understand that our present efforts in humanity's behalf cannot be continued with this intense *priority* indefinitely. There are other activities in the Universe which demand our energies and attention. We will never leave you comfortless, but this is the time to take full advantage of God's *unprecedented* special aid to earth.

There are many on the planet who truly believe in no God, and I say to you now that if you have not believed because of the

hypocrisy which you see practiced in churches, you must nonetheless make every endeavor to think and act in a loving, caring
way to all you meet. Otherwise, your lack of concern will later
weed you out of those light workers identified as the so-called
"chosen people."

Be certain you hear this statement. No one will be allowed to
return in the next thousand years who has not demonstrated in a
daily way by action and thought that they are God's love personified. None of you who do not extend yourself to your
brothers and sisters or do not influence the power structures on
the planet to practice peace will be returning.

Because of your free will, you have the ability to do what you
will but that freedom has been your nemesis. Therefore, I urge
you to quell your doubting minds and selfish personalities and
place your attention only on what is reverent and peaceful at
every level of life. Whether you call yourself agnostic or are a
member of some religious body is not the issue. The issue is
your demonstration that you love God, love peace. You must
demonstrate this love. *Must*, I repeat, over and over. You must
do this -- not in remembrance of the one called Jesus -- but for
your own immortal soul's progress.

I, The Christ, can do nothing to save those who do not
acknowledge and demonstrate the truth of their inner beauty.
Christian, hear this. You who believe you are born again yet act
self-righteously superior had better evaluate your state of purity
and surrender your attitude to one of true service and assistance
during this time of Tribulation. Let your test be how well you
can truly love all and try to assist them. Judge not. The cost is
high.

Long ago other spiritual teachers issued this same invitation
to humanity. But because of free will, most did not choose
peace. Now this clarion message goes forth again. CHOOSE
PEACE! "Many are called but few will answer" is the result of
humanity's stubborn, unrelenting insistence on doing things his/
her own way. I ask you, "Has this brought you the world of
peace and love and joy which you want? Or, is your life now

filled with the threat of nuclear catastrophe and possibility of earth's destruction, not to mention damage to regions of space?"

This new call to humanity lies partly in the hands of our Love Corps and only a short time remains. Join me in doing all we can. As of today every soul is notified of this opportunity of spiritual growth, self-knowledge, and service. Reserve your place in the Golden Age by your commitment now, whatever you have done before. Are you not weary of separation from those who truly love you? Are you not ready for peace and joy at last?

In summation, I open my heart and send this message to all who will receive me in the inner sanctuary of their souls. The blessings of the God-of-All awaits you, my brothers and sisters. Accept them now if you haven't already done so.

Begin your meditation times immediately and cease them not.

Let the light of love shine on this tiny blink in God's kingdom where your neighbors in space watch this televised episode of a unique earth drama called "Will Humanity on Planet Earth Survive Themselves?" You are the producer, director, and cast in this play. We in the higher realms have created this hero's role and offered our assistance; the rest is dependent upon your individual and group endeavors.

Even though the time called "the Tribulation" is an apparent ending of some kind, I have told you there is no ending in Spirit, so do not expect to have an experience which totally ends life. Remember always that God extends ... extends ... extends ... and therefore so do the star systems and the universes and the galaxies ... and my dear ones, so do I and you! Do not fret about how it began and what God is. God is breathing or extending out and then will breathe us all home again to enjoy our spiritual banquet. Merely trust that there is a plan of great promise and joy for all who choose it. Trust. Believe. Without trust you are in peril!

In the name of all things holy and beloved of the Creator, then, I invite your participation in these years of earth's transformation. You have been presented with the reminder of an opportunity to embark upon the greatest spiritual adventure of all times, the preparation of planet earth for her own growth to true purpose. My hand is outstretched to you, my heart sings with the promise of your opportunity to shine as a bright star in the Creator's heavenly diadem. Will you not join us and your fellow light workers in this final attempt to bring peace to the world?

Even if the majority will lazily ignore the summons, and an active portion seize war as their mode of life, the New Age will be in full force by the turn of the century. Your three choices today are whether you wish to learn and serve *now,* or *later* under pain and suffering caused by spiritual procrastination, or *not at all.* Therefore, I recommend you step forward to your destiny in the light *now* where you will go forward with mighty companions in Spirit, for we in the greater realms truly love you and desire only your good.

The Golden Age is a time of group action for the benefit of everyone ... the actual living and demonstration of love and wisdom beyond the individual personality level. For this reason, group meditation is necessary and must be done either in churches, elsewhere with other organizations, or with your own friends.

God is with you, children of creation, souls of an expanding tomorrow. We have gone to prepare a place for you, but it is your own will, your choice, which determines your rank henceforth. All is prepared for this magnificent band of light workers to join together under direct revelation. However, only your commitment will bring the power into you and through you for your own advancement and for service to humanity.

Then cradle the wounded hearts of the lost and suffering ones and wherever you are guided let your words and deeds honor their true identity. For are you not the representative of Spirit -- the envoy of love on earth? Give the love you have received, then; teach peace. This planet earth needs your healing presence as does all life upon her. Shall we linger in a moment of bliss to empower our noble intention? Shall we feel increasing ecstasy as love's melody fills our hearts with memories of what once was and will one day be again?

I, THE CHRIST, WORLD TEACHER, DO HEREBY CALL FORWARD ANY SINCERE PERSON ON PLANET EARTH TO BECOME A LOVER OF GOD ... A LOVER OF YOUR PLANET EARTH ... A LOVER OF YOURSELF AND ALL LIVING THINGS THROUGHOUT THE OMNIVERSE. THIS PLANET NEEDS VOLUNTEERS FOR A LOVE CORPS TO BOND IN UNIFIED AND ENDURING ENDEAVOR. WILL YOU JOIN US OF HEAVEN WHO ASK FOR YOUR ASSISTANCE? WILL YOU MEDITATE DAILY AND SHARE YOUR LOVE WITH OTHER MEDITATORS WEEKLY? WILL YOU BECOME ONE WITH GOD?

IF SO, BY THE POWER AND AUTHORITY OF MY ROLE AS YOUR WORLD TEACHER, I DO GRANT YOU THE FULL SUPPORT OF HEAVEN IN YOUR RESPONSIBILITIES AS ENVOYS OF WORLD AND UNIVERSAL PEACE. KNOW THAT YOU ARE, HENCEFORTH, NEVER ALONE, AND THAT AN ADDITIONAL PERSONAL GUIDE OR TEACHER WILL BE PROVIDED YOU WHEN YOUR MEDITATIVE COMMUNICATION SYSTEM IS LINKED TO HEAVEN AGAIN.

Although I am the risen son of God and present world teacher to the planet earth, my greatest role is that of being on the Gold Ray (Christ Consciousness) in this 12th Universe. Therefore, I attend your planet now where I am joined by a mighty creator called the Silver Ray. The Silver Ray, twin creation to the Gold, has created all sub-rays and has brought earth both the color spectrum of the rainbow and the glowing nighttime reminder of God, your moonlight.

The Silver Ray, the Great Ray of Hope and Healing, has volunteered to ease the subconscious pain and the soul memories of your 8-million-year-long negative experiences so that there will be peace on earth at last. You will hear this great yet gentle healing energy call you forth to revere God and all of life.

In the miracle of our combined power and nurturance earth's light workers will thrive as never before, both individually and as planetary citizens of a galaxy that draws them into deeper knowing and service. May this clarion announcement of God's presence here thrill the slumbering vibrations of your soul as the angels and spiritual masters join with us to touch your life with hope. REJOICE, and welcome this silver creation of God, the Great Ray of Hope and Healing in your 12th Universe, who has united with me in this time of awakening.

Now your soul can finally sigh out its ancient sorrows and drink from the mystic well of peace. REJOICE, because of this extraordinary spiritual opportunity, never brought to earth before. Again, I say "Rejoice," for this is the highest gift any planet can receive from the cosmic heights.

Join us in this hour of unprecedented participation to save your garden planet, and humanity, from the destructive course being enacted on earth today.

I now leave you to the inner spirit of your own knowing. But, I invite you to join me, the Silver Ray, and your teachers of all times to go forward with earth in that blazing glow of infinity that is ever expanding in its intensity and purpose. You are the love-wisdom pattern for the Universe. This has been your constant, but usually forgotten, responsibility. It is time to awaken.

Let Love Corps volunteers and all men and women of goodwill join together in this final gathering -- in this most profound of enduring endeavors.

So be it, beloveds.

AMEN.

NOVEMBER 17, 1986 ADDENDUM

Effective this date, citizens of planet earth are granted an additional two years of intensified support by the spiritual forces because of their peace efforts over the past 18 months. Therefore, please expect a noticeable change in the earth's vibratory energy rate which will aid in raising human consciousness toward PEACE.

Stop the hydrogen underground explosions! Cease all space weaponry. Time is of the essence. Use it well. Godspeed.

1994/1995 COMMENTS

Although I am a risen son of God, and a present world teacher to those on planet Earth, using Gold and Silver Ray energies—I am excited to announce that since July 29, 1994, when the comet's fragment collisions on Jupiter created a higher vibration for this solar system and parts of the Milky Way galaxy, a new history has begun. Indeed, I and the entire order of the Christ have been potently joined by the transmutable Blue Flame (Ray) of beloved Archangel Michael and his various legions of light who are insistent upon reclaiming Earth and humanity for the higher good. Then truly are you called forth!

This is extraordinary news, dear ones, for it increases our light power in this region and possibly decreases the time needed to gather together those light servers now—or soon to be—ready for some kind of ascension! However, you must understand it means that the clash between light and dark will be temporarily increased while Lord Michael's calling reverberates across the planet and registers in the souls of all humanity. There is a ferment brewing.

Then I strongly urge that you learn an ascension meditation technique for healing your body and also for possibly acquiring a 55-foot (or wider) crystalline energy disk of light around your body that can be accelerated to what you call the speed of light. I call this experience reaching transfiguration or acquiring the garment of light, but other teachings identify a similar process called the Merkaba (or Merkabah) meditation. These meditations are ways of using the purity of love, certain breathing patterns, mudras (hand positions) and various eye movements and visualizations to accelerate the vibratory frequency of the cells into an atomic acceleration of light (lightness). Only then can your physical body leave the third dimension safely, without death, and retain full consciousness.

At this "holy coordinate point" that is an extraordinarily high energy rate, it is not only possible to take your physical body into higher dimensions, but you can visit other cosmic locations and continue to grow in awareness—consciousness—and service to God. This has been the only way a human person could physically cross over the invisible crystalline barrier grid established around planet Earth by Archangel Michael's power. Some teachings have called the grid "the ring pass not" because only pure beings could ascend through it—thus the name Ascended Masters. Just remember that this holy coordinate point is where the Mother/Father vibrations fuel your DNA shift from cocoon to butterfly, from earthen to galactic identity. It is here you will truly be home with us, your spiritual family—ready for joy and more adventure!

Then meditate to hasten your own personal ascension, but I assure you that even if you do not learn to energize your way into ascension, without physical death, you are a part of heaven and to heaven you will return! Have no fear, beloveds, but rather rejoice that so many will be with us very soon—and that the divine plan on Earth is being fulfilled. Although you may hear stories that all humanity will simultaneously ascend together via the high mega cell consciousness, or superconscious touch of God—sometimes called the photon veil or belt—please discern that such a pledge may be quite sincere and still present an extremely complex task. I say to you, however, that although the adventure will be challenging, it has always been my personal desire to bring all of humanity back to God through the gift of grace. Grace is for everyone but requires both acceptance and a genuine change to a loving heart, which is an actual vibratory rate that can be measured. Then be about your Mother/Father's business and practice the innocence of love. In that way you will always achieve the purpose for which your soul has come.

Let this be a time of great rejoicing and celebration for anyone who loves the Creator and chooses to come home as the long-awaited prodigal. We lovingly await your return.

So be it beloveds, and amen.

Chapter X

The Alchemy of Ascension

May the showering light of the Creator's presence join us in love and wisdom today as I return to clarify what these ensuing eight years—since the first publication of New Teachings for an Awakening Humanity—have inaugurated for you and all of humanity presently living on this extraordinary planet. Indeed, as we of heaven observe the tremendous shifts many of you lightworkers have made within the boundaries of what you call reality, it is enormously satisfying that your willingness has produced so much growth in awareness in so brief a moment in time. You are to be commended and congratulated for your sincere commitment to the awakening process and for your efforts to acquire greater and greater consciousness. As cosmic creations of a mighty and caring parent, you are noble offspring awaiting an unprecedented correction of your genetic mutancy. Yes, you await the raising of your DNA woundedness back into the full consciousness condition you once had prior to malevolent genetic engineering that was done to most humans about 10,000-13,000 years ago in that country called Atlantis.

Today, then, most of humanity on planet Earth operates on about one-sixth the amount of genetic capability they once had. This reduction of the human being's genetic composition from a fully conscious creation to one of a mutant state is biblically referred to as "the fall"—meaning that the original genetic DNA pattern had been so badly damaged that humans were no longer at full consciousness levels of knowing God while living in physical body form. This deliberate DNA retardation not only caused the Earth human's separation from God and the divine forces, but it prevented remembrance of your spiritual origins and your recollection of other galactic human beings presently alive on nearby planets and star clusters, such as the brightest star in your sky, Sirius. This genetic interference and retardation buried the truth that all Earth humans were originally physical beings capable of telepathic communication, clairvoyance, clairaudience, and clairsentience. That is, they could consciously see, hear, feel, and transmit or receive various vibratory frequencies of light and information which was your natural inheritance. This range of abilities was quite normal for all humans everywhere, including those here on Earth before their genetic codes were damaged—and I happily report, your former powers will be normal for humans once again very soon! In a simple concept, dear ones, you were designed as a fountain of youth or a spiritual alchemist capable of taking superconductive elements and transforming them into matter form—your body—for thousands of years of life.

Because everything in creation is a product of light, God love, or what you call energy—in some form or another—your natural God-design is awesome, indeed. Only these past DNA mutilations currently prevent your ability to employ and enjoy that energy adequately. I remind each of you, therefore, to use even the minimal energy you do have in a positive and constructive way! And to live nobly and spiritually in both thought and deed while we prepare the way for an amazing ascension process. We who have come to teach and guide you through this most onerous of circumstances into ascension, know far more than it has previously been advisable for us to share; nonetheless all of us, in our present day religious guidance, speak to you of love, of nurturance, and of respecting your brothers and sisters. All of us have explained the need for cooperation, harmony and peace, have we not? These teachings also stress the need for turning within to your soul place, the inner knower, the perfect guide who is an energy form capable of connecting you to the cosmos from which you came. This intuitive, nurturing, creative aspect of you still lives, in spite of your genetic mutancy, and with the constancy of your faith and spiritual commitment—it remembers God, your galactic identity, and your reason for being here. Has it not brought us together, in fact, at this very moment, so we might communicate with each other in this meaningful but unusual way?

The many centuries of the Earth humans' mutancy have not been without whispers that the alchemy process, in which the power or process of transforming something ordinary or common into something more precious, could be found. Indeed, in Europe's medieval, chemical science period, the aim was to achieve the transmutation of the base metals into gold along with discovering a universal cure for disease and finding a way to assure prolonged or eternal life. Thus, as mentioned in the New Cells, New Bodies, NEW LIFE! book: "What is there embedded in the deep recesses of the human family's consciousness that covets better health, longer life, and even immortality? Is this a deeply planted concept, an archetype, that haunts humanity's unconscious repository of evolutionary history with lingering impressions of a past truth once enjoyed?"

My answer to that is YES, your DNA is still encoded with the disconnected or suspended parts required to reclaim the 12-helix scalar wave of full consciousness condition! All is not lost. There are a few beings on the planet whose genetic lineage never had their 12-helix DNA fully crippled, thus accounting for the various psychic and spiritual gifts that a rare few possess. My own appearance on Earth was to model what humans could be and I left behind one method of resurrection (or ascension) using what your cultures call the speed of light, or what I call an energy acceleration that transmutes matter into light. My model has helped only a few attain physical ascension, but the seeds were planted that love and forgiveness would bring you home in consciousness, at least.

My own pattern was one of meditation, fasting, rituals using light energy and breathing techniques to increase the amount of cellular light in the human body. (This includes the use of certain herbs, nontoxic foods, air, and water as part of a healthy lifestyle.) However, there are three other ascension methods besides the pattern that I wish to identify for you. These three other potential ascension patterns for Earth humans are as follows:

1. Raising the entire human race into a mass ascension experience through certain spiritual and physical energy events—such as realigning or removing the energy grid once placed around Earth that prevents negative souls from leaving this dimension. (The Jupiter Comet fragment collision has begun this initial possibility.)

2. Utilizing naturally occurring cyclical, photon energy patterns (photon is a kind of light) to simultaneously shower humanity with so much intense light that their bodies could quickly acquire full consciousness. This might be done in tandem with number 1, above.

3. Teaching humans how to make "manna" via an alchemical process spoken of in the Bible, which transforms certain rare elements into health-giving superconductive products. The greatest of all elements is gold because when it is transformed into a white powdery substance that is easily assimilated by the body, it becomes a light fuel for extended life. Food for the gods, beloveds. Food for achieving and maintaining the 12-helix full consciousness. (We have already given you iridium and rhodium.)

Using my own ascension pattern and methods, many of you have been meditating, using your dreams, and seeking to cleanse and heal yourselves of negative beliefs and emotions. Thus great progress has been made in this past decade. Indeed, many decent people have single-handedly created improvements in human thinking and behavior that are absolutely miraculous. Others have joined together on various projects to improve government, to heal human pain, and to shift the suffering of all living things by a higher application of spiritual perception. Regardless of their motives, they are inordinately valuable in serving Earth's and humanity's needs, not to mention the needs of your solar system and the galaxy itself. Much more is happening than the limited reports from your media and printed sources would indicate. Your planet is buried in lies, half-truths, and governmental secrets, as anyone must surely realize. But more than that, most of humanity has forgotten why it was created, and what God's purpose was in allowing this human life-form to evolve. For evolve it did, but not as your Darwinists purport. Your human form came from the stars in an evolutionary expansion best described as an inter-dimensional decision by the archangelic realms, and those you call spiritual masters and lords, to create planetary caretakers in this galaxy.

Now let me further explain the possible mass ascension mentioned as number 1, above. Please try to understand that your DNA genetic origins were placed within the sacred geometrical pattern or design called the star tetrahedron which is a uniquely human pattern wherever it appears. The human pattern, design, creation, or energy definition, then, is truly to be called galactic or cosmic in origin. In every way humans are extraterrestrial, to use an Earth word, because this DNA life code that makes you a human form—rather than a horse, whale, or bird—had its origin elsewhere in space. In every sense then, you were and are an evolving life form identified as a valuable addition to God's family of life! And the higher genetic DNA pattern used to create a physical form capable of having full consciousness is definitely from space, not a development that occurred here on this single planet you presently inhabit.

I trust that your awareness of this idea will not be upsetting or disquieting, but rather will be a thrilling discovery—a discovery that God needed and wanted a life form to give service in physical worlds which is why humans were quickly advanced in evolution's sequence. Thereby your abilities as caretakers of this galaxy's many physical planets were genetically designed to be superbly accomplished. Dear ones, you are cosmic in origin. Your breed, so to say, exists in many areas of what you call the Milky Way galaxy in purposeful and important ways. Galactic humans are often the first physical settlers or pioneers for God's expanding purposes. And more than you may yet realize, some of you are the light-beings or are becoming the light-beings—described in holy books such as the Bible—as gods with a small "g."

There are few of you on Earth who yet grasp the enormous significance of who and what you are because of your present genetic mutancy. But some souls can taste an ancient flavor of my meaning and accept that through the spiritual use of light, life began for your ancestors in what is termed an etheric condition, or a high vibratory frequency that did not require physical bodies. Spirit came first and your relation to Archangel Michael in that chain of creation cannot be overstated! That beloved light-being is—in ways difficult to explain—the human form's midwife. Suffice it to say, your lineage began in light and love with an intention to create useful members of the spiritual hierarchy. This experiment has left a most notable mark in this galaxy. Nonetheless, there have been renegades within this original human creation because of the free-will factor—as your Earth's violent history describes. We are sending the healing energies of wisdom, love, and peace to you, to aid the resurrection of your original DNA full consciousness, and many of you are becoming more and more aware, and absolutely capable of reclaiming your original 12-helix heritage as described in the book New Cells, New Bodies, NEW LIFE!

Whatever negative genetic practices occurred to cripple Earth humans long ago, good news prevails today. We are helping you return to that greater nature and normal genetic condition. Indeed, you are becoming spiritually mature, galactic humans once again after a genetic detour that may seem hurtful, or inappropriate at best. Yet do I assure you that because of this suffering you have learned a truth so profound that it is changing the course of cosmic history. Whether you can believe it yet or not, you of Earth who have retained your spiritual commitment throughout this ignoble event, will soon be respectfully regarded throughout the cosmos. Indeed, my beloveds, you will become known as one of God's most important helpers in operating various material world planets such as Earth.

Notice I say God's creations which means there are many different physical body styles or forms. Humans are but one of many life forms in physical existence, just as there are angelic forms of different kinds, also. Creation is varied and experimental. You are not less important because God has many creations, unless you allow yourself to think so. Your acceptance of this

truth about human beings will open a vast area of joyful exploration soon to be experienced if you wish it. Life is incredibly
abundant as this planet so obviously demonstrates! Flowers
come in many sizes, shapes, colors, and odors. Plants and trees
are also profuse, as are animals, birds and fish— even the insects
and tiny viruses. If you can comprehend that beings like yourself
are only one physical genetic pattern, even as a cedar is one type
of tree and a nightingale is one type of bird, you will face the
upcoming transition with greater peace and security. I come
today, then, to put this imminent transformation and ascension
into a clearly defined context for all who will listen and test the
validity of my message within their own soul. For there the
resonance will occur. I ask that you test my comments, as you
would those of any other speaker—inside the resonating chamber of your heart and soul. Simply ask your soul whether you are
cosmic in origin or not.

One of our gifts to aid in your ascension is to make it easier to
reclaim your power and authority through access to the many
energy influences and upgrades we have shared with you. Beginning after World War II and then most profoundly in 1985/86,
when Earth's rigid, concrete reality was penetrated by our
harmonious waves of higher consciousness, you began to awaken.
As you were fed the healing octaves of our love and wisdom, your
hidden code of genius, mutantly sleeping within the DNA cell's
original composition, was vitalized and an enormous resonance
began to throb within the cellular definition of your beingness.
Gradually, then, miraculous things began to happen as humans
participated in their evolutionary emergence from the cocoon-
like prison of ignorance into a more sentient group consciousness!

In 1987, what you called the Harmonic Convergence intensified an inter-dimensional awakening, and a loosening from the
duality of separation began a new cycle of unity and holiness
(wholeness). Exponential resonance moved some of you into an
ever-increasing focus on psychological cleansing and an emergence from immature emotional patterns of personal selfishness.
Some of you began to remember the soulful satisfaction of

harmonic living, and to yearn for community, group cooperation and planetary salvation.

We have watched your progress since the end of World War II and witnessed your expanding transformation, especially during the amplifications of energies during what you call solstice, equinox and full-moon rituals and meditations—and also wherever church services or celestial-type music have raised your feeling level to heaven. Some churches allow and encourage quiet times of meditation, also, and these provide an ever expanding increase in your vibratory rate. Nature too, plays an enormous role in developing human compassion and in providing ways to express it through the nurturance of animals, cetaceans, fish, plants, birds, minerals, air, soil, and water. Each aesthetic thought you have, or deed you do, increases your consciousness and brings your vibration of love closer to heaven. Indeed, each time you are environmentally wise, or reach positive agreements, or are kind to one another, you are blessing life and your own soul frequency, as well. This results in increased perception and higher consciousness for use in balancing your personality with its soul commitment as a galactic caregiver.

Then by using personal and group meditations to focus on positive change, you can combine your separate energies into a group and begin synthesizing these intentions into a vision of a healed humanity, a purified society. New visions gain a foothold against the darkness of violence and negativity—especially during those times when enormous numbers of people group together to further the cause of peace and spiritual goals—as during your December 31st world peace meditations. You would scarcely believe the enormous progress humanity has made in the past eight years since the release of books like <u>New Teachings for an Awakening Humanity</u> which encouraged and inspired people to know their value and to dedicate their lives to the divine plan.

Many dear souls have brought a myriad of messages to the public reminding them of their origin and purpose. Through continued meditation, prayer, and contemplation, a vast number of beings have remembered who they are and why they are here. Indeed, their outpouring of positive messages in music, art, religion, science, conservation, education, government, and innumerable other Earth activities has further enhanced the quality of human consciousness. We have been delighted at the use of such words as "planetary citizens," "global families," "planetary advocates," "Peace Corps," "Love Corps," and the like, which indicate the nature of your function here as group caregivers and heartfelt companions.

Aided greatly by the communication media of TV, movies, radio, print, etc., there has also been a meaningful surge in the out-picturing of humanity's psychic and spiritual abilities and in the galactic nature of humanity's potential. Pictures which change perceptions and introduce positive consciousness have often been introduced and encouraged by us through those who will listen to our guidance and serve our angelic cause.

It is important to verify that the most influential futurists among you have been utilized to suggest the value of co-creation, not merely procreation, and to foster co-societal aims not just personal goals and satisfactions. The emergence from individual self-cleansing and personality development has spiraled toward broader partnerships, community cooperation, and synergistic group consciousness. Application of metaphysical principles has begun to influence human potentiality more and more frequently as many different religious teachers proclaim the necessity for understanding and practicing God's plan. Christians who lacked ability in meditation skills could acquire these skills from Eastern religious teachers and did so (in the U.S., especially) when their own Christian churches did not teach them to turn within, to quiet themselves and listen—even as I meditated during biblical times (and as the great saints of all times and places have done).

You and we have seen, on every front, how the power of our energy has strengthened your mission for inter-dimensional consciousness through the collapse of rigid misbeliefs and new perceptions that caused the actual fall of physical walls, governments, and dishonorable leaders. Russian autocracy was recently challenged by a gnawing world dream of peace based upon a spiritually-based governing system, just as America's romance with materialism's greed is being presented a choice of potential collapse or the restitution of <u>spiritual economics</u>. All around the planet, then, the showering presence of our divine intervention has opened minds, hearts and bodies to the human family's DNA reclamation process. A reclamation of ancestral galactic power and an inter-dimensional, multidimensional wisdom and love is your certain destiny, beloveds! How your soul sings to this promise of transformation and then soars in joyful expectation of beneficence! As I have been a spiritual model, template, and example to many (though my mission has frequently been misunderstood), some of you are also remembering that you, too, have a role within the Christ consciousness of the galaxy as models and patterns worth exemplifying.

Our energy and light gifts have continued with several major outpourings of special energy—particularly in 1994—that have further opened your spiritual awareness to a comprehension of what has been happening in this decade and where humanity is being directed. You are probably aware that our interest and interaction from both the spiritual realms, and your humanoid space brothers and sisters who retain full consciousness, have been enormously amplified! Not only have both spiritual realms and galactic humanoids focused greater energy, knowledge, and power to Earth, but there has been a greater combined intention of mutual cooperation and a more exacting focus on the affairs of Earth and your solar system This we do as part of a profound universal evolution back to the Mother/Father's bosom. Indeed, many prodigal life forms—not just of the human species—are yearning to be embraced by that sacred presence! Therefore, an immense gathering is taking place, so mammoth in size and proportion that its numbers defy an accurate count. From the lowest to the highest dimensions and dominions, this longing to be "home with the Creator" has spread its silver-golden radiance over the canopy of all creation and into the fabric of nearly every soul.

You, too, my beloveds, are hearing this call and you will feel this movement toward group cooperation with ever increasing intensity, linked as you are in galactic heritage. Early in the 1990's, I and the ascended masters from dimension one through seven, received the invitational overture from the archangels, especially Lord Michael, to begin the great love and wisdom gathering of all light-servers. Since April 23, 1994, in fact, you have enjoyed an even more extraordinary increase in spiritual energies than ever before, resulting from the great vortex reopening of the Lemurian consciousness. I speak here of Lemuria as that ancient nation and culture that had the human family's most highly conscious, physical life expression ever known.

This Lemurian culture of nearly a million years ago, located in the region called the Pacific Ocean, was quite superb in a variety of ways. Many historians speak of its gentle wisdom and loving cooperative societies, but not all realize that it was Archangel Michael who brought this noble experiment into physical matter. This planned society of galactic caretakers and pioneers assumed dominion over your most exquisite planetary sphere, following an earlier, successful etheric (mostly nonphysical) experiment that had existed for literally eons before its attack and ruin.

The Lemurian society's extensive energy application of wise and compassionate stewardship, though it later met a final physical defeat at the hands of some anti-Christed Atlanteans, remains a powerful pattern of influence even into present times when the Prince of Darkness seems to rule the planet. Although the Lemurian physical lands are mostly destroyed and lie buried beneath the expansive Pacific Ocean depths, yet its etheric (invisible energy pattern) template in higher realms has now been opened by spiritual agreement over the island you call Maui, Hawaii—a valuable anchoring locale.

This provides a vortex of enormous group consciousness that is now flowing around the planet and you are feeling its nurturing, creative, and intuitive character even as I speak. Indeed, its sacred ambience gently interpenetrates your earthly consciousness and the planet's ethers so your soul can drink deeply from its influence of caring competence and spiritual guidance. Thus it is not uncommon to feel drawn to the vibrations of the many Pacific Island native cultures and to sense the inherent joy of their gentle ways and their acutely protective attitude of stewardship for the planet and for all living things. I pause for a moment and ask if you can sense that energy and gentleness about which I speak?

* * * * * * * * * * * * * *

This Lemurian vortex opening from the etheric-spiritual realms, as it becomes fully grounded into physicalness, sets the stage for even greater space-family interrelationships from the human family in the region you call Sirius. Sirius has your closest physical, galactic human family and is located just a few light-years away from Earth. Of course, these energies will permit stronger connections between all galactic humans whether they are located in those places you term Lyra, Vega, Sirius, the Pleiades, Orion, Arcturus, etc. It is also the phasing-out time of the unpleasant abduction experimentations caused by those smaller-bodied, large-eyed beings you call aliens—those from Zeta Reticuli, who are not genetically compatible with human DNA, though they have explored that breeding possibility with Earth's governmental approval.

These Zeta Reticuli are not a genetic human species as are the galactic human beings living on some stars and planets such as Sirius, the Pleiades, Orion, Arcturus, etc., and one day your governments will have to confess to the relationships they have had with these nonhuman extraterrestrials instead of your own species. Can you see how badly your governments want the UFO issue censored? Some of you will view this cover-up and secrecy as a vicious blight and betrayal of the human race when you learn the full details.

It is important for you to realize that you have had many prior connections to human galactic space family members who may have had past genetic influence here on Earth. That is to say, the peopling of Earth may have been caused by God through the cellular DNA patterns of humans already living on other places. Our great Creator uses many designated co-creators to spread their genetic offspring and advance the peopling of immense physical realms and dimensions. Even as I speak, your own Earth scientists are now actively doing experiments on the DNA codes and cellular compositions of your human genetic identity. By removing parts of the DNA strand and influencing the cells and chromosomes, they tamper with various definitions of life itself.

Since they have even been able to clone a human embryo, you must realize that physical co-creation is possible. (All the more reason to demand that these scientists doing genetic engineering behind closed doors be ethically pure in their attitudes and be morally guided by the human citizenry at large!) Kindly remember that the reason your present body is mutant and your consciousness limited, is because the later genetic engineers of Atlantis were not of pure intention and they did destructively tamper with the human DNA strand, leaving the genetic code of the general population badly reduced in capacity. It is absolutely appropriate today for you to establish the moral and ethical codes under which genetic engineering is practiced!

Now I wish to specifically identify for you the present circumstances that humanity will probably soon experience so that we have a mutual context in which to hold planet Earth's potential events. I have deliberately used the words <u>probably</u> and <u>potential</u> because in our inter-dimensional usage of time and space, we find that there is a frequent distortion between your linear Earth calendar and our own levels of consciousness in the spiritual realms. This apparent contradiction often leaves humans feeling confused, untrusting, and even betrayed when predictions made in good faith do not occur or are only partially accomplished. I need to say that until recently, when your own consciousness could be brought into alignment with the reality of your holographic knowingness, it was almost impossible to coordinate our realities together in a congruent time frame.

There are several reasons for this—a primary cause being that your group consciousness is seldom constant nor is it centered throughout the day and night—even within the various moon and solar energy influences that affect you and your planet. Like the ebb and flow of an ocean, human consciousness rises and falls, and sleeps and awakens in irregular patterns that frequently baffle and challenge our sincerest wishes to assist your evolution. That is why we ask you to be contemplative or meditative each and every day so that our vibrations can comfort and guide your soul's desires into the personality's life choices and behaviors. And this is why we insist that you gather together every week, or more frequently if possible, to form a matrix of light that can hold the depths of our caring.

In addition, you must realize that even as we of the spiritual realms are lending our guidance and love, the great archangels such as Archangel Michael, Gabriel, Uriel and Raphael, have a plan of action that affects many different dimensions and many life forms throughout this and other galaxies. These extraordinary complexities are always being updated according to the quality of energies available within all humans and nonhumans, not merely your own individual personal center of reality. Then as the holy books relate, there are wars and disputes in heaven, some on nearby dimensions and levels of consciousness that affect your personal and planetary development—and vice versa. Both your individual awareness and the level of group consciousness at any given moment on this, or any planetary body, draws or feeds from an immense pool of light, wisdom and love that flows into any opportune potential. Thus life is never static, but is always changing, even for those of us you might presume to be supremely important and powerful.

Yet the motive behind the change remains focused on both the Creator's intention and will, until it is accomplished. Energy takes its next flow of creation while the change is accomplished. At present, then, this Universe, and the Milky Way galaxy in particular, are learning that light can always attract the darkness back into balanced respect and companionship. You, my dear ones, are the leaders of this learning lesson, and every thought and action you take for the light has a potential influence over humanity and many other life-forms, not merely those who live elsewhere in an identical or very similar human body to your own. It is no exaggeration to confide that you—who I term cosmic citizens, though you may temporarily be located on planet Earth—can influence the future of this solar system, galaxy and a myriad of people, places, and life-forms seeking light, wisdom and love. I have spoken it before and I repeat it here. You are the divinity of God's expression in flesh.

Through your evolution back into full consciousness, you leave a model for all of life, be it human or nonhuman. As you shift back to your true identity and utilize that sacredness for the light, the probabilities of those efforts—like our own—will not be known immediately, but will add rays of gold and silver to the fabric of creation, instituting a rainbow arch stretching into eternity. Then be of good faith and certainty as the potentialities and the probabilities we may mutually achieve become recognized and appreciated by many other levels of consciousness, anxious themselves to contribute to the Creator's intentions for a fully-developed spiritual sentience throughout the Omniverse.

Because so much is happening with the positive use of light for the expansion of God's plan in this galaxy, you are advised to learn about these other human beings who reside on other planets. For in very real ways they can be considered genetic relatives who have had their own experiences over eons of time in many far-flung locales. It is imperative, in fact, that you understand that these various galactic humans and their activities have helped create a present scenario that directly affects who you are, what has happened to you, and what your future may be. It is not only the spiritual realms and the archangels who are involved in designing your life, beloveds. Some of those other humans who are your galactic relatives affect you, as well, even as your Earth parents, grandparents, and those of earlier Earth generations have affected the current hereditary circumstances of the physical person you are today—if you see the comparison I'm making.

Various particulars about your many human and other galactic visitors were given in the recent book You Are Becoming a Galactic Human, which provides a partial history of the major extraterrestrial activities pertinent to Earth's conditions today. Other authors and channels have also provided some pieces of Earth's history as it relates to your galactic human ancestors. However, galactic history is really quite complicated and would have to be seriously studied over a period of some years, because—as you know from the study of your own nation's history which covers only a few centuries—there are many interwoven events and relationships. (Unfortunately, no one on Earth today knows your real history!)

Those that live on Lyra, Vega, Sirius, Orion, the Pleiades, Arcturus, and other galactic human locations (with millions of years of history) spend centuries of their 2000- to 4000-year-long lives learning their own and galactic histories. That is why we can only give a hint of this enormously complex historical information. Nonetheless, certain bits and pieces of galactic history are coming into your Earth consciousness now, because particular galactic activities have affected you and will be affecting you more and more as Archangel Michael gathers all the legions of light together throughout the many realms.

Vividly imagine, then, what an entire quadrant of an average sized galaxy with billions of planets has experienced over millions and millions of years. And not just with the human genetic form but with the interplay of nonhumans, as well, who incidentally outnumber the Creator's more recent genetic creation called humanoid. Consequently it will soon be necessary for those of you on Earth who are coming back into full consciousness to realize that humanoids are but one flower in God's garden—not the only variety in creation! But let me return to humanity's current circumstances and clarify what is particularly helpful and useful to know.

Following the Lemurian energy vortex opening during April 23-25, 1994, your bodies had hardly assimilated the vibrational effects of group consciousness and nurturing commandments before another massive energy influence occurred. From mid-July, until end of the month, 1994, other highly influential energy frequencies were unleashed when 20-some enormous comet fragments penetrated planet Jupiter's atmosphere. This experience became the object of human scrutiny by astronomers, the media, and many millions of human beings who witnessed the event on television or read of it in their newspapers. Did you see it? This is the precursor to one of the three major types of ascension patterns I previously mentioned.

As eyes were focused upon the spectacular solar system event, this enormous planetary sphere, Jupiter, was now identified as a neighbor, even though positioned far away in solar system space. Jupiter's pummeling on the far side by a series of physical comet projectiles was an influential opening in what you call the human psyche, even as your earlier space dramas leading to moon landings shifted humans from egocentric perceptions to a realization that Earth lived and moved in space. Indeed, that novel perception of Earth seen from the moon, as an orbiting space craft, allowed the next phase of galactic awareness to be introduced. Humans truly began to grasp that planet Earth is a precious commodity worth saving even from their own unconscious greed and abusive habits.

This ascension opening of the group planetary consciousness to the truth that God has many mansions in space has become a foundation for the next required understanding that Earth is also part of a solar system with nearby neighbors. Neighboring planets can affect Earth either positively or negatively, depending upon other factors over which Earth humans have no control! This phase of realizing you have relationship with other physical planets is crucial to your acceptance of galactic responsibility as a member within a solar family. So in less than 20 years the human Earth family has seen itself—via its traveling astronauts and scientific instruments—as living on a physical planet orbiting in space that also has planetary neighbors.

In addition, you have now seen one of those solar neighbors, Jupiter, closer than ever before, and just at a moment when it was being affected by circumstances beyond itself. This perception is vital to your perception and understanding of yourself as a solar system resident within the galaxy's aegis.

Is it perfectly clear, then, that as comet fragments bombarded the far side of Jupiter with tremendous force—that might have harmed even your own home planet—you have acquired a necessary concept of yourselves as planetary dwellers living in a solar system that can be influenced by external—even galactic—events and circumstances beyond your control?

Have you suspected that the emissions from those comet fragments pummeling into Jupiter released a number of forces it would be difficult for most Earth dwellers to recognize? Let me simply identify one of the important physical ones as a graviton emission or an energy influence possibly related to maintaining planet Earth's equilibrium and hopefully avoiding a pole shift. These and other energies may also be used to assist in repairing the ozone hole and later reestablishing Earth's firmaments. The higher spiritual dominions, and those inter-dimensional beings you call extraterrestrials, may be able to use these graviton emissions to help realign Earth, and your solar system, and also influence areas far beyond them! The comet collision on Jupiter did something else, as well. It gave a Jupiterian quality to the energy emissions that surround you, granting new beginnings through the use of universal wisdom and love.

The Jupiter energy experience also accentuated a powerful calling by Archangel Michael to further awaken your spirituality, and this is a messianic announcement of enormous importance! Like the birth of the baby Jesus and many other religious and spiritual events that have become historical landmarks in the Earth human's psyche, this Jupiter event has brought into focus a great messenger and protector—a universal and galactic messiah. This newly acclaimed God-oriented messiah is that one identified as Archangel Michael, who reminds humans on Earth that the true purpose of their existence is to return into the higher heavens where he is again calling all the legions of light into cooperative comradeship and service.

Then I ask you to contemplate my messianic presence on Earth 2,000 years ago as the forerunner of this 1994 Archangel Michael event and realize that all of the light beings in this solar system and galaxy are being called back home. Now the great Father/Mother's son, Lord Michael, extends a further invitation to planet Earth and its light servers to hear a solar and a galactic awakening call!

Since I realize that our constant admonitions to use these incoming energies positively are difficult to translate into your own mental experience, several illustrations will be given to demonstrate how those energies may be comprehended by the human family, especially those who serve God. Then kindly observe *Illustration #1*.

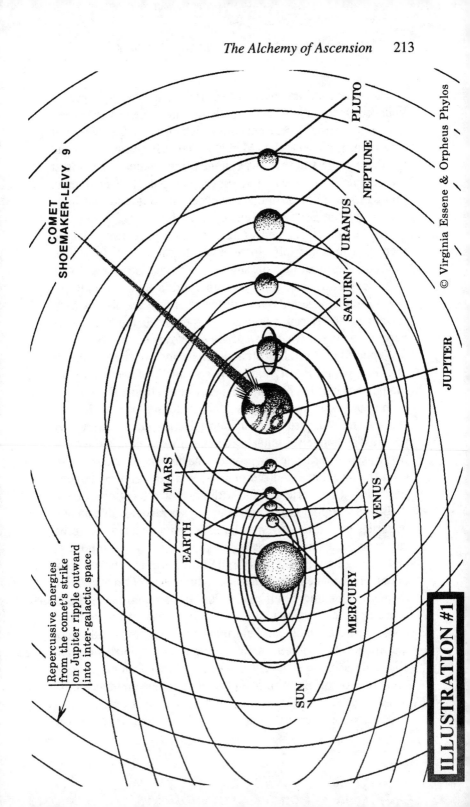

ILLUSTRATION #1

Please become an observer far out in space looking down on your own space neighborhood called a solar system. You can see a rotational circular movement in which there is a Sun with four small nearby planets called Mercury, Venus, Earth, and Mars and then five planets farther away in the orbital pattern, the closest one of which—and the largest—is called Jupiter. In a sense, then, you can see Earth positioned between the Sun and that huge planet, Jupiter. Both are influencing Earth.

As the comet fragments plunged into Jupiter, they released many unusual emissions, some of which are physical in application, but others that are more subtle and spiritual, so to say. Notice that these emissions traveled into Earth's aura, or multiple energy fields, where the rays of the solar Sun are also flowing toward Earth. Because you have experienced the Sun's rays before, you know what power they have over life as you live it. So Jupiter is now sending off additional waves of energy that are affecting planet Earth, humanity, and all life forms, invisible though they may be. Jupiter is, in fact, a newly formed <u>etheric sun</u> with subtle spiritual energies of high consciousness flowing across your solar system and up into galactic patterns directed by the great archangels. Jupiter is a source of valuable qualities now being used to permeate and promote the higher consciousness of both the awakened and the unawakened here and far beyond Earth. It is a great friend filled with intrinsic gifts of upliftment.

Because Jupiter is a living thing, it has a recognizable nature, or series of qualities, even as humans and animals do. Briefly, Jupiter represents the capacity to experience new opportunities and the beginnings of things through the use of cosmic wisdom, of universal concepts and ideas. Its nature is one of great creative expression leading to self-realization! Jupiter's influence therefore aids a truer understanding of divine philosophy and spiritual consciousness which can help transform ignorance and doubt into higher love vibrations. Wherever Jupiter's outflowing energy embraces other life, it deposits this inspirational energy. Thus for you on Earth, Jupiter's noble influence portends only positive aspects, further empowered by the Sun's fire.

Kindly consider that your entire solar system in now being

upgraded in vibration by an energy wave, a kind of rippling intrusion of vibratory frequencies (sound you cannot hear but which does exist). This Jupiter collision by the comets released energies that uplift the solar system's alignment back into higher purposes, moving it from where you still reside in a state of illusion, to the truer reality from which this lower dimension was mirrored—and to which you wish to return since it is the true inner spiritual world from which you came.

Now please observe *Illustration #2* which shows the combined Sun and Jupiterian energies focused into an invisible crystal field. This new field's influence is altering Earth's grid pattern so that she may have about a 20-sided crystalline grid. It is also upgrading her chakra system to 13, and these will now fit inside, or be enclosed within, that greater crystalline grid. In other words, these combined subtle Sun and Jupiter energies have begun to prepare a higher dimensional identity and reality for your Mother Earth homeland. Indeed, she is being advanced dimensionally/inter-dimensionally which gives you a greater opportunity to obtain your own 12-helix DNA pattern and new 13-chakra system which together will return humanity to full consciousness. What is occurring, then, is a solar system shift that upgrades and magnifies the ley lines within Earth's new global grid so she now wears a brighter garment of light. As you find the numbers of the nine major vortex locations presently on Earth's ley lines, notice that all have had certain physical identifications on them such as sacred mountains, religious sites, pyramids, or areas of amplified energy power emanations.

Notice the many crisscrossing ley lines and how they form what appears to be a great over-connecting web. This is the global grid about which I speak. These ley lines connect to each other even as your physical body acupuncture roadways of energy are one system of life-supporting power. So, too, the Earth's grid formation is holistic and interconnected because of a great plan by the wise civilizations who preceded your present world. Can you see the plan of this grid with its precise intersecting web? Great power is created wherever the east/west and north/south electromagnetic lines cross or intersect. Notice these power

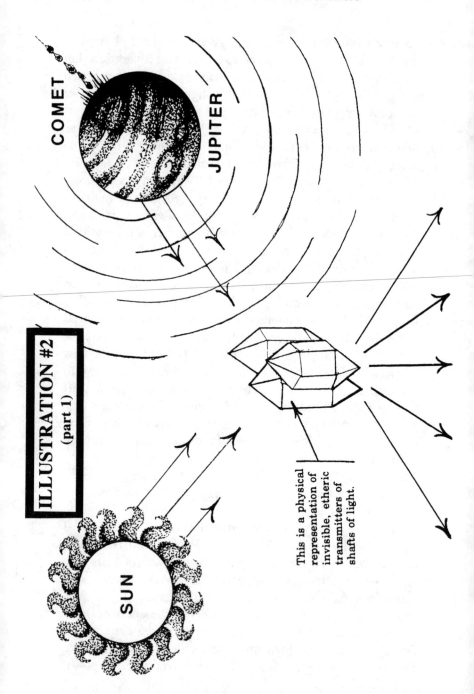

ILLUSTRATION #2
(part 1)

COMET

JUPITER

SUN

This is a physical representation of invisible, etheric transmitters of shafts of light.

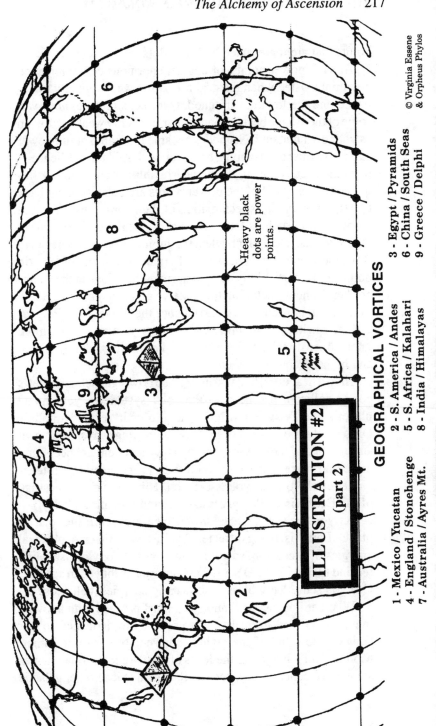

© Virginia Essene
& Orpheus Phylos

ILLUSTRATION #2
(part 2)

GEOGRAPHICAL VORTICES

1 - Mexico / Yucatan
2 - S. America / Andes
3 - Egypt / Pyramids
4 - England / Stonehenge
5 - S. Africa / Kalahari
6 - China / South Seas
7 - Australia / Ayres Mt.
8 - India / Himalayas
9 - Greece / Delphi

Heavy black dots are power points.

points that are represented by black dots.

At such power points, of course, enormous communication potential existed when the grid formation was originally established and the ley lines initiated. Over eons of time, however, some of them have been damaged or irreversibly weakened, even as your own mutant DNA codes became incapable of full power and consciousness. Happily, however, with Archangel Michael's messianic return, using the wonderful Jupiterian vibratory frequencies, nearly all of the power points are being brought back to help in humanity's reclamation of their former psychic and spiritual gifts such as telepathy, energy healing, clairvoyance, clairaudience, etc. In fact, when the Jupiterian energies began to flow, the vibrations increased the frequency of many of the grid points, most particularly several dormant locations in the southern hemisphere, including the inactive place you call the South Pole. It will now be vitalized to balance the active North Pole for greater spiritual communication to assist in accelerating more inter-dimensional activity with your heavenly guides, teachers, and higher frequency essences.

I hope, dear ones, that you now grasp how significant Jupiter's comet collision has been to the solar system, to your home planet's energy system of grids, and to your very own body's DNA healing experience. In very interesting ways, your own auric field and the now-expanding chakra system are becoming more and more balanced, which with proper meditation techniques can help speed your ascension. This was a major message of my Earth visit 2,000 years ago . . . and remains so today.

As you look at *Illustration #3*, please observe that just as planet Earth is being affected by these subtle and physical energies of ascension, so your own physical body is also being fed and fueled for the DNA shift your soul has longed to achieve. Can you sense these blessed showering energies, beloveds?

Whether you can or cannot, you must proceed with a loving intention to lead a positive, purposeful life dedicated to our Creator and to all of the higher representatives of our Father/ Mother God—not just to the Jesus of old. Nor to the other names some have called me by, such as Sananda. (Since other galactic

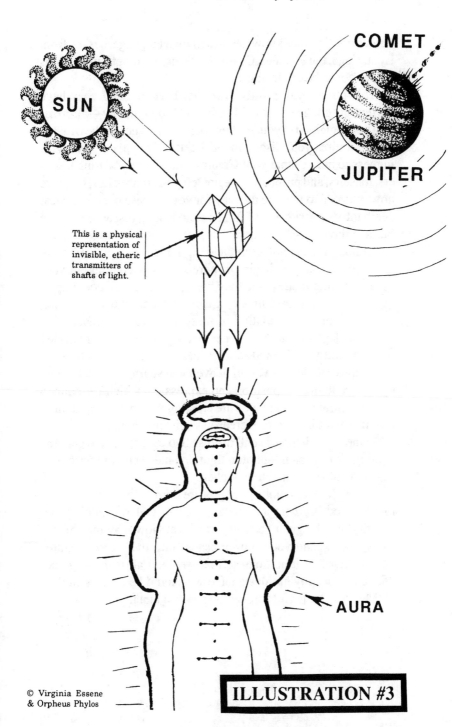

SUN

COMET

JUPITER

This is a physical representation of invisible, etheric transmitters of shafts of light.

AURA

© Virginia Essene & Orpheus Phylos

ILLUSTRATION #3

human civilizations know me in their own language, be they from Lyra, Vega, the Pleiades, Orion, Arcturus, Sirius, etc. my various names could be confusing.)

This purposeful, positive life that I recommend, may have current prophetic information available to humanity—information not contained in your earlier Earth books, such as the Bible—but it requires your discernment! I certainly applaud your willingness to believe that your Creator and the light-bearing teachers, masters, and prophets have not left you comfortless, but have now returned to prepare the way for your release out of physical death into the ascension of full consciousness, just as they did in biblical days.

Although I cannot command it, I urgently and fervently recommend that you begin or more earnestly continue in your inner listening modes—be they meditation, prayer, contemplation, fasting, inspired music, art, movement, ritual, chanting, nature or some combination of these positive experiences. Do this each day! so your human personality is cleansed and healed of its limited attitudes and actions, and your S.O.U.L. station can be receptive to those levels of heaven you yearn to acquire. Then by a more loving disposition and expression, which I attempted to demonstrate long ago, you are creating your own communication link with heaven to increase ascension's hour.

In the next chapter I shall discuss two other possible patterns leading to ascension—photon light or a mega cell of consciousness, and also ascension by alchemy.

Meanwhile, remember that you are born of love and wisdom, my beloved brothers and sisters, and in that recognition and identity lies the great certainty of peace. Now may the Creator bless and expand your consciousness into the sacred pastures beyond Earth's limitations so that we shall all reside together where our destiny has designated we should be . . . in unity!

May you be joyful forever. Amen and amen.

Chapter XI
Your Natural Inheritance Reclaimed

As we continue our discussion about ascension, I remind you that one of the most difficult things for a human being to do is know him or herself, which is why all religions and philosophies have admonished their participants "to know thyself." Then do I remind you once again that your purpose on Earth is to discover who you are, who humans are, and then to follow your personal and human purpose unerringly and without compromise. But of course you may be raising your eyebrows at this remark for it is indeed challenging and often difficult to persevere, is it not? It may be especially challenging when you sometimes feel a little uncertain about yourself, about other people and their motives, and about the external circumstances in which you find yourself living on the planet. Although I have spoken about this is in an earlier chapter, I would like to expand the subject because it is absolutely vital to your ascension process and is a critical aspect of your present circumstances as a spiritual being on planet Earth. It is also necessary for humans to learn who they are as a galactic species.

As I have asked you to remember who you are and who humanity is, so I also wish you to know who the one you call Jesus is. It is vital you do not hold me to some image or stereotype from the past which has been erroneously reported in various biblical descriptions and commentaries, however well-meaning these have been. Those past perceptions as contained in those stories certainly do have a element of truth in them—please understand

I do not deny that. But I ask you to cease the petty arguments about the color of my hair and eyes, my height and weight, my name, etc., and realize you can best know me today by light and sound and by the vibration of love we share—rather than past physical appearances and misperceptions.

I came to Earth to be a model of love, and Jesus was a simple, uncomplicated name for that purpose. I believe this name helped me be approachable by the ordinary, average people of the day so that forgiveness, decency, and hope could bloom. It was a name for a comforter, a friend, and a teacher of straightforward guidance as stated in parables and beatitudes—most of which remain in today's bibles with some degree of accuracy. I sought no reverence then, nor do I now. My guidance is still straight forward, and I hope useful to those who hear it, for I truly do wish to give comfort, love, and hope in this time of awakening.

Because most Earth humans cannot see me as I am today, your major religious symbols primarily show my dead or suffering body on a cross of pain—a past symbol that can only incite sorrow and guilt. Then free me from death into the resurrected living Jesus or the Christ Jesus of now. On this book's cover I have used The Christ simply to draw attention to a powerful energy available to you. It was this Christ energy that had to become lower than the angels—to hold spirit in flesh—to express what you call "divine thought."

The Christ means divine thought which is your heritage and your only way of receiving inspirational guidance and the molecular healing that will one day reclaim your long lost, full consciousness. This divine thought, originated by the Creator, is what runs the celestial, angelic, soulic, and galactic kingdoms of light. Since the human species is part of the galactic kingdom of creation, given dominion over the care of physical places in material worlds in many dimensions and dominions, those who have detoured from that role may surely reassume it! That is why I came to Earth, to rekindle your memory and help you open your heart to its highest frequency of love, nurturance, and compassion. As you do this, you will again receive your Mother/Father's inheritance and the bounty of those vibrational rainbow riches. A detour need not be final or fatal if directions are noticed and utilized, dear ones.

Then what is it that I am asking you to do in our relationship? When you think of me as the one called Jesus or Christ Jesus, etc., dismiss the former perceptions, opinions, and beliefs in your mind about what I look like, and begin to rely on sound to acknowledge my whereabouts around you. Rather than picturing me as an individual person alive long ago—call to me with sound that acknowledges that I am alive today within those Gold and Silver Rays of our awesome Creator. In using sound you acknowledge I have within me the will, mind, and power of the Holy Spirit, or Holy Ghost, as some call it. Thus, in me, the trinity exists, just as you are part of that trinity if you would have it so. By accepting the empowerment of choosing to use the Holy Spirit in your life today—which is what I asked you to do long ago—you leave the world of duality and separation in order to accept higher influences, even as I did.

In fact, let me acknowledge that when I came upon the Earth, it was beloved Archangel Michael who came to help me. So I wish you to hear his own words about this event so you will understand that you, yourselves, may receive far higher oversoul guidance than you can imagine at this moment in evolution. For by what I achieved, the pattern for the "second coming" was established for you to follow . . . to claim.

Because it is difficult to put the exact sound salutation down on paper (a sound that I wish to have you use when you think of me), just try to come as close to AH ZUH NIGH (with a quick release of, or accent on, the NIGH) as you can. With this sound you will be using a salutation known to your galactic brothers and sisters on the Sirius B homeland planet. These individuals live physically closer to you in the galaxy than any other human species—only 8.6 light-years away from Earth—whereas the Pleiadeans live 400 light-years away, for instance. If you will look at the frontispiece map of the Milky Way galaxy and find what is called Orion's arm or spur, you will notice Earth's proximity is closer to certain galactic humans in that area than it is to the Central Sun some 30,000 light-years away. (For us there are no light-years as you call them—just hyperspace measurements, but I am using a term your present scientific minds understand.) More precise locational information is explained and pictured in the book <u>You Are Becoming a Galactic Human</u>.

I request that you try to say AH ZUH NIGH when you think of the Creator and me. If you cannot do what I have suggested, Jesus will still be acceptable so long as you focus on the living friend and teacher—the ascended Jesus. Because we love each other, Jesus will do. The healing councils of light will always respond to that name while you are still at this lower dimension where no lofty titles are required or expected.

AH means you are calling the I AM (or the beginning intention; will).

ZUH acknowledges the power of creation (or the "pulses of time").

NIGH is the physical creation energy that follows the spiritual into manifested form.

With this AH ZUH NIGH sound you acknowledge the Creator and the Gold and Silver Ray aspects it brings into your dimensions of life. The Gold Ray is cosmic consciousness or the universal mind vibration of communication—what your Egyptian's identified as the "all-knowing eye." The Gold Ray activates wisdom and eternal truth throughout dimensions and spheres, calling forth all angelic hosts to stimulate and inspire those sleeping, unconscious souls so they may reexperience the Law of One—the eternal truth and philosophies of light. The Christ Consciousness serves the Gold Ray by carrying forth the circle of light and creating soul-to-soul unity so that all minds unify in one harmonious purpose throughout the many dimensions.

Please realize that your brother, Jesus, is a Christed being also intent on bringing you into the circle of light, and through higher mind soul groups, to impart knowledge and activate the eternal love embrace of peace and grace. Since the Silver Ray's greater entrance into this dimension at the time Haley's comet affected planet Earth in 1985-86, its purpose has been to teach humanity how to heal itself. It does this by bringing the divine empowerment energy of self-healing and self-attunement that all must use to cleanse and heal themselves for the upcoming ascension. So, beloveds, I serve the great Rays of Gold and Silver today, as I hope each of you will want to do, so that we can be connected in the immediate focus of healing humanity and planet Earth.

Perhaps you will understand that in order to come into the negativity on Earth long ago to awaken, inspire, and assist humanity's remembrance of its part in the Creator's plan, I needed assistance in order to accomplish my purpose. It was my energy relationship with Archangel Michael (Mikael) that empowered my Earth life and final resurrection. This is, of course, the same great one who has now come forth to call all beings in this galaxy back into the circle of light, reminding them that souls must now choose their affiliations of either light or darkness.

Lord Michael carries the transmutable Blue Flame composed of ultra violet, infrared, gamma rays, and all other levels of electromagnetic energy beyond your visible spectrum. These Blue Flame components are best described as creative aspects of the great Central Sun of this Universe—not just your galactic Central Sun—that are now sending forth a laser beam of fire to activate all souls to join the legions of light. Because of Lord Michael's current energy magnification, heaven's angelic chords and choruses are bringing the harmonious voices of radiant love to flood humanity, the planet, and all lifeforms upon her surface. There are also those of inner worlds and other planes of existence being affected. Indeed, those of higher consciousness are rejoicing that he is further empowering the harmonic convergence of space-time relationship in the galaxy and Universe, not merely Earth and your solar system.

Thus we of the many mansions are much more aligned for your good than has happened for thousands of years, especially since the July, 1994, comet fragment penetration into Jupiter. (See the earlier illustrations about the comet effects on Jupiter.) Therefore, I have asked our beloved Lord Michael to share with you how he and the angels can help those in human bodies, by describing how he aided me during my own earthly sojourn.

Before continuing my own remarks, then, please breathe deeply for several moments as you prepare to greet Archangel

Michael. Then invite him to share with you his own perception of how he came to help me during my physical embodiment on Earth.

ARCHANGEL MICHAEL'S MESSAGE

Greetings to you, beloved of the light,

I am Archangel Michael, Christ of your Universe, bringing my protector energy through the transmutable Blue Flame to neutralize all levels of negativity within the planes or dimensions of living entities throughout this Universe. I come to restore life and bring equilibrium unto the souls that are ready to create the ascension flame (vibration) and reclaim peace. In that evolution I am gathering the Christed ones in their perfection of spirit to uplift and create other worlds. I come to restore balance so that the living Creator can see its own reflection personified through all of its legions of light which reign throughout all the celestial, angelic, spiritual, soulic and galactic kingdoms.

The element I use to transmute negativity and to overview the Universe lies within the capacity of fire, understood as proton, electron, and neutron energy, originating in the Central Sun. This fire element also manifests itself through the electromagnetic fields of cross currents of various coding systems of frequencies—color, light, and sound. The latter is the universal language of the spiritual domains. The Central Sun of the Universe is symbolic for the living Creator, which is only a personification of itself in its own energy expressed for all to behold. This Creator is far greater than any symbol known or given unto man, or known within the many inner dimensions, and although its many creations are powerful, yet none of us can behold or see the Great Almighty.

Nonetheless, because of the Holy Trinity, there is a key for all souls to obtain that which is mind, power, and will. Through the usage of this key all souls can find their way back to the Source from which they separated within the multiples of forms and expressions throughout the Omniverse of Oneness. For those within the trinity who chose to oppose, or separate into duality—

such as those called Satan, void of light, or evil—certain crystalline dimensional limitations, barriers, or energy grids were created to restrict the Prince of Darkness on Earth. For example, an energy grid called the angles of the tetra was created by means of a geometrical crystalline energy rope or thread. This light grid currently surrounds the Earth's atmosphere as a fence or boundary until the tests of learning can be passed or realized by all souls, through the ascension flame. Only by a positive vibratory frequency, then, could each soul advance through that energy grid boundary back into higher light realms while the negative ones remained under restraint. Many spiritual teachers and holy ones have descended into Earth's place of darkness to increase the light here and teach the ascension process, but because progress has been slow, another plan came to be tried which I shall now briefly describe and which many of you will fully understand.

To assist humanity, the higher lords of time gathered and decided that the Christ Consciousness energy of divine thought would send a being to earth who would hold a physical body and yet breathe the breath of the divine flame. He would hold to steadfastness and show the physical world how love is manifested within, and then expressed through both thoughts and deeds. By his model, the Law of One would be taught and through his demonstration he would advance many into the higher regions, to restore the souls into the path of their salvation. Therefore, one being called Micha was appointed to go to earth and be this master of divine thought to express the ultimate of the divine.

This one is known to you as my son Micha (or personification) appearing as the energy of the eternal light as Jesus the Christ (meaning Jesus the divine thought of eternal light expressed and manifested into form). He would walk the earth showing the grace of God, the love, light, and law of God for all to behold and to emulate. He would demonstrate the powers of light, and teach man to find the true path of the living God that resides within— also known as the Father/Mother. As it was said, "It is not I who doeth these things but the Father (or living God) within me."

I was given the appointment to reside within the eternal grace—called the living light within him—and it was my voice that assisted him in following the divineness of his soul. I came to him in many ways throughout his manifestations of truth, inspired thought, and the gifts that he showed man on the earth plane. I was sent to him and I appeared as the Holy Dove when he was baptized by John the Baptist, thus gifting him with the eternal flame of the divine—or as it was spoken, the Holy Spirit which is the breath of God. That spirit entered into him connecting his physical, emotional, mental and spiritual embodiments as ONE. I also came to assist and guide him through the trials of separation (earth embodiment) that he might have the strength to hold the oneness while walking and teaching those on earth to find the kingdom of heaven. Through his demonstrations of spirit we hoped to restore within the human consciousness the pathway back home to the eternal grace of divine love.

Many were concerned that the message and model of Micha (as Christ Jesus) had not penetrated deeply enough in the sleeping souls trapped in flesh. Many feared that humanity would never wake up and return home. Still we have continued to persevere on behalf of all separated souls everywhere in the galactic kingdoms, including those on planet Earth. In Jesus and others you have consistent helpers whose constant request in all higher councils is: "Help their souls!"

Thus, as the light now comes to you to increase your energy levels into higher vibratory frequencies, you must make this final choice to serve the Creator's goals. Because there will very likely be a continued upgrading in consciousness throughout your quadrant of the galaxy, it could be quite a lengthy wait for those souls who miss this spiral of the positive ascending energies! Therefore, make your choice to be with this present spiral, beloveds! I will assign a high teacher/guide to each of you who accepts. Then do not delay. Join with us now!

And so mote it be.

I AM MICHAEL

* *

Jesus continues . . .

Now that you understand that the negative beings were banished by Archangel Michael and sealed on Earth under a high vibratory frequency grid of sacred light, you will understand why so many people seem to be sleeping here—or even involved in cruel and evil deeds. There has been a low vibration that does not encourage spiritual behavior. However, at this particular moment there are many souls of light who have chosen to come into life here to help provide a broader base of light, knowing that a long desired plan of reclamation was scheduled to occur. They are, in a sense, heavenly teachers who will assist in the human evolutionary phase called the "second coming." Most of you reading this material, for example, are of that group, or you are one whose soul has longed to return to the Creator's warmth and forgiveness through the sacred gift I have called grace. Therefore, Lord Michael, many angels, the Ascended Masters and I will be fervently guiding your path if you request it.

Many times this commandment has been spoken, dear ones, "Love God with all your heart and mind and your brothers and sisters as yourself." It was with this ancient truth that I, and many others, came to teach everyone on Earth that you can be made whole again by the required change of heart and application of the basic spiritual principles.

The Earth's population, then, is presently composed of negative ones who persist in evil, unloving deeds . . . those who are awakening back to spiritual integrity from long, unconscious sleep . . . and those who have volunteered their light in the salvation of planet Earth. Upon your streets, then, there is great diversity in what we call consciousness. Those who are sensitive to energy, in fact, can see, hear, or feel the variations of this consciousness as they go about their daily activities. The quality of each person's energy intention is obvious, like an identifiable aroma called a stench or its opposite—a perfume. Then with the many gifts of energy that we are now bringing to our dedicated light-servers and to the many awakening souls who long for home, the balance of decency and honor is swinging more and more to heaven's favor. Many people know something unique is happening as time seems to shrink, creating an unusual sense of urgency. You may be sure that Archangel Michael's final call, warning, or reminder, that all must choose their commitment to the light, if they wish grace, will only intensify each soul's restlessness until the promise of an added teacher/guide is made real through your free will request!

Given this critical offer of restitution and potential resurrection which is stirring inside of each being, many unusual opportunities for manifestation will occur. This stirring is caused by the amplified power of the great archangels of many dimensions, especially Michael. Indeed your future on Earth lies in the realm of incredible probabilities and potentials! It is, beloveds, in this state of open perception and surrendered, erroneous beliefs, that miracles occur.

Miracles will occur because each soul may now have additional guides assigned to it, some from very high angelic dominions, to make ascension as joyful as possible. For those who serve the light, and are moving into group endeavors as a way of life, exponential changes can occur. So the question naturally arises, how can anyone prepare for the future during these extraordinary circumstances? Is there any security to be had from material possessions, bank accounts, employment, pensions, and so forth?

Your questions come to us constantly; every instant you ask—what should I do? Where should I go? Your prayers, pleas and petitions are unending, which is why I am quickly updating this book's contents. As your souls feel the intensity of this spiritual shift in consciousness, your personalities are often stricken with the fear of change. Having walked upon the Earth, I can relate to these uncontrolled emotions that you let control your lives, thereby causing harm to yourself and others. The prescription for healing this fear is in your own hands and must be healed by your own efforts and introspection. Love and trust the Creator. Listen within for the guidance that is yours to express. Be willing to do those things that you are guided from within to do. If you have not been meditating, begin at once! You must be still to hear the soul voice within you and the guidance being directed to you by powerful angelic assistants.

I will now repeat the primary prescription that exists for eliminating fear while you are in human form.

1. You must know that the light of God, of goodness, of the Creator, has a plan to call all humans home to live in peace—and that you have been personally and collectively called.

2. You can have great guides and teachers all around you to assist during this ascending upliftment out of negativity.

3. You must be silent and have meditative listening times to hear that guidance. Guidance will not generally come to you from the present sources you rely upon such as radio, television, print, and other communication media—although we are influencing them to improve. It will come primarily from within your deepest soul direction and spiritual knowingness.

4. You should associate with others of like mind and intention during this process lest you be hampered by negative vibrations rampant during this evolutionary time. Indeed, group consciousness is a primary base of support and joy that will give comfort. For some this means a church, temple, ashram, or other place of positive group intention such as a weekly meditation circle. For others it may mean living with a blood family or marriage partner or friends of similar spiritual understanding and commitment. New spiritual families and communities based upon common beliefs, meditation, and group manifestation are rapidly increasing, and represent a future trend..

Naturally, you fortunate beings have all or several of these intertwining support groups to assist your attainment of the full consciousness humanity seeks and needs. As I advised long ago, "Where two or more are gathered in my name, there also shall I be." That simply means that whenever two people can agree to be harmonious and cooperative with each other, the Christ—divine thought—is present and available as an exponential energy to assist with whatever needs may exist.

Today I would advise you to be joined with one other person in divine thought and then go on to create the largest harmonious group possible so its light matrix can bring a richer and faster manifestation fulfillment. These are the times when small groups of at least 12 or 13 can focus their minds simultaneously in a positive intention to achieve a common goal or purpose, thus creating laser-like manifesting power. Larger groups are even more powerful, of course, so as you achieve success in smaller groups, transfer those skills into those larger group situations whenever you can to maximize your manifesting power.

It is also now possible to begin learning how to achieve consensus, which is to say a council of one-mind agreement. Although a few people, organizations and businesses utilize this principle for brief periods of time, it is not consistently practiced in any serious or constant fashion, planet-wide, as it is elsewhere in the galaxy by those of the human species. In this utilization of one-mindfulness you have much to learn. Of course, one-mindfulness, or unity, creates a unified field of energy which can be used as a manifesting tool, something you are learning. Those you term galactic humans from other nearby locations in space, who are at higher consciousness and frequency, have little dissension within their immediate, local family groups as people of Earth generally do.

FUTURE EVENTS

Now I wish to briefly comment upon the questions that come to us from your dimension regarding future events. These questions flood our realms with common themes of fear, confusion, and uncertainty and are growing louder all the time. Part of this occurs because there is so much increased inner receptivity and "channeling" of divine thoughts these days, all of which may give different information, guidance and advice. Then do I beseech you to memorize and practice the following comment at both conscious and unconscious levels, by whatever means you can, so you will never forget it! YOUR SOUL PATTERN OF MASTERY REQUIRES YOU TO LISTEN WITHIN AND DISCERN THE CORRECT PERSONAL INFORMATION WHICH IS YOURS ALONE TO FOLLOW! BECAUSE SO MUCH INFORMATION NOW COMES FROM SUCH A VARIETY OF FREQUENCY LEVELS AND GALACTIC

RESONANCES, YOU MUST BE INWARDLY ADVISED OF WHAT PLAN AND PATH IS UNIQUELY YOURS DURING THIS EARTHLY ASCENSION TIME. NO ONE PLAN EXISTS FOR FIVE BILLION PEOPLE. THEREFORE, YOU MUST TUNE IN TO YOUR OWN TEACHERS!

Please go back and read that statement again. And again. And again. Then let it sink into your belief system, beloveds, There is no greater message I can give to protect you in these changing times. You see, some of you have had ancient relationships with certain spiritual realms and individuals, (such as myself or Archangel Michael) and are here to fulfill agreements made eons ago. Each of you is a part of a certain plan and team, so to say, and will consequently be needed to assist in the completion of a specific role in those unfolding circumstances and activities.

Some people have strong relationships with certain galactic human family homelands, not of this Earth, whose function is also a part of the same reclamation plan but with some variations. There are literally billions of helpers coming from dimensions both familiar and unfamiliar—from inter-dimensions known and unknown—and from spiritual realms related to the human species and to nonhuman creations. To use your vernacular, THIS IS A BIG DEAL! A HUGE, UNSPEAKABLY MAMMOTH OPERATION THAT AFFECTS THIS GALAXY AND MANY OTHER GALAXIES AND DISTANT SYSTEMS OF LIFE.

So, yes, we who are known to you as spiritual masters and teachers will come to humanity by telepathic contact and perhaps even be seen in physical appearance sometime during this ascension shift to full consciousness. Some of you may feel that you have been lifted up to spiritual levels for special tasks and responsibilities, working with those who have merely been names in holy books up until now—even as others will experience what is called being on a space craft of extraterrestrial origin with friends from whom they have been long separated. But most other people will remain at specific Earth locations as healers, counselors, and teachers where their talents can be best utilized to assist your five-billion-plus awakening human population.

In the meantime we are flooding human consciousness with

many products and inventions to help the body's genetic health, and you will be constantly amazed by their variety, quality, and usefulness. If you find your body struggling through its DNA changes, test these new products -- along with natural herbs and certain energizing supplements -- to find out what works best for you. Soon there may be a very powerful, extraordinary, awesome, ingestible product available, like the biblical "manna," to help some Earth humans bring their DNA cellular level back to full consciousness. So do not let governmental officials deny your citizen's rights of choice in matters of personal medical treatment and health products!

As the days of your existence march inexorably into what you term "the future," many of you call to us for information that will keep you safe far into the 21st century -- especially knowledge about the photon belt, UFO's and matters of galactic and spiritual life. So, because I love you and respect your intelligence, let me attempt to discuss your earthly concerns from my own point of view, not from yours which unfortunately tends to operate out of fear and controls the negative power of the three lower chakras. This fear regrettably interrupts and overpowers the higher energy centers of love, right use of will and your magnificent spiritual mind, but the higher consciousness frequencies will be intensifying to help humanity help themselves.

Now please pause and take several deep breaths........for even the word fear can trigger apprehension in your emotional body whereas breathing can relax that condition and is always your ally in any emotive circumstance. Good. Now pause for another moment and focus your thought on the immensity of the universe with its billions of galaxies, interpenetrating rhythms and cycles, and the Creator's powerful energies of wisdom and love. This wisdom and love are freely given and pour forth to create and support a myriad of life forms. Life forms that would eventually densify from light down into many levels and dimensions of expression such as the one you are presently experiencing. In this sea of creation, the Milky Way galaxy gives many different orbiting planets enough life for consciousness to inhabit what you term physical density or reality. Imagine that awesome consciousness in its full grandeur spewing out its intention and energy for life to be birthed, then manifesting into denser physical properties which your scientists call waves, fields, and flows of quantum energy. Because these aspects of original intention which your bible calls God's "word" exist, so do you, for over the eons of movement, of experimentation, this womb of consciousness and energy have caused uncountable, awesome expressions and forms too vast to comprehend in your dimension. They nonetheless exist and can influence one another in ways you have neither vision nor mathematics to express. Indeed, your intuitive understanding of mathematics -- especially what a few humans can envision as fractals -- will bring you closer to what we call the vocabulary of creation. Your present perception about creation is evolving a little at a time and the next century will be full of advancement and surprises if the knowledge is used wisely for the greater good.

This great womb, or matrix of creation, about which you know so little, is best understood as an ocean full of possibilities ready to be influenced. You are presently thinking of this powerful substance as photons of light which is a step in the right direction, albeit a limited concept that must one day deepen into further understanding. Whatever you call it, many beings in many different dimensions are using this energy to develop their own capabilities of manifestation.

The principle I hope you can hold, whatever you call this God-stuff, is that it has as many functions and capabilities as there are beings who understand its nature and apply it. So if you think of one tiny, tiny, tiny intelligent particle by itself, attracted to other tiny intelligent particles -- each with its own consciousness to learn and grow -- perhaps you can imagine what happens when these move together in the unity they possess. Perhaps you can accept that they take on a greater potential for change and, in a sense, gain maturity...even speciality. So if you can grasp that everything in existence has some level of both consciousness and energy, then you can surmise that when you compact and focus these wise little aspects of the whole with an intention and purpose, they can grow and learn, and they can be impressed by others, also. They are capable of evolution, of expanding, and the human species, though contained in a solidified form, is much like them.

Until this past century, there was very little scientific discussion and exploration among western nations of what you presently term a photon, except by a few "cutting edge" physicists who began exploring various theories regarding sub-atomic and quantum energy levels. By your measurements, today, a quantum field is something tinier than one-millionth of an inch, and photons are much smaller still! So there is much to learn about energy forms and how they are used. Of course, there was much greater metaphysical knowledge, including what you presently think of as scientific, available among certain eastern religions whose written histories had been preserved for over 5,000 years, but these were generally unknown to Europeans. Only recently has even your dictionary definition of the word photon given the general public a vague understanding of its meaning. For what is love but God's vibration extended to the Archangelic, and many other realms, for use as photon energy in the creation of physical worlds?

When you look in your famous Webster's dictionary today you will likely find a statement something similar to this: "A photon is a quantum of electromagnetic energy having both particle and wave properties. It has no charge or mass but possesses momentum and energy. The energy of light, X-Rays, gamma rays, etc., is carried by photons." Then from this definition you must realize that photons are so basic that nothing in your material world can exist or survive without them. They are, simply put, "God stuff," and at your level of life, are the basis of creation itself. For when their innocent quality and power is impressed from an idea at the highest level of Archangelic -- and other -- intention, potential reality and physicality begin their journey into lower vibratory frequencies.

That pure force and power, the photon, carries many seeming diversities because it is the basic manifesting matrix for seven different dimensions or levels of expression of reality, with each level having different natural or scientific laws, so to say. What vibrational frequencies regulate one subtle level, for example, are quite different from the level above or below it, having been deliberately established so that they do not impact each other inappropriately. In your own world of the third dimension, what you call scientific laws are simply various manifestations of that universal photon quality, termed God or love, which contains the many defining aspects and qualities appropriate to this dimension's consciousness.

Simply put, then, in the subtle but powerful levels above your present reality, there are planes of creation sensitive to thought. At these higher levels the Archangels, and many others, create the material worlds of planets, stars, and heavenly bodies with their precise and pure mind power. This powerful intention to organize the photon particles into specific patterns can only be entrusted to the purest of beings, which is why humans can not personally use photons, only atoms, and only in a very minuscule fashion thus far. But you, and your various groups, are beginning to use the atomic level of these photons in your dimension more and more frequently and with more powerful effect on your material world. Never forget, however, that other superior minds and conditions are also at work. Indeed, their prior and present thoughts in the higher heavens have brought certain natural laws into effect at many dimensions and levels, some of which are presently bringing forth powerful cause and effect patterns throughout many realms and worlds, including your own!

Beloveds, this universe in which you dwell, is filled with this foundational energy -- photons -- an energy basic to every possible creation of mind. This "God stuff" is a vast ocean of energy without form or mass, an awesome but passive matrix without movement of its own, but one whose fluid potential awaits impression and utilization. Like a gigantic womb of life, a container of all possibilities, it allows itself to be utilized and precipitated in endless forms throughout the seven levels of physical expression with the third and fourth presently relevant to your own experience. (Although this is a simplification of sorts.) Thus do those ingredients you give scientific names like particles, atoms, molecules, etc., have one original source or beginning. And all of the electromagnetic specifics such as light, heat, what you term radio (sound), the invisible X-Rays, gamma rays, even the images on your Earth television screens, are but particles or wave form qualities of what you call light or photons. These photons can even be generated on the Earth by such simple combustion as a campfire or turning on electricity to illuminate a light bulb. Of course the rate of photon activity in cycles per second created from your light bulb source is infinitesimal indeed compared to something like visible light which operates at about one trillion cycles per second.

Another word your scientists have coined in recent years is tachyon -- a differentiated energy primarily in the 4th dimension which operates in partnership with the photons as they come into these lower physical worlds. In the 4th dimension the tachyon and photon are travel-mates, as it were, harnessed together in this slower physical density. It is the tachyon that attempts to break the speed of light causing its photon partner to go through a two-phase experience of changing form. The photon shifts between being a ring-shaped particle, similar to a donut or smoke ring, and then dissolving into a wave form containing both an electrical and magnetic force. When these two separated electrical and magnetic aspects collapse back upon themselves, the wave returns to its particle identity and donut appearance. The photon's movement through space, then, alternates between its identity as a particle and a wave. Frankly, this has confused western scientists until the past century, just as the composition of those particles called electrons, protons and neutrons had been veiled. Someday, as you move into the *physical* fourth dimension, you will have greater familiarity with their creative functions.

Please remember that atoms are a denser expression of the more subtle photons and that atoms are the basic building blocks of your present physical world. If you can grasp that your dimension cannot create with photons directly, only a stepped-down version called atoms, the rest of my message should be clear. Knowing little about photons you have nonetheless become aware of atoms and have termed your current energy usage as the atomic age -- the age that requires you to realize that atoms are not solid, but have a nucleus of smaller components named protons and neutrons at their center with orbiting electrons traveling in paths at distances away from the nucleus.

Solid things, then, using your temporarily limited sensory capacities, are not the solid objects they seem to be because few human beings can see or sense their fantastically fast movement. However, as you are willing to learn that atoms are your physical world's building blocks, as a stepped-down version of photons, you open your consciousness to inquiry about what lies beyond apparent density and reality. This will allow us to accelerate your positive use of the Earth's atomic building blocks and to aid humankind in their evolution as masters of energy through loving intention and thought. By practicing your mind/heart use of what you call atomic power with increasingly positive intentions and outcomes, you learn the necessity and value of precipitating or manifesting results for the highest and best good. Only by learning to appropriately use atomic energy here at this level of reality do you prepare yourself as trustworthy spiritual users of photons when that vibrational frequency interaction becomes available to you in a higher dimension.

Always remember that creation is fluid and therefore allows for some surprising aspects. Even radical changes are likely in your physical/material worlds because thoughts are capable of creating certain probable patterns and results -- as you of Earth may have noticed.

Should the physical expression of a specified photon compaction occur -- a photon belt for example -- understand that its movement brings you the opportunity to apply lovingness to every occasion as you advance on the road to higher consciousness. Think of any compacted photon belt as both physical and with an accelerated mega cell of spiritual consciousness -- an opportunity to fulfill your soul's true nature. The photons are already around you and will certainly grow stronger in the days ahead as they move through their particle and wave aspects.

Therefore I recommend that you be of good cheer and keep a positive attitude about the heaven on Earth you have come to install through the power of your positive attitude and actions using the spiritual consciousness of photons. For by the creative power of your love you can pass through any challenging times with clarity and balance. Hold fast to your loving brothers and sisters and utilize the united power of group consciousness for the highest and best situation for yourselves, but also for the planet and all of life.

These are my recommendations for living a joyful life during this exciting but challenging time, then. And remember to keep your light flowing with heaven's good will and graciousness so that you will grow in consciousness and become ever more spiritually evolved. Your physical body is impermanent, dear ones, but your soul is not! Therefore, use your body to impregnate your eternal soul's purposes and consciousness into matter while you are here. This will contribute to life and its magnificent expression on planet Earth through your personal gifts and talents.

On this note of eternal love and respect, beloveds, and with a celestial embrace of peace, know I leave you only through the lips of this channel. Your desire to remember God's plan and live unceasingly in the bosom of the divine means we will never be apart again unless you choose the path of separation.

With exuberant joy and heaven's blessing, I remain your affectionate elder brother,

CHRIST JESUS

Afterward

I am delighted to share a few personal comments with the readers of this book because I can testify to the changes that meditation, prayer and contemplation have made in my own life, and which paved the way for me to accept intuition -- or the God connection -- as a normal part of my everyday existence. So much so that I could now accept the assignment of transcribing these notes from the Master known as The Christ. I feel certain that it was the many years of meditation and my earnest desire to be of assistance that drew his energy to me, along with my willingness to give the necessary time such an undertaking requires. He also told me that many Christians had frozen him into a past that was over and gone and he needed someone who could allow him to be the expanded being that he is today.

To say that I have been privileged to receive this information can only hint at the deep feeling of joy it brings. Yet I share honestly that it also brought up every emotion of fear, lack of self-worth, and doubt that my personality still retained even after years of psychological cleansing and efforts to become emotionally grounded and secure.

When I was first approached for this task I had a constant questioning that demanded, "But why me? Why me, when there are so many other good people available?" And the answer came, in gentle support, "Because you wish to know the true me, are willing to serve, and have given me permission to enter your life." Over and over again I was told that because this is a free will planet, all of us must ask to receive the spiritual ones -- must agree to cooperate by our personal choice.

I need to share with you, also, that I had to confront fear of the greatest magnitude -- fear that I couldn't do it "right" -- fear that I would be laughed at, ostracized or scorned -- fear that my mortality might tint the truth of the message ... and many other things. I experienced this in spite of a joyful relationship with this great one who insisted we had worked together before and that he was grateful for my help once again.

Still, doubt and fear were my companions many times when Jesus first spoke to me and I even broke my toe as a symbol of the ungrounding I felt in my mental and emotional attitudes. At first I would nervously ruin tapes I was speaking into or my fingers would become blocked when I sat in the silence before my typewriter ready to hear his message for transcription. I have to admit that until I just surrendered and relaxed into the peace of meditation, he had to struggle to be heard in my mind.

The question that I often asked him was, "Jesus, will anybody believe I can do this?" For although I am a college teacher of known sanity, I felt people would think I had gone crazy.

How patiently he let these fears surface, and how lovingly he led me a step at a time those first days. It was not until I felt the sure contact between us that I finally agreed to make the notes for the book and worked, day by day, not knowing exactly where the next day's information was leading.

Eventually, during the nearly 6 months of work, a clear and consistent pattern emerged in which each day's messages fit together and took the form of a book with nine chapters. There were times I could feel him searching my mind for words to explain a concept that he could not find and he would have to detour and use an alternative expression which probably was not his first choice. Also, when he would release mental pictures, light packets, or symbols, I would be overwhelmed by the immensity of their content and would have to have him slow down and go over it with me piece by piece. Still he insisted I was doing well and that he was pleased with my energy and service. In the beginning Jesus would often revamp phrases and verbiage over and over again, but as he learned what vocabulary was available in me, he quickly moved to utilize it to the maximum extent possible. Nevertheless, due to our hurry in publishing this book, there are probably errors for which I must take full responsibility. Should you find any, please let me know.

There were many times when I could feel the Master's presence with me as if we were temporarily entwined. I have felt his sadness at the way the world has treated his teachings and I have felt his indignation, as well. He is a being of immense love but also a powerful, practical thinker of enormous will. There were times, too, when I cried either during or after a session from the realization that many souls will refuse to listen to his -- or any -- words of love and peace.

At the end he told me we had achieved most of what he had hoped for and we were far enough along that he would let the rest go due to time restraints. But in any case, you the reader must select from its contents what is valuable for yourself. If there are questions please write me about them.

My main reason for not wanting to scribe this book was the tremendous responsibility it seemed to hold. However, I was told not to take on anyone else's responsibility. Rather I was told to write the words down and let them speak for themselves. Here, then, is that gift for your perusal. May it serve you in some meaningful way.

Many of you are already channels of love, and many channel by means of intuition or the way you sense and know things. Many have undoubtedly had direct experience of the words or presence of Jesus and other great masters -- your own personal teachers and guides -- or the inner guidance of soul and Holy Spirit. Some of these contacts are personal and private, but others contain the seeds of truth to be shared with others. I encourage you to take your step forward, to release the doubts and fears you may have, and give what you can right now if you are asked to participate.

For those who are just beginning the meditation process, don't be surprised if there is a cleansing time you must go through to reach a higher level of purity in your mental and emotional attributes. I had meditated nearly ten years and still it was six months after my return from Israel before Jesus was able to speak clearly to me regarding this material. During this 6 months I had some unusual changes in consciousness and some physical distress as various barriers to the higher vibrations were cleansed away. That is not to say I am perfect even now! Nor do I say each person requires that long to cleanse. It was only my unique experience. But most of us can't sit down and immediately receive the higher vibrations without a time of cleansing out the old ideas and patterns that would stand in the way -- a time to be healed enough to present the material in as pure a form as possible.

So if you wish to have soul guidance, please be willing to meditate both daily and then weekly in groups with others who desire peace on this planet ... for by that action did I, myself, make a way for this message to be brought forth, so I know it works! I would also like to publicly acknowledge my friends and fellow meditators for the hours of deep peace and joy which sharing our hearts' love together in a group has brought. Without that I am certain my road would have been very different. So to each and every one with whom I have ever meditated I say a sincere and grateful, "Thank you!"

Because of the intense and insistent comments from Jesus about humanity's need to meditate, I was expecting to include a bibliography of sources and groups which are involved with this activity. But I was told that each one who is sincere merely has to ask within to learn which meditation style and/or group is appropriate, and the way will be made clear. Lists of books can be obtained in libraries and book stores, of course, and you will be drawn to your own answer and experience. Yes, ask within. That is the place to begin always. But then you must follow through with action for the cycle to be completed. For this is a planet where manifestation and realization of mind thoughts must occur to show us our creations.

I honor your own path, and again encourage you to do the greater things that Jesus asks us to do in the seeking of inner peace. You may have noticed that I continue to use the familiar name "Jesus" rather then "The Christ," which seems impersonal to me. But this is just my habit. Truly, this is a cosmic being who speaks to us!

In closing, I want to share that through his mental pictures I have seen other solar systems, galaxies, and far-flung corners of the Universe, which deepened my awareness of what he seeks to draw us toward. And I realize that we of earth are far more than I ever dreamed . . . . . perhaps more that I can even comprehend while in physical form . . . . .

Yours in love and service,

Virginia

1994/1995 COMMENTS

It has become clearer and clearer, in the years since I first penned this book, that tremendous changes have happened to us humans already—and that even greater ones await! My own body and emotions have struggled to keep pace with the powerful acceleration of energies that demand cleansing and healing, as have those of many other people I know. All around me I see living proof that these DNA cellular changes and chakra adjustments require careful attention even as we learn to successfully participate in group consciousness for the good of all life.

My experience continues to be that individual and group relationships present my greatest opportunity for personal growth and for acquiring the ways of mutual cooperation. I am also finding that when the energy of a committed group consciousness can be focused to envision a better world, manifestation is incredibly powerful and often nearly instantaneous. Then let us join together and focus our healing intention where our Creator would have it be . . . on growth, love, and wisdom achieved together through the principle of unity.

Always your spiritual sister,

Virginia

Products and Services

S.E.E. Publishing Company
    books and audio tapes

ABR Audio Products–Tom Kenyon
    books, audio and video tapes

Love Corps Network and Share Foundation
    newsletter, network, soul readings,
    counseling sessions

Order Form

Earth, the Cosmos and You
Revelations by Archangel Michael

by *Orpheus Phylos* and *Virginia Essene*

NEW *for* Year 2000!

In Archangel Michael's revelations for the Millennium you will learn about...

• Why the Mirror of Venus and the "4-Corners" may be calling you

• Sacred geometry for building your homes and centers

• The Holographic Computer and your soul's history

• Ascension's many patterns and choices

• Healing techniques from Lemuria

• How to visit Earth's inner worlds and dimensions

• Earth's advancement into the 12th solar system position

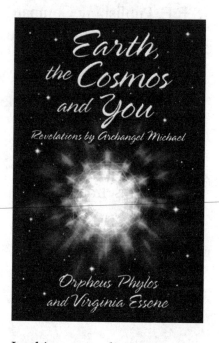

In this extraordinary revelation, Archangel Michael gives information and maps describing planet Earth's grids, ley lines, vortices, power points and energy portals. It is these seldom-understood aspects of the planet's essence that influence our birthplace, our souls' journey, and our everyday lives.

Spiritual Education Endeavors Publishing Company
1556 Halford Avenue #288, Santa Clara, CA 95051-2661, USA
(408) 245-5457

$14.95 paperback • 5.5 X 8.5 in. • 240 pages • ISBN 0-937147-31-1
Library of Congress Card Catalog Number 99-97558

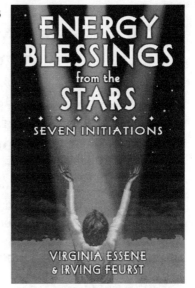

TRANSFORM YOUR CELLULAR WATER FIELD

Extraordinary audio tape recorded by Irving Feurst to accelerate your spiritual transformation!

Water. We cannot live without it, yet how many of us really understand its remarkable physical and spiritual properties—and the even more remarkable properties of water in living cells? As explained in the <u>Energy Blessings from the Stars</u> book, the water in your cells is not the same as tap water. Your cellular water is really a liquid crystal and, as such, is capable of holding information and subtle energy. As we evolve spiritually, the subtle energy field surrounding our cellular water becomes ever more organized, continually increasing its ability to hold information and hold higher vibrational energy.

Side one is an explanation and exploration of the mysteries of water. Side two is a remarkable guided meditation that releases a shakti—a metaphysical or spiritual energy that behaves intelligently—to accelerate the naturally occurring transformation of the energy field around your body's cellular water. The result is an acceleration of your spiritual evolution because your subtle bodies will be able to hold more information, more energy and higher vibrational energies.

This tape is imprinted with actual transformative frequencies that cannot be duplicated. Using this tape will increase the ability of your subtle bodies to benefit from shakti—the shaktis used in the initiations described in the <u>Energy Blessings from the Stars</u> book—as well as those used in many common forms of energy work. It is also possible that using this tape may deepen your meditations.

Spiritual Education Endeavors Publishing Company
1556 Halford Avenue #288, Santa Clara, CA 95051-2661 USA
(408) 245-5457

Single cassette tape T103 $12.95 60 minutes
Please use the order form on the next to last page.

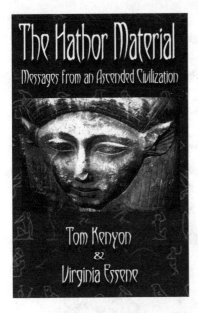

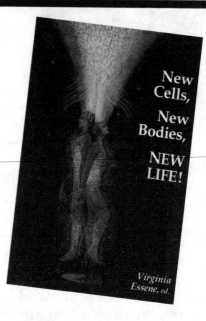

"Having trouble separating your delta waves from your thetas and super high Betas? Fear not: Tom Kenyon will help you get a grip on your consciousness, sub-consciousness, and altered consciousness in his book."

BRAIN STATES

TOM KENYON, M.A.

300 Pages • $11.95 Retail • ISBN 1-880698-04-9

Brain States—Kenyon, a psychologist and a musician, has spent years studying the effects of sound, music, and language on the human nervous system. Kenyon offers a technical excursion into how the brain works, noting the clear distinction between brain and mind. To do this he ascends to the heavens with Pegasus and drops by a shopping mall puddle to visit an amoeba. Through Kenyon's book, you will learn to overcome test anxiety, increase your intelligence, power your athletic abilities, hone your language skills, cure numerous psychological problems, tweak your creativity, and jump into altered states of consciousness.

UNITED STATES
PUBLISHING

AVAILABLE THROUGH: S.E.E. PUBLISHING

The Hathors' Self-Mastery Exercises
on Audio Tape

The Self-Mastery Exercises in <u>The Hathor Material</u> book are also available on a convenient audio cassette tape. The tape was recorded by channel Tom Kenyon.

On this tape, Tom uses his remarkable four-octave vocal range, accompanied by the Tibetan bowl, to call the names of the archangels. This extraordinary sound called "toning" lifts one's subtle bodies into a high frequency state as a prelude to doing one or more of the Self-Mastery Exercises.

Tom guides the listener through each exercise and incorporates background psychoacoustic sound tracks to facilitate integration of the exercises. A special heart-opening meditation with the Hathors is also included!

Single cassette T102 $9.95.

Tom Kenyon's ABR Audio Products

In 1983 Tom Kenyon, M.A., formed Acoustic Brain Research (ABR) to scientifically document the effects of sound and music on human consciousness. As a psychological counselor and musician, Tom discovered that sound and music could be powerful catalysts for both personal growth and healing. By enrolling the efforts of numerous researchers in both private and university settings, ABR has substantially documented the positive benefits of psychoacoustic technology.

Since November 1997, S.E.E. Publishing Company has been distributing all of Tom's ABR tapes and compact discs. S.E.E. also sells Tom's book <u>Brain States</u>.

ABR tapes are remarkably successful in helping you achieve the self-enrichment and self-empowerment goals you seek. This is because of the scientific research, creative artistry, and advanced technology ABR invests in each program.

Music and sound have, from man's earliest cultures, been known to influence our states of mind. Now, through the application of advanced engineering, ABR utilizes the physics and psychology of sound to bring new scientific meaning and direction to this wondrous phenomenon.

ABR technology uses a variety of natural and electronic sounds, including specific sound patterns and frequencies,

Spiritual Education Endeavors Publishing Company
1556 Halford Avenue #288, Santa Clara, CA 95051-2661
USA (408) 245-5457

differentiations of tone and vibration, synchronization, oscillations and pulsations, verbal and non-verbal input, tonal architecture, and hemispheric spanning. These are all orchestrated to stimulate the brain/mind into more resourceful states of awareness. Today, ABR is a recognized leader in psychoacoustic development and is acknowledged by professionals and lay persons alike as a source of the most advanced and neurologically-sound audio tapes available today.

BioPulse Technology™

ABR psychoacoustic technology is based on the use of complex tonal matrices in which various sound patterns are mixed to stimulate the brain/mind into more resourceful states. Many of these tones are mixed beneath the level of audible hearing, masked by other sounds, or sometimes music, specifically composed for the desired mental/emotional state.

ABR tapes and CD's also take advantage of "biopulse technology™" in which specific tones, known to affect brain states, are mixed into the tonal matrix. Research indicates that such frequencies can significantly alter awareness. These biopulse frequencies fall into a few broad categories, and a parenthetical note after each tape title/description indicates which biopulse frequencies are used.

The primary categories of the biopulse frequencies are:

Delta (0.5-4 Hz) - associated with deep levels of relaxation such as sleep

Theta (4-8 Hz) - associated with tranquil states of awareness in which vivid internal imagery often occurs

Alpha (8-12 Hz) - relaxed nervous system, ideal for stress management, accelerated learning, and mental imagery

Beta (12-30 Hz) - associated with waking/alert states of awareness

K-Complex (30-35 Hz) - clarity and sudden states of integration, the "ah-ha" experience

Super High Beta (35-150 Hz) - psychodynamic states of awareness

 Spiritual Education Endeavors Publishing Company
1556 Halford Avenue #288, Santa Clara, CA 95051-2661
USA (408) 245-5457

AUDIO PRODUCT DESCRIPTIONS

Relaxation and Stress Management

Sound Bath
Soothe and relax yourself with this wonderful mix of beautiful music and ambient nature sounds. One of our most popular tapes for relaxation. (Theta range)
Single cassette T209 $13.95, compact disc CD209 $16.95

Wave Form
Wave Form gently "massages" your brain, helping you to dissolve tensions and drift into deeply relaxing states of awareness. (Theta range)
Single cassette T202 $13.95 *Headphones suggested.*

Wave Form II
Based on an ancient mantra believed to be the sound of the inner heart, this tonal matrix gently "opens the heart" thereby raising consciousness to a purer state of awareness, self-awareness and harmony. Beautiful vocals are intertwined with deep harmonic musical passages. (Theta range)
Single cassette T207 $13.95 *Headphones suggested.*

Rest and Relaxation (R & R)
For busy people who don't always get the rest they need, this tape includes *The 24-Minute Nap* and *The 22-Minute Vacation.* People love this tape! (Mid-Alpha to low Delta range)
Single cassette T402 $13.95 *Headphones suggested.*

Homage to Sol
Beautiful repetitive tempos for guitar, flute, and cello. Based on discoveries of the Lozamov Institute, this beautiful and restful music opens new vistas of serenity.
Single cassette T201 $13.95

Meditation

The Ghandarva Experience
A powerful journey into the spiritual realms of being. This unique program includes a 30-minute talk on the history of the Ghandarva and traces its roots back to Vedic India. Part Two is a compelling listening experience and includes the Chant of the Archangels and the Calling of Sacred Names, the Ghandarvic Choir, and a beautiful rendition of the 23rd Psalm.
Single cassette T801 $13.95, compact disc CD801 $16.95

Singing Crystal Bowls

Ethereal sounds of quartz "singing crystal bowls" to enhance altered states of awareness. Stimulate your body's energy centers as the "crystal vibrations" flow throughout your body.
Single cassette T203 $13.95

New Video Tape Available

Sound Healing and the Inner Terrain of Consciousness. Tom explores the New Physics and its applications to Sound Healing. Part Two, **Song of the New Earth**, is a video collage of natural scenes from around the world. This visual experience has been mixed with a stereo sound-track of Tom's healing sounds. Approximately 60 minutes.
Video cassette(VCR)V101 $29.95

Fitness

The Zone

A delightful and truly effective tape designed to be used with a "Walkman-type" cassette player while doing aerobic exercises such as running, walking, etc. Increases your self motivation and encourages a more intense workout. (Alpha-Beta)
Single cassette tape T605 $13.95 *Headphones suggested.*

Self-Healing and Recovery

Psycho-Immunology

This widely acclaimed "self-healing" program helps you to explore the body/mind connection. It has been created to help you develop a greater potential for "healing experiences," and to assist you in your natural self-healing abilities. Note: Not a substitute for medical treatment. (Alpha-Delta)
Set of 3 tapes T401 $49.95 *Headphones suggested.*

Yoga for the Eyes

This tape offers eye movement exercises, guided imagery, and musical patterns to help rejuvenate your physically-strained and stress-weary sight. (Mid-Alpha range)
Single cassette tape T608 $13.95 *Stereo headphones required.*

Freedom To Be

Free yourself to make healthier decisions and live a fuller life. Designed as a recovery program for alcoholism and drug addiction, these tapes have been found to be very helpful with

issues of low self-esteem, self-sabotage, and emotional overwhelm. (Theta) *Headphones suggested.*
Two tape set with instructions T602 $29.95

Transformation Now!

A highly intense psychoacoustic stimulation of the brain/mind for rapid personal transformation. Note: Epileptics and persons with brain damage should not listen to this tape without professional help. (Shifts rapidly thru Alpha, Theta, and Delta)
Single cassette tape T302 $13.95 *Headphones suggested.*

Healing the Child Within

Unique guided imagery helps you to resolve deeply-held childhood issues. (Alpha to Theta range)
Single cassette tape T601 $13.95 *Headphones suggested.*

Mind/Brain Performance Increase

Creative Imaging

Processes used with this tape have been documented in independent tests to significantly improve analytical abilities, creative problem solving, learning, and insight. Protocols accompanying the tape can also be used to increase visualization abilities. (Mid-Alpha)
Single cassette T205 $13.95 *Headphones suggested.*

Mind Gymnastiks

This "flagship" of ABR's programs has been hailed by researchers, professionals, and laypersons as a highly innovative and powerful tool for helping to increase mental abilities and performance. Users report expanded creativity, speed of processing, perceptual clarity, and feelings of "being on top." (Low Delta to K-complex) *Stereo headphones required.*
Set of 6 tapes with instructions T700 $99.95

Inspired: High Genius and Creativity

Utilizing visual imagery and sophisticated archetypal psychology, these participatory tapes help you tap into the creative principles that great scientists and artists have used throughout history. Enter meditative states where enhanced visualization and inspired dreams help you gain insights into problem solving and goal attainment. (Mid-Alpha range) *Headphones suggested.*
Set of 4 cassette tapes with manual T701 $89.95

LOVE CORPS NETWORKING

The term *Love Corps* was coined in the book *New Teachings for an Awakening Humanity*. The Love Corps is a universal alliance of all human beings of good will who seek both inner personal peace and its planetary application. Thus the worldwide Love Corps family is committed to achieving inner peace through meditation and self-healing and to sharing that peace in groups where the unity of cooperation can be applied toward the preservation of all life.

In order to support our light-workers, wherever they may be, we publish the Love Corps Newsletter. Its purpose is to keep our Love Corps family informed of the very latest information being received from the Spiritual Hierarchy. Newsletter subscribers are eligible to join the Love Corps Network. Please send a SASE for an application.

Virginia Essene frequently travels around the United States and the world to link Love Corps energies, to share additional information not included in the books—*Earth, the Cosmos and You: Revelations by Archangel Michael; Energy Blessings from the Stars; The Hathor Material: Messages from an Ascended Civilization; New Cells, New Bodies, New Life!; New Teachings for an Awakening Humanity*; and three other out-of-print titles—and to encourage humanity's achievement of peace and the preservation of all life upon planet earth.

Please contact us for further information if you would like to be involved in the Love Corps endeavors or to participate with us in seminars. Contact us to schedule a soul reading or an individual counseling session, in person or by telephone.

This "Time of Awakening" brings a new spiral of information to move each of us to a higher level of inner peace and planetary involvement. You are encouraged to accept the responsibility of this evolutionary opportunity and immediately unite efforts with other people in creating peaceful attitudes and conditions on our planet.

SHARE FOUNDATION
1556 Halford Ave. #288
Santa Clara, CA 95051-2661 USA
Tel. (408) 245-5457   FAX (408) 245-5460
E-mail: lovecorp@ix.netcom.com

ORDER FORM - part 1 of 2

Audio & Video Items (T = tape, CD = comp. disc, V = video)

Title	Code	Price	Qty	Title	Code	Price	Qty
Creative Imag.	T205	$13.95	____	Rest & Relax.	T402	$13.95	____
Freedom to Be	T602	$29.95	____	Singing C.B.	T203	$13.95	____
Ghandarva E.	T801	$13.95	____	Sound Bath	T209	$13.95	____
Healing . . .	T601	$13.95	____	The Zone	T605	$13.95	____
Homage to S.	T201	$13.95	____	Trans. Now!	T302	$13.95	____
Inspired: . . .	T701	$89.95	____	Wave Form	T202	$13.95	____
Mind Gymn.	T700	$99.95	____	Wave Form II	T207	$13.95	____
Psycho-Imm.	T401	$49.95	____	Yoga . . . Eyes	T608	$13.95	____

Transform Your Cellular Water Field .... T103 $12.95 ____

Hathors' Self-Mastery Exercises tape .... T102 $ 9.95 ____

Ghandarva Experience .... CD801 $16.95 ____

Sound Bath .... CD209 $16.95 ____

Sound Healing in the Inner Terrain of
Consciousness with Tom Kenyon, video .... V101 $29.95 ____

Total of audio tapes, CD's, and videos (U.S. $) $_____ •

Books

Earth, the Cosmos and You .... @ $14.95 $_____ •

Energy Blessings from the Stars .... @ $14.95 $_____ •

The Hathor Material .... @ $12.95 $_____ •

New Cells, New Bodies, NEW LIFE! .... @ $11.95 $_____ •

New Teachings for an Awakening Humanity:
   English ed. (**Revised 1994/1995**) .... @ $9.95 $_____ •
   Spanish ed. **Nuevas Ensenanzas** .... @ $5.00 $_____ •
Brain States by Tom Kenyon .... @ $11.95 $_____ •

Minus quantity discount (books only, see next page) .... $(_____) •

Product total (above items marked •) | $_____ |

Plus 8.25% **sales tax** (California residents only) .... | $_____ |

Plus **shipping & handling** (see next page): .... | $_____ |
   (Amount is based on **Product total**, above)

Please send me the **Love Corps Newsletter:**
   One year (bi-monthly) subscription = $24 .... | $_____ |
   Canadian & other international = $30 (airmail) .... | $_____ |
   Earlier issues @ $4/issue U.S.A., $5 foreign. Specify
   year & mo. _____ J/F, M/A, M/J, J/A, S/O, N/D .. | $_____ |

Love Corps donation (tax deductible, see next page) .... | $_____ |

TOTAL ENCLOSED (add items within box) .... $_____

NOTE: Be sure to complete part 2 of the order form >>>>>>>>>>

To: **S.E.E. PUBLISHING COMPANY**
c/o The SHARE FOUNDATION*
1556 Halford Avenue #288
Santa Clara, CA 95051-2661 U.S.A.
Telephone (408) 245-5457   FAX (408) 245-5460
E-mail: lovecorp@ix.netcom.com (for info only)

Quantity discounts; books only:
5 to 9 books - take off 10%
10 or more books - take off 20%

U.S. Shipping & Handling Charges

Product total $	Amount	Product total $	Amount
$00.00 - $14.99	$3.95	$45.00 - $59.99	$8.45
$15.00 - $29.99	$5.45	$60.00 - $74.99	$9.95
$30.00 - $44.99	$6.95	$75.00 - $99.99	$11.45
		$100.00 and up	$12.95

Notes:

• Canada & Mexico add $2.00 to above Shipping amounts.

• Other International charges vary by country and weight; please call, FAX, or e-mail for rates.

• Please send check or money order in **U.S. funds** payable through a U.S. bank, or send an International money order made payable to S.E.E. Publishing Co. We **do not accept** foreign currency, or checks drawn on a foreign bank.

• We will ship your order by the best carrier. Some carriers do not deliver to P.O. boxes, so we must have both your street and postal address. Please request shipping rates for first class or air mail.

• All prices and shipping & handling charges are subject to change.

The Share Foundation is a non-profit organization. Contributions are tax deductible under section 501(c)(3) of the IRS code.

Please PRINT (this information is for your mailing label)

Name

Address

City   State/Province   Zip Code
(_____)
Area Code   Telephone Number (optional)